"iGen—the post-Millennial generation born after 1995—is different, and their education needs to be different, too. But how? Marching Off the Map answers that question for educators, parents, and coaches. Along with a broad view of this generation's strengths and challenges, it presents strategies immediately useful for reaching them, from lengthening their attention span to using imagery and narratives. Marching Off the Map is the much-needed road map for the educators, parents, coaches, and youth leaders interested in guiding today's students."

Dr. Jean Twenge, Professor, San Diego St. University and author of *iGen: Why Today's Super-Connected Kids Are are Growing up Less Rebellious, More Tolerant, Less Happy--and Completely Unprepared for Adulthood*

"Profound, insightful, and compelling! Tim Elmore's best work! Marching Off the Map challenges us all to become champions for our young people. A brilliant tapestry of research, personal stories, and strategies for change necessary to impact generations to come. A must read!"

Dr. Michelle McGrath, Executive Director, Wisconsin Association of School Councils

"Tim Elmore's Marching off the Map is an insightful and thought provoking book to help us ignite students to learn in a brand new world. It provides new practical solutions to "why we must change, what must change and how we must change". I am a great admirer of Tim and Growing Leaders, who have been instrumental in leadership development in our athletic program for almost a decade. This is an important must read for all who lead young people."

Kevin Almond, Executive Associate Athletic Director, University of Alabama

"Now more than ever, we must find new and innovative ways to actively engage students in their educational and leadership development. Dr. Elmore continues to share his insight and passion for students with this timely resource. This book sets a strong contextual "why," with a clearly defined "what," followed by real-world action steps to truly impact the next generation of leaders."

Josh Bledsoe, Chief Operations Officer, National FFA (Formerly Future Farmers of America)

"As a career coach and writer, I witness everyday the far-reaching effects of parenting and education on how we grow, develop, and thrive in our lives. I also see how negative, limiting messages and experiences can hold young people back from reaching their highest potential. I'm a huge fan of Tim Elmore's work, and his new book is a powerful guide full of vital information for teachers, parents and employers who are committed to doing their part to support young people to thrive in a new world."

Kathy Caprino, *Forbes* Contributor, Career Success Coach, Leadership Trainer, Speaker

"Standardized learning in a customized world is simply not working, and Dr. Tim Elmore's revolutionary new book, Marching Off the Map, is all about charting a new course! Grounded in provocative research and loaded with practical application, Tim captures the essence of why transformative change is vitally important in how we lead, teach, and parent this unique generation of learners. This must-read book creates awareness, reveals a sense of urgency, and inspires a unified call to action that has the potential to profoundly change our world."

Leslie Smith, Head of School, Orange Lutheran High School, CA

"We are living in dramatic times. Almost 30% of the planet is connected and communicating with a tool created by those who are younger than us. We may feel lost about how to lead, but Tim Elmore's has given his life to mastering this issue. His experience and insights are a great place to start--not only in understanding this emerging generation, but to fearlessly meet them there."

Jason Russell, Co-Founder, Invisible Children, Producer of Kony 2012, CEO of Broomstick Engine

"Marching of The Map offers tremendous insight into our changing world and how we must respond to it. As educators, we must shift our approach to meet this next generation where they are, and they will certainly come to us significantly different then any generation. Tim Elmore and Andrew McPeak do an excellent job of bringing this issue to light."

Gene Smith, Vice President and Director of Athletics, The Ohio State University

"This book is a must read for those who want to better understand how different generations approach life. It not only makes a compelling argument about why we need to change the way that we interact with the younger generations that is based on extensive research, but also offers actionable steps that we can take to bring about that change and challenge students to give their best effort. As an educator and researcher, I am always looking for better ways to challenge students to make a positive impact on themselves and others. As I read this book, I immediately found things that I could use to better understand and motive the younger generation.

"In my profession (college professor and administrator), I have seen the differences in the generations who have moved through the university. I look for ways to engage the students each year and have noticed the changes in the students over time. This book articulated those changes and brought clarity into the behaviors that I have observed over my career. As I read Marching Off the Map, I wanted to be sharing it with others who are currently engaged in crafting the Next in Engineering Education as well as with my professional society who are trying to figure out how to engage this generation of engineers."

Dr. Mary Lynn Realff, Associate Chair for Undergraduate Programs, Georgia Institute of Technology

"Once again, Dr. Elmore provides a must read for those committed to helping young people succeed. The insight and applicability highlighted in Marching Off the Map offers a practical framework for those interested in helping students prepare for college, career, and civic life."

Cory Epler, Chief Academic Officer, Nebraska Department of Education

"Marching off the Map reflects Tim's latest efforts to help our leaders, parents, teachers, and coaches impact the next generation. Tim's work has impacted so many homes, schools, athletic programs, and businesses working with young people because of his research-based content and more importantly his tremendous heart for developing future leaders. His passion for leveraging the strengths of future generations is contagious – and his books are must-have resources for anyone developing young people."

Kyle Stark, Assistant General Manager, Pittsburgh Pirates

"Tim Elmore and Andrew McPeak's new book, Marching off the Map, is critically important and illuminates profound research to impact the lives of Gen Z, educators, parents, employers, mentors and communities. The imperative to forego the status quo and embrace and navigate change for students has never been more apparent. Marching off the Map should be required reading for all those invested in positive outcomes and solutions to ensure the success for every child, adolescent and young adult."

Dr. Judith J. Pickens, Former Senior Vice President of Programs and Youth Development Services, National Boys and Girls Clubs

"Marching off the Map is a 'call to arms' for educators, as well as coaches, employers and parents. In this book, Elmore give educational leaders the background research and insight to make the case for restoring learning to our schools. He reveals the pitfalls of standardized tests to the overburdened teaching community but, at the same time, offers timely solutions for helping educators lead students as we march into uncharted areas of engagement – areas which have the potential to enhance learning. Where many books highlight 'all the problems with' or 'all the excitement of' the emerging generation, Elmore once again gives us a balanced perspective for mentors and educators in our time. From teachers to superintendents, from principals to senators, leaders at all levels who will decide the climate in which students learn should read this book. Through cogent argument and relentless examples, Tim reveals the timeless truth that education takes place in the context of relationships. For those who hope for a better education for our children, Elmore and McPeak give direction to help foster genuine education through relationships in our homes, schools, colleges, universities and the workplace. Woven throughout this book is the optimistic realism that we can lead coming generations to maturely take their place in history – improving the world, solving problems, and serving people beyond what we currently imagine for them."

Dr. Galen Turner, Academic Director for Computer Science, Cyber Engineering, Louisiana Tech University

"Dr. Elmore has once again challenged us to think about our students and the way they learn. Marching Off the Map reminds us all to take risks and try new techniques to help inspire our next generation of leaders."

Brad Cohen, Author of *Front of the Class: How Tourette Syndrome Made Me the Teacher I Never Had,* Administrator, Addison Elementary School

"As a leader and administrator in higher education, I'm always looking for ways to better inspire, connect and invest in the lives of others, especially our student-athletes. My friend, Dr. Tim Elmore, struck gold (again) with Marching Off the Map. This book provides us the "navigational beacons" for our journey to engage Generation Z and their experience as lifelong learners. You'll gain a clear understanding of how this generation could shape the future and/or how the future could shape them."

Joseph R. Castiglione, Sr., Vice President and Director of Athletics, University of Oklahoma

"Dr. Elmore provides a forward-thinking and research based approach to challenge high level educators and coaches to change our mindset in order to stimulate learning in an ever changing culture. He offers practical ideas and insights to inspire a winning approach to helping youth and athletes succeed."

Jason Biles, Director of Performance, Houston Rockets

"Tim Elmore has been a guide for many coaches, faculty, staff, parents and students over the years. Marching Off the Map is an insightful addition to his guidance, as he enables us to peer into the future to see what students will need as they graduate. I recommend his work to anyone who cares about preparing our young for adulthood and leadership."

Sandy Barbour, Director of Athletics, Penn State University

MARCHING OFF THE MAP

INSPIRE STUDENTS TO NAVIGATE A BRAND NEW WORLD

TIM ELMORE

with ANDREW McPEAK

Poet Gardener
PUBLISHING

Published in Atlanta, Georgia, by Poet Gardener Publishing in association with Growing Leaders, Inc.
www.GrowingLeaders.com

ISBN: 978-0-9966970-6-4
Printed in the United States of America

Library of Congress Cataloguing-in-Publication Data

Dedicated to the educators, coaches, employers, youth workers and parents who are already marching off their maps to prepare young adults for an unknown future. You set the pace for the rest of us.

CONTENTS

PART THREE: HOW MUST WE CHANGE?

TAKE A QUIZ
Do You Tend to be More "Old School" or "New School?"

Before we begin, I'd like to invite you to assess your leadership style with students. Circle the number that tends to be the most accurate description of your current style of leadership and communication. Obviously, your most helpful answers are your most honest ones, describing how you approach connecting with kids today.

1. **When it comes to a classroom, it is the teacher's job to instruct students, creating the most comprehensive lesson plans and explanations on the subject.**

   1   2   3   4   5   6   7   8   9   10
   No   YES

2. **When I have conversations with students, I try to create space where they don't feel they have to take a scary risk, a place where they feel comfortable and familiar.**

   1   2   3   4   5   6   7   8   9   10
   No   YES

3. **As an experienced teacher, coach or leader, I believe my number one job is to find a pedagogy, or style, that I challenge kids to acclimate to; they must adjust more than me.**

   1   2   3   4   5   6   7   8   9   10
   No   YES

4. I believe students must adapt to the rigors of didactic learning and critical thinking, so I don't normally use stories or visuals when I communicate.

1	2	3	4	5	6	7	8	9	10
No									YES

5. I don't take a lot of time to keep up with all the cultural changes taking place today. I keep my nose to the grindstone and continue doing my job, the best I can.

1	2	3	4	5	6	7	8	9	10
No									YES

6. I have a difficult time with change. I like to find a routine that works and stick with it. Each year, I try to challenge kids to make shifts to my style.

1	2	3	4	5	6	7	8	9	10
No									YES

7. I think our world is too full of screens and portable devices, so I prefer to not let kids use technology when they're with me.

1	2	3	4	5	6	7	8	9	10
No									YES

8. Kids are unfocused, so when I am teaching students, I find I do most of the talking to prevent them from getting distracted and to help them move forward.

1	2	3	4	5	6	7	8	9	10
No									YES

9. One of the biggest challenges I face when it comes to young people is their short attention spans. They just don't pay attention to anything that's too long.

1	2	3	4	5	6	7	8	9	10
No									YES

10. I do the bulk of the work, when it comes to preparing to teach students. My job is to captivate and hold their attention with my lesson plans or message.

1	2	3	4	5	6	7	8	9	10
No									Yes

11. I don't spend time looking to see what former generations did to prepare kids for adulthood and career. I spend my time looking forward at the future.

1	2	3	4	5	6	7	8	9	10
No									Yes

12. When teaching kids, I believe the most effective line is a direct line, so I get straight to my point. I don't mess around with the "why"; I go right to the "what."

1	2	3	4	5	6	7	8	9	10
No									Yes

Tally your score: _____

Turn the page to discover whether you're "old" or "new" school.

SCORECARD

If you were honest, your score will reflect how you approach most of the major themes of this book. If you are an educator the questions are most relevant, but I believe parents, coaches, employers and youth workers can apply these themes as well. Here is my suggested scorecard for the quiz you just took.

If you scored...	Then you are likely...
12 – 36	A very savvy and highly skilled teacher, communicator or leader for this next generation. Keep doing what you're doing. They need the balance you bring.
37 - 61	Effective at knowing what a 21st century student needs, but may still over-function (or under-function) and diminish their growth. Seek to improve where you can.
62 – 86	An average leader for this new generation and will need to apply yourself to both understand and empathize with who they are and what they need from you.
87 – 111	A bit of an "Old School" leader who got stuck in past methods or traditions. To connect with today's young, you must learn new approaches and pedagogies.
112 – 120	An unashamed "Old School" leader who may have been around a long time, but also may be losing your effectiveness. This book will challenge you to grow.

CHAPTER 1

WHAT IF THE FUTURE COULD TALK TO US?

Three significant cultural changes beckon us to become pioneers.

Stop worrying about what you have to lose. Start focusing on what you have to gain.

—Anonymous

I recently spoke to a mom whose son, Matthew, is 25 years old. She told me about a conversation she had a month earlier with Matt's former high school principal. They are close friends and the principal was grieving over the fact that Matt was still unemployed, living at home and suffering from mental health issues. In the conversation, the principal acknowledged a vital shortcoming:

> *I felt the need to write you today about our children. They've been on my mind...*
>
> *Now that both our kids are older...I hate to admit that we're getting used to higher levels of anxiety and depression in them. I deeply regret our adult children are addicted to screens and meds to help them cope with life. I'm disappointed that we didn't teach them emotional intelligence and social intelligence; work ethic and resilience; vision and leadership. These are basic skills my parents taught me, but I'm afraid they're not getting taught at home or at school these days...*
>
> *I want to apologize for the part I may have played in Matt's developmental problems. Like too many other school leaders, I carried a narrow definition of education. During the last fifteen years I felt it was all about test scores, and keeping up with Finland and Singapore. As I look back, it appears the more we pushed them academically, the more we failed at teaching them life.*

Wow. That's quite a confession.

But this principal is spot on. Matt is among the millions of young adults who are languishing instead of launching their careers. He moved back home after leaving college early; he lacks ambition and is wandering in his life choices. He feels too insecure to ask young women out, and is insecure about most of his adult decisions. He is, indeed, addicted to his meds as well as his video games but plays them as a coping mechanism for his depression. If you asked him, you'd discover he wants to do something significant with his life, but isn't into starting small or at the bottom of the ladder. He hates the phrase, "You have to pay your dues." With so much to offer, Matt isn't in the game yet.

Matt's sister, Zoe, is 16 years old. I met her last year when she was a high school freshman. She likes to listen to Vampire Weekend. She enjoys playing "Pokemon Go." She loves posting memes on social media. She's been known to binge watch "The Unbreakable Kimmy Schmidt" on Netflix. She's played on a soccer team for years. When you meet her, you quickly see she's gifted, savvy and beautiful. After one conversation, however, I recognized she's full of angst, caring far too much about what others think of her. She's overwhelmed with the five screens in her life, which is where she discovers what others think of her. She's confused about her identity. She sees herself as gender fluid. And she's stressed about what her future will look like. In fact, I'm deeply concerned for her mental and emotional health. As we talked, I realized she didn't even know how to ask for help.

After a conversation with Zoe, I also knew she was different than Millennials, (like her brother Matt) who make up an older population. She's part of Generation Z and there are millions like her. I was reminded how important it is for us, as caring adults, to prepare today's kids to be ready for an unknown future. Zoe feels the adults in her life just don't understand her. She and her peers are different.

Which means—we may need to change.

Matt and Zoe have a younger sister named Savannah. She's in the sixth grade and is a bit different than her older siblings. Like Zoe, Savannah doesn't remember a day without social media. As an 11-year old, however, she's addicted to it. She admits it. She says she can't go through a day without it. If her parents take her phone away as a punishment, Savannah quickly sends her passwords to her BFF's so she can keep her

Snapchat streak going, via friends. She takes Adderall for her ADHD because her parents say she has a hard time focusing. Savannah loves theatre arts and wants to be an actress or a dancer in her career. She loves watching "New Girl" on TV and does so, at times, to "get away from all the ****" going on in the world.

Like many middle school students, Savannah has been exposed to far more trauma around the world than she needs to know. She is already promiscuous with boys and has done some sexting (text messages with photos of her naked body). It's how she meets boyfriends these days. She is convinced, however, her mom and dad have "no idea what's going on" in her life.

Savannah's a younger member of Generation Z, who appears to be slightly different than the older members of that generation. The fact is, change happens so rapidly, that even within a generation, young people can experience very different realities, depending on how social media and technology shaped them as they moved into their tween years. To say that their world is different than ours was growing up is an understatement.

After conversing with educators over the last several years, these observations are not rare. Many recognize that simply continuing what we've done in the past will not get us to our goal. The future will not merely be an extension of the past. Too many end their careers in regret or exhaustion, like Matt's high school principal.

This book is about moving into unknown territory as caring adults, and leading the way for the younger generations behind us. It's all about inspiring students to learn in this brand new world. Whether you are an educator, a parent, a coach, an employer, a youth worker or just someone who cares about kids, this book was created to help you chart the course into the future.

WHERE IS HISTORY TAKING US?

If you've ever visited Walt Disneyworld or Disneyland, you've likely experienced the fast-paced ride, "Space Mountain." It's a roller coaster in the dark. The first time you ride this zany thing, you have no idea what's coming—but it's coming fast. There are spots of light, but mostly obscurity. You find your car swerving around bends you didn't know were there, or dropping fifty feet in a virtually pitch black environment. It's what makes the ride fun. Space Mountain can be described with four words:

- SPEED
- CURVES
- DROPS
- DARKNESS

Those are also four words to describe our journey into the future.

We are moving at breakneck speed as technology is unveiled faster than ever. We can't fully see what's up ahead. We can only guess. Our population and culture is becoming more pluralistic with each passing year. We meet different generations and ethnicities we aren't familiar with. There are bends in the road we didn't see coming. People get scared more easily and sometimes do strange things when encountering different contexts or people. Like Dorothy in the Land of Oz, the world is no longer black and white, or predictable. It's in full color and it's odd and inexplicable. It feels like we're traveling into uncharted territory.

The fact is, we are.

How Technology is Evolving

No one would disagree that technology is defining how we live today. What we often fail to recognize is how rapidly it transforms our lifestyle. The Singularity University Conference is an annual event focusing on the "exponentially accelerating technologies" that impact several global industries. After attending the 2016 S.U. Summit, German blogger Udo Gollub summarized some fascinating predictions made there.

"In 1998, Kodak had 170,000 employees and sold 85 percent of all photo paper worldwide. Within a few years, their business model disappeared and they went bankrupt. What happened to Kodak will happen to lots of industries in the next decade—and most people don't see it coming. Did you think in 1998 that three years later you'd never take pictures on paper film again? Yet digital cameras were invented in 1975. The first ones only had 10,000 pixels and didn't gain traction. So as with all exponential technologies, it was disappointing for a long time, before it became mainstream in only

a few short years. This will now happen with Artificial Intelligence, health, self-driving and electric cars, education, 3D printing, agriculture and jobs."[1]

Welcome to the 4th Industrial Revolution. Welcome to the Exponential Age. "Software and operating platforms will disrupt most traditional industries in the next 5-10 years. Uber is just a software tool. They don't own any cars, but they are now the biggest taxi company in the world. Airbnb is the biggest hotel company in the world, although they don't own any properties."[2] This is a preview of tomorrow.

Ever heard of 3D printing? "The price of a cheap 3D printer came down from $18,000 to $400 within 10 years. In that same time, it became 100 times faster. All major shoe companies started printing 3D shoes. Spare airplane parts are already 3D-printed in remote airports. The space station now has a printer that eliminates the need for the large amount of spare parts they used to need in the past. [As 2016 ended,] new smart phones now have 3D scanning possibilities. You can then 3D scan your feet and print your perfect shoe at home. In China, they have already 3D-printed a complete 6-story office building. By 2027, 10 percent of everything that's being produced will be 3D-printed."[3]

"When pondering a business opportunity, I must first ask myself: "In the future, do I think we will still need that?" If the answer's yes, I must work on how to make that happen sooner. If it doesn't work via my phone, I should forget the idea. Any idea designed for success in the 20th century is probably doomed to fail in the 21st century. We must recognize that 70-80 percent of jobs will disappear in the next 20 years. There will be lots of new jobs, but it's not clear there will be enough new jobs in such a short time."[4]

"How about everyday life? There is already an app called "moodies" which can tell the mood you are in. By 2020 there will be apps that can tell by your facial expressions if you are lying. Imagine a political debate where we know whether the participants are telling the truth or not! Many currencies will be abandoned. With Bitcoin becoming mainstream in 2017, it might even become the future default reserve currency."[5]

"Right now, the average life span increases by three months per year. Four years ago, the average life span was 79 years, now it is 80 years. The increase itself is increasing and by 2036, there will be more than a one-year increase per year. So we all might live for a long, long time, probably way beyond 100." [6]

How will education change? *"The cheapest smartphones already sell for $10 in Africa and Asia. By 2020, 70 percent of all humans will own a smartphone. This means everyone will have much the same access to World Class education. Every child can use the Khan Academy for everything she needs to learn at schools in First World countries. Further afield, the software has been launched in Indonesia and will be released in Arabic, Swahili and Chinese soon. The English app will be offered free, so that children in Africa can become fluent in English"* within half a year. [7]

How does all this affect the way we prepare our students, employees and children?

How Childhood Is Evolving

Technology isn't the only element changing today. Educator and cultural critic Neil Postman explained another challenge we face.[8] He argues that childhood, as we've known it historically, is disappearing. Kids today are exposed to media (television, movies, news, entertainment, music) without boundaries. Thanks to technology, information streams into their lives 24/7 and often has no filter on it, even for young children. When we determined not to censor content in the media, we had no idea (understandably) how it would affect our kids. We're removing the opportunity for them to experience innocence and wonder. However, because they're still maturing emotionally, socially, cognitively and bio-logically in their first 25 years, we have now begun to witness a strange paradox in our young:

- The extinction of childlikeness
- The extension of childishness

Consider what the non-stop, infectious flow of information is doing to our young. Since they are exposed to so much adult information, so early in their lives, they can prematurely lose (1) their sense of innocence,

(2) their sense of wonder and (3) their sense of trust. Their childlike outlook diminishes as they watch both adults and peers bully each other in cyberspace; as they're exposed to adult images on television and YouTube; as they trade in spontaneous "Capture the Flag" games for participation in adult-supervised competitions; and now have less to look forward to in adulthood because they've already experienced so much in childhood. Games are no longer about "play" but "reputation." They've seen the under-belly of society during their elementary school days and are jaded and skeptical by adolescence.

Simultaneously, however, this information does not necessarily translate into maturity. Knowing a lot of data doesn't equal growth. Postman puts it this way: "the tie between information and action has been severed."[9] So, a student can graduate from all levels of school, even with good grades, but be emotionally or socially behind. Biologically, the graduate is an adult. Emotionally, the graduate may be unprepared for the adult world. During the years of 2010 to 2015, somewhere between 60-80 percent of our kids moved back home after college.[10]

During those same years, approximately eight percent of Millennials brought their parent to a job interview.[11] Between 16 and 27 percent of young adults in America will be arrested by age 18.[12] 13 percent of them (ages 20-29) are unemployed.[13] The average debt for Millennials between ages 25 and 34 is $21,000.[14] A 2012 report by Joel Klein and Condoleezza Rice reveals that 75 percent of our youth were not even eligible for the military due to obesity, criminal records or failure to graduate.[15] Far too many university deans mourn this dilemma by saying, "Knowledge doesn't equal maturity. Giftedness doesn't equal maturity. Influence on social media doesn't equal maturity." Our kids may no longer be childlike, but they often continue to be childish.

I call this "artificial maturity." In my book by that title, I explain that too many of our young are over-exposed to information far earlier than they are ready, yet they are under-exposed to real life experiences far later than they're ready. This causes them to appear mature—they know a lot—but too often it is artificial, not authentic. They can continue to act like a kid, especially if they come from affluence, where gadgets and parents have enabled them to avoid responsibility. Once again, this sends them into adulthood unhealthy and unready. They are savvy yet naïve. [16]

A few years ago, Jake Halpern and Company surveyed high school students and asked: What would you like to do in life? Given multiple choices, their responses were telling:

- 9.5 percent chose a chief of a major company.
- 9.8 percent chose a Navy SEAL.
- 13.6 percent chose a United States Senator.
- 43.4 percent chose the personal assistant to a famous celebrity. [17]

Becoming an assistant to a celebrity was their top answer! Wow. What does this say about the psyche of American youth? Is it that they don't want the pressure of being famous, but are happy to assist someone who lives that fairy tale lifestyle? When it comes to performing, many want proximity to the limelight, but not the pressure.

We must find a way to lead our young into the future, preparing them for anything life might throw at them. This will require us to teach and lead them with different methods than we currently employ.

How Adulthood Is Evolving

At the same time the information age offers our children adult knowledge, without boundaries, it is also affecting the adult population—you and me.

You've likely noticed that across the board, in most industrialized nations, the concept of adult authority is diminishing. Teachers experience less respect from their students than they did in past generations. It is the same for parents and their children; civil servants, (i.e. law enforcement) and citizens, coaches and their teams or employers and their staff. In short, the respect of elders by the young has shrunk. You might argue that this isn't all bad. I agree. Blind submission to authority can be lethal. I also argue, however, that this may be occurring, in part, because our expectations of adult character have diminished. We've lowered our standard for adult behavior.

If you think our kids are pitifully impulsive on social media—just look at the adult population. (Remember the two presidential candidates in the 2016 election?) If you think teens are addicted to Facebook, just study the hours their mothers spend on it. If you think young athletes on the Little League baseball field act childish, just look at their dads. The behavior of adults and children has become more and more similar.

Society has baptized "youthfulness." We want to look young, feel young, dress young, talk young and act young. We argue with our children's teachers. We push our kid's coaches to get them special treatment. We're not good at delaying gratification, and we frequently don't keep commitments we make . . . very much like children.

The result? Adulthood has lost much of its aura and authority. And deference to one who is older has become rare. There is a greater disregard for rules and a greater degree of "discipline problems" in schools. I believe it's partly our fault as adults. Case in point. When my children took part in a community theatre program, I became embarrassed by the conduct of the parents. It wasn't the child actors that behaved so immaturely, it was the "stage moms." Over time, I found myself using the phrase: "Let's keep the 'drama' on the stage" or "Let's all try to 'act' like grown-ups."

It was both sad and shameful.

Do you remember a commercial for Ivory Soap decades ago? It involved a mother and her daughter standing side by side. The goal for the television viewer was to guess which one was the mom and which was the daughter, because they both looked so young. Bingo. Too often, this is a picture of our culture today. We can't tell who is the adult and who is the child.

- Children act more like adults, in many ways (savvy and skeptical).
- Adults act more like children, in many ways (impulsive and emotional).

We try to look, act and feel so young; we fail to offer our children a picture of what an emotionally healthy adult looks like. Perhaps our twenty-somethings don't act like well-adjusted adults because we haven't given them a good model to follow.

People do what people see.

Perhaps respect for elders is rare because we haven't earned it. Instead of challenging kids to act like adults, we are emulating them. Social media has conditioned adults to be "caught up" on information but "dumbed down" by the information. This doesn't help us sustain our civilization well at all.

If you look at the numbers, one reality stares us in the face. By and large, the Baby Boomer generation (of which I am a part) did not do a great job preparing their children for adulthood. With some exceptions, of course, millions of us chose to be a "pal" rather than a "parent" to our kids. Or, we decided to be a "helicopter" hovering over them, making decisions for them and disabling them from launching into adulthood well. As several university deans have told me, "26 is the new 18." All of these young adults grew older, but too many of them did not grow up.

A Vu Jade World

The fact is, we are moving into what Harrison, Day and Halpin call a "Vu jade" (vu-ja-de) world, which is the opposite of a "deja vu" world. This new world is where leaders realize "I have never been here before, I have no idea where I am and I have no idea who can help me."[18] In this kind of a period, leaders feel what Patrick Lagadec described as "*Terra Incognitae*," a "world unknown and uncharted."[19] Dr. Len Sweet says we are not merely experiencing an era of change but a change of era.

Do you remember Sergei Krikalev? He's the Russian cosmonaut who the Soviet Union sent into space on a shuttle back in 1991. While circling the earth in the space station Mir, his worst nightmare was realized. His country went out of business. Wow. As fellow citizens struggled to form a new country (the Commonwealth of Independent States), Sergei was stranded in space…for a record ten months! Yep. You read that right. After 311 days, the staff finally returned to the control center and brought this "space victim" back home. Just imagine, however, how his world had been rocked. The Soviet Union was gone. The Commonwealth was birthed. Mikhail Gorbachev was gone. Boris Yeltsin was president. And Sergei's salary— which was once in the 95th percentile of Soviet salaries—could now barely buy a Big Mac at the Moscow McDonalds.[20]

What a picture of our world today.

In less than one year's time, life can fundamentally change. The way we live, connect, shop, bank, work and self-identify can all shift swiftly, sometimes before we can evaluate if things are really better or not. Change brings both gain and loss. And for those of us who lead our young, it means we cannot afford to be sleeping at the wheel.

This forces us to look at outcomes we hope for, not merely inputs we've been practicing for years and years. We must first ask: what destination do we need to help this emerging generation reach, and then ask: how can we help them get there? What outcomes are essential that can inform our inputs?

It's a new world requiring new maps. Are you ready?

SETTING EXPECTATIONS

It's been said that life is pretty much about managing expectations. I agree. So at the start of this journey—I wanted to offer some guidelines for what this book can be expected to accomplish and what it does not propose to do. The goal in writing the book is to furnish you with a compass for the future.

Just as Christopher Columbus set sail for India, but ended up in North America and assumed he'd call the natives "Indians," I believe history is progressing into new realities we didn't see coming. We could mistake where we are. We might misname the natives we find living in the future. Like Columbus, we may have assumed we'd arrive at one destination, but in reality, we're heading toward another. It isn't necessarily bad, but this book is about facing the new reality and capitalizing on it. We want to help you leverage tomorrow the best way possible.

There is much we can discover.

Our education strategies haven't been sufficiently productive, our parenting strategies haven't furnished positive results and our kids are graduating unready for life after school. I know your work is difficult, whether you educate them, employ them, coach them or parent them. I am hopeful this book will show you how we can change—for their sake.

I enlisted the help of my colleague, Andrew McPeak. He is a wise Millennial, part of today's emerging generation of adults and someone who keeps his ear to the ground on trends and students. He facilitated all of our focus groups with young teens and helped to research the finer points of this book. I even asked him to write the chapter on "Modern Day Map Makers," which illustrates the changes we believe we must orchestrate as we lead this younger generation.

In this book, we'll usually refer to this new generation as "students" because as of now, they are still in school. They're not yet full-fledged adults and in their careers. That will happen soon and we hope this information prepares you to lead them well. While we are writing to a larger audience, we will use this language.

The Travel Guide

This book is accompanied by a *Travel Guide*. The guide is your personal app. It is for you to write in, to interact with, and to develop an individual plan for your work with students. This book you're holding contains the ideas and questions, but I hope you'll leverage the "Travel Guide" to create your own personal "map" for the future.

You will notice we've tried to be "pracademic." The content you'll read is research based, but in addition, we offer practical ideas on how we can respond to the data. There will be studies to interpret and steps to take. We've tried to be solution-biased. Again, you can record your own reflections in the "Travel Guide."

While I've written this book for educators, our audience is any adult who cares about the emerging generation:

- Teachers
- Parents
- Employers
- Coaches
- Administrators
- Counselors
- Non-profit executives
- Pastors

I'm actually very hopeful about the role they can play in human history. I believe they'll be a generation who improves—even transforms—society. I believe this, however, with one condition. I believe they can reach their potential if, and only if, we rethink the way we're leading them. If we will change our ways, they will change our world. I actually believe this.

Last December, a six-year-old kid told me he didn't believe in Santa Claus. I smiled and asked if his mom ever told him about St. Nicholas visiting children on Christmas Eve and surprising them with gifts. He looked at me blankly and replied, "Yeah, she says that. But she lies to me about other things, too." Skeptical and savvy at age 6. It's time to travel into this new world, where kids are uncertain yet hopeful.

They desperately need a compass from you.

CHAPTER 2

HOW DO YOU MARCH OFF A MAP?

We must march to places with new maps when our familiar ones are antiquated.

Do not go where the path may lead, go instead where there is no path and leave a trail.

—Ralph Waldo Emerson

We live in a day that conditions us to seek safety. We are safety conscious and teach our children to be safety conscious. We have safety policies, we wear pads and helmets, we buy insurance plans and we retain attorneys all to lower the risk of harm.

Years ago, I had surgery done on my abdomen for a hernia. It was a first for me, and the doctor told me to enter the next week with caution. I was to avoid anything that could damage the incision. A week later, I sat in the upper deck at a San Diego Padres ballgame. I love baseball and felt I was safe there. After all, what could happen in the upper deck, right? Unbelievably, I was hit by a foul ball, in the first inning, less than six-inches away from that incision. I was stunned.

Needless to say, I lived through that ordeal. And I got myself a foul ball. But I also got myself a life lesson. There is no completely safe place on planet earth. If that Upper Deck in San Diego wasn't safe for me that night, nowhere was safe.

OUR PURSUIT OF SAFETY AND SECURITY

As ridiculous as it sounds, that ballgame was a threshold for me. Everything became clear about my natural inclination to seek safety and security. It was a picture. Since then, I've reflected on my life and realized that whether I was pursuing risky ventures or withdrawing to some hiding place from the dangers of the world, I could not dodge risk. I can never totally sidestep peril; no one can avoid or prevent all harm. Life is not neat; it is messy. And the sooner I embrace that, the better off I will be.

Over a six-year period of time, I was involved in seven automobile accidents, hit from all sides of my car. In two cases, my car was turned into an accordion, mashed together in the front and back. These were all on safe roads—not on bridges or cliffs.

I've been detained in communist Romania (during Nikolae Ceausecu's reign) as a Type 1 diabetic, and had my insulin confiscated. I was just traveling through the checkpoint, but it became traumatic. This was supposed to be routine.

Later, I was in a small plane crash in New Zealand. The airplane dropped 120 feet to the ground, as we crash-landed on a field. Needless to say, it was a bit of a miracle the four of us in that aircraft survived. While it gave me a chance to address the entire Kiwi population on the national news that night, it wasn't the trip I planned.

I've had a knife held up to my neck, as I tried to serve the homeless, near a downtown soup kitchen. I felt the blade and heard the colorful vocabulary of the perpetrator as he threatened me for being on his turf. I was just trying to feed some hungry people.

Yep. I've drawn one clear conclusion about life. No matter how hard you look, there is no absolutely safe and secure place that's invulnerable to the threat of hazard. Further, our human pursuit of security sabotages our ability to change, or take appropriate risks. It can actually make us irrelevant.

This book is about advancing into territory that's new and unfamiliar. As humans, most of us don't do that well, especially as we age. We naturally seek out safe, comfortable and familiar places. We tend to be creatures of habit. And when we construct our habits and conquer our daily procedures, we feel better about ourselves. After all, who doesn't want to feel like they've mastered their career?

So we create "maps" or paradigms with which to live by. Good or bad, they can become unbreakable habits. We push life to the subconscious level, where most of our day requires no real thinking. It's a routine. At first, it feels like we're in sync; we sense we're in the groove. Over time, however, we get stuck and don't notice. Sadly, we can mistake a "rut" for a "groove." Too many of us have built ourselves a hut in a rut.

WHAT MARCHING OFF THE MAP LOOKS LIKE

Do you remember reading about Alexander the Great, in history class? He was the famous warrior who was born to King Philip II and Queen Olympia. His parents had him tutored by Aristotle, so he was cultured and educated from boyhood.

He lived from 356 – 323 BC, and during his tenure of leadership, he garnered the support of the Macedonian Army and began conquering territory across the known world. He united Greece, reestablished the Corinthian League and conquered the Persian Empire. In fact, he took his army and marched east, conquering everything from Greece to India. He became King of Persia, Babylon and Asia. There seemed to be nothing he could not conquer.

"Alexander the Great and Porus" - Fontebasso, Francesco (18th Century)

What's little known today is that Alexander was notorious for frustrating his soldiers. Why? Because he was not satisfied to merely conquer the known world. He continued to march into unknown territory where his men had never traveled before. There were no maps. In fact, he transformed some of his soldiers into "map makers"— requiring them to draw new maps as they discovered new lands, sketching out the rivers, the hills, the plains, the mountains and the valleys. Can you imagine? They literally had to draw the maps as they marched.

This had to be both exhilarating and frightening. They mapped as they marched. They penned as they progressed. They were training as they were traveling. They had nothing else to leverage. It would have been useless to continue using old maps in this new territory.

This is where we live today.

Matt, Zoe and Savannah (from chapter one) all not only live in this new world, they're growing up in it. This world has overwhelmed them, and they're now attempting to find ways to navigate it and cope with it. Many from their generation have a "love-hate relationship" with it. And they need guides to help them make progress. As you stand in front of your classroom or your own children—you are, in a sense, Galileo. You are Magellan. You are Christopher Columbus. You are Lewis and Clark. You are Neil Armstrong. Ready or not, they need you to play this role.

Our world is both expanding and shrinking. Our past maps and methods are antiquated. Like it or not, we're moving into unfamiliar territory and many think it's too difficult to explore. We have fallen in love with our old maps.

We may be educators. We may be athletic coaches. We might be employers or parents. But while it sounds cliché, our kids today are growing up in a radically different world than we did, and it's time for new maps to guide them into this new territory. It is silly for us to continue to assume our old maps, drawn a century ago, would be sufficient for the new places we're treading each and every day. If it's any consolation, this has never been easy, for any generation.

Even in ancient days, people loved the familiar. Folks didn't embrace new "mapmakers" like Copernicus, or Newton, or Galileo. Even Christopher Columbus couldn't get funding from his own country for his trip. They assumed the world was flat. Yet, since his day, new maps have expanded rapidly. Especially since the Enlightenment, change has been happening on a growth curve that makes most people shudder. Discoveries are made and yet, they are questioned and shunned. The unknown produces fear in us.

Have you seen a map from antiquity? Often, the maps were colorful, graphic and descriptive of the current landmarks across the terrain.

Many would actually include pictures within the maps. What we frequently fail to notice, however, is what would appear in the upper corner of those maps. Take a glance at the one I've included here. Do you see what's in the upper right-hand portion of this map?

"A Map of the Norwegian Sea" (1539) Olaus Magnus

It's a dragon or a serpent.

Mapmakers would include a drawing like this to communicate the message: Over here—this land is the known world. But up there—we don't know what exists. It's unknown territory. Be afraid. Be very afraid.

It appears that over the centuries, humans are not too different:

- We embrace the familiar and the routine.
- We love the comfortable, secure and the safe.
- We migrate toward what's predictable and easy.

PIONEERS AND SETTLERS

Making new maps is an art we must learn. In fact, in the upcoming chapters, we'll journey into why those maps are essential for a new generation of kids growing up today. We'll examine what the new terrain looks like on the horizon. We will survey some of the mountains we'll have to climb to reach our desired destination. And, we will even meet some new "map makers" who can help us get there.

This book is designed to help you recognize what changes you must make to lead and equip a new generation of emerging adults who live in the corner of the map:

- For educators, our role must change as we teach a generation of students who don't need adults to get information.

- For parents, our role must change as we raise kids in a time of terrorism, economic recession, racial unrest, underemployment and ubiquitous technology.

- For coaches, our role must change as we train young athletes who have eight- second attention spans, and may arrive at practice with little resilience or grit.

- For youth workers, our role must change as we mentor students who may have few life skills or values because adults either over-functioned or were absent.

- For employers, our role must change as we onboard young employees who may have never had a real job before, and may ask when "spring break" will be.

Are you ready for this?

I believe adults today can be divided into two groups, in terms of their disposition. The two groups can be described in this way:

1. **Pioneers**—Those who explore and pave the way for others.
2. **Settlers**—Those who move ahead only when they know it's safe.

I believe the vast majority of human beings fall into the "settler" category. We'd rather wait until those pioneers or early adopters try the new "territory" and ensure the terrain is safe and functioning before we step forward. We play it safe. The pioneer is about risk. The settler is about routine. Every one of us leans toward one or the other, but I want to unashamedly nudge you toward becoming more of a pioneer.

Why?

Our kids today need us to do so. We can't afford to adopt an idea five to ten years too late. By that time, it's outdated and we'll lose a percentage of them. We can't finally become acquainted with their social media world five years into it. It will change by then. We cannot recognize what's "trending" five years too late; it will no longer be trending. They're certainly moving into new territory, with or without us, adopting new apps for their phone, new social media connections, new ways to communicate, even new morals where expediency—not ethics—rule the day.

I must warn you, however, that becoming a pioneer is definitely risky. Pioneers are usually the ones with arrows in their back. (They've been shot by settlers who can't understand their strange new tactics.) There are no guarantees of success. But, I can certainly guarantee failure if you remain a settler. Settlers will be left in the dust as the young people we lead disconnect from us and find others they can follow to new places. Or, they will forge ahead with no mentors at all.

It's an understatement to say that both Millennials (young adults) and Generation Z (adolescents and children) do not want to "settle" for what's happened in the past. They want progress. They don't want to exclaim "Me too!" as they repeat what someone else has done. They want to say, "Me first!" as they attempt something no one else has done. In 2000, Neil Howe and William Strauss were among the first to publish research on the Millennial generation in a book entitled, *Millennials Rising*.[1] In that book, they noted that one of young peoples' greatest fears was that they would "settle" for a career or a lifestyle that was mediocre or unexciting, as their parents' generation had done.

I enjoyed the series of TV commercials that DirecTV broadcast in the early part of 2016. Did you see them? The television ads were called, "The Settlers." They showed a modern neighborhood in a typical American town, where a 19th century family had moved in and were using a horse and plow, wore old-fashioned overalls and didn't have the luxuries that most families enjoyed. When a young boy runs out into the field, he finds his dad and asks him why they must settle for cable TV and experience lower customer satisfaction. The dad, sitting on a wagon replies, "Because we're settlers, son. We settle." After interacting with a neighbor who's enjoying our modern world, the father tells his son, "Now go churn us some butter, and then make your own clothes."

After talking to students about this commercial, I found it's a humorous picture of how the young see our world. Believe it or not, they perceive an older generation settling for less; for the less effective and the antiquated, when an entirely new world is available. They assume we are just "settling." Perhaps every generation of youth in the last century has assumed their elders were old-fashioned. This is why I believe we must cultivate one significant skill set in ourselves:

We must be able to either adapt to the new world that's emerging, or we must explain why a timeless virtue or value is still relevant in our 21st century world.

Do you have this skill?

I think it's important that we reveal both the new realities that are emerging in culture, as well as the timeless principles that have existed for centuries that we must help kids embrace. Both are essential. Adults must enable the students to leverage what is new, yet at the same time, hold on to what is ancient, yet valuable. We must be both timeless and timely. So, our job as we serve the next generation is two-fold:

- **To adopt or adapt.** We must seize what is new and help kids leverage it well.
- **To explain and equip.** We must relay to them the timeless ideals every generation needs.

Both of these tasks are paramount for adults to master today. On the surface, they appear to be oxymoronic. They don't seem to go together. We're usually good at one or the other. I believe, however, we must possess both skill sets. We must help kids grasp new skills for the future world they'll be living in, but also hold fast to old skills that never go out of style, such as integrity, discipline, and empathy. We must hold on to what's timeless and yet promote what is timely for the young around us. They'll need both trending hard skills and traditional soft skills to succeed in life.

Let me illustrate how one writer blended the timely and timeless to communicate, entertain and teach. In August 2015, the musical "Hamilton" opened on Broadway. In it's first year, it was nominated for an unprecedented 16 Tony Awards and won eleven of them. How could this happen? The music, lyrics and script are written by a relatively young Lin-Manuel Miranda. I believe Miranda's genius lies in the fact he combined both a timeless story of rags to riches leadership, with the timely genre of rap music. It's stunning. Yesterday's story; today's style. Timeless and timely.

By mastering both tasks, we actually become a pioneer. We become the rare breed who can teach the importance of both the past and the future. We value both. You might call this person a progressive-conservative. Or, a conservative-progressive. We are reaching backward and forward at the same time.

Why Do Our Young Need Pioneers with New Maps?

Let me now build the case for pioneering. In my book, *Twelve Huge Mistakes Parents Can Avoid*, I list a handful of reasons why we often feel like a foreigner as we work with this new generation. In short, it's because they represent a generation of "firsts" who are inaugurating so many new realities in our world.

This is the first generation that:

1. **Doesn't need adults to get information.**
   Consider how this difference changes the role of an adult. Because information is everywhere, we are no longer brokers of data. They don't need us for information, but for interpretation. We must help them make sense of all they know, by giving context to the content. The task isn't to access data, but to process data and form good decisions.

2. **Can broadcast their every thought or emotion in real time.**
   You see this every week. Thanks to Twitter, Snapchat and Instagram, your kids can send messages to huge populations who matter. They are the new PR for your school or department. Some posts actually get famous…good or bad. Most, however, have not been equipped to harness the megaphone in their hands.

3. **Has external stimuli at their fingertips 24/7.**
   Because a portable device is in their hand, they receive outside stimulation any time they're bored. Many don't think well on their own. This outside entertainment may have reduced their internal motivation. They've never had to motivate themselves. They depend on a screen to push them. We must equip them to find it within.

4. **Are socially connected at all times, but often they connect in isolation.**
   This is the most connected generation in history—but perhaps the one who's experienced the least community. They're rarely disconnected, yet they are lonely because their connection is virtual—in isolation,

on a screen. Their empathy, soft skills and emotional intelligence are lower because of it. They'll need those skills for life.

5. **Will learn more from a portable device than from a classroom.**
This one is a game changer. The portable device they hold in their hand is now the compass that guides them, not their teachers. They'll consume more data on this device than through any other means. It may be inaccurate or damaging, but it's available and they are digesting it. They'll need us to help them navigate this tool.

6. **Uses a phone instead of a wristwatch, camera, wall calendar or board game.**
Students no longer manage their lives the way we did growing up. Their phone tells time, provides entertainment, takes pictures, gives directions, connects with friends and broadcasts their messages. Designed to make life simpler, this non-stop information center has made them the most stressed out generation to date.

It may go without saying, but today's young population is also the first generation that adults cannot say: "I know exactly what you're going through." The world has changed so rapidly, we really don't know exactly what they're experiencing. My parents could not prepare me (as a parent) to raise a child with a portable device in their hand—because they never had to do it themselves. Sometimes I'm in a world without a relevant map. Think about where the future is migrating for a moment.

In his groundbreaking book, *The Inevitable: Understanding Twelve Technological Forces That Will Shape Your Future*, author Kevin Kelly paints a picture of life in thirty years:

- "You don't own a car, or much of anything else, paying instead to subscribe to products and services as you need them." (Think Uber.)
- "Virtual reality is as common as your cell phone. You talk to your devices with a common set of hand gestures." (Think Star Trek.)
- "Practically all surfaces have become a screen, and each screen watches you back. Every aspect of your life is tracked by you or someone else." (Think The Matrix.)
- "Advertisers pay you to watch their ads." (Think The Jetsons.)

- "Robots and Artificial Intelligence took over your old job but also created a new one for you, doing work you could not have imagined back in 2016."
- "Ultimately all humans and machines will be linked up into a global matrix, a convergence that will be seen as the most complex event up to this time."[2]

BUILDING THE BRIDGE AS WE CROSS IT

When Margaret Mead died in 1978, she was the most famous anthropologist in the world. She helped to shape our understanding of culture and how all aspects of human life were connected. While controversial, she helped ordinary people grasp cultural anthropology during the 20th century. During the latter part of her career, she wrote about modern society—and how it was changing the very way we live. My friend, Rob Hoskins, reminded me of her conclusions over lunch recently and we discussed how prophetic Mead was in her evaluation of our world. In her book, *Culture and Commitment: A Study of the Generation Gap*, Mead recognized that history has given us three distinct periods of cultural growth.

The Post-Figurative Society

For many centuries, people grew up in a post-figurative society. This period was marked by tradition. In this era, adults had already determined how life would be for their children. Not much changed. Parents and family prescribed almost everything—from who the child would marry, to where they would work, to what they would do, to how they'd continue the customs and norms of their society. For millenniums, society would simply perpetuate the customs of the past. Previous generations dictated how life would look for new generations.

Some refer to this as the Agricultural age. The primary way people made a living was out in the field, with crops and livestock. While there were trades like blacksmiths and shoe cobblers, most worked the land outdoors. The critical element that differentiated you was your muscles. It's how we got things done.

The Co-Figurative Society

As modern times emerged, nations experienced the Renaissance and Enlightenment. Humankind began to question the simple perpetuation of customs, traditions and ways of life. Gutenberg's printing press increased education levels. Reason ruled the day. This leveled the playing field for young and old. Both became involved in who the young would marry, where they'd live and what they would do vocationally. Humanity moved to a co-figurative society, when, because change was in the wind, everyone (adults and emerging adults) had to figure out life together. Everyone was getting used to new discoveries, communication and characteristics that marked their day.

During this period, which lasted for centuries, the Industrial age was born. People began to make their world more efficient. Both science and industry progressed as devices were introduced to increase proficiency. It was about speed and volume. The critical element that differentiated you was your machines. It's how we got things done.

The Pre-Figurative Society

Today, Mead suggests we are living in a pre-figurative society, where change is occurring so fast that adults have almost nothing to offer kids in terms of how to deal with new realities. In fact, the kids are figuring life out as it comes to them. Often, a young person understands the "new norm" sooner than adults do; they adapt to new technology, new patterns and paradigms that surface with the new technology and frequently march into new territory before their elders do. Sadly, this makes it difficult to lead our young, and can make us feel irrelevant as leaders. Adults can feel ill-equipped to guide children, as kids embrace the paradigm shifts more quickly than they do. Our time period is marked by innovation and adaptation.

In this period, which has only been around for decades, we entered the Information age. Not only do we enjoy mass communication from radio and television, but personal interaction through computers and portable devices. Data is everywhere because it can be produced and shared by everyone. The critical element that differentiates us is our minds. That's how most of us make our living and get things done.

But, wait. There's more.

I believe, we've only begun to taste this pre-figurative world. Over the next two decades we'll experience an astonishing transformation of our lifestyles and expectations. In fact, I believe we are now entering what we might call the Intelligence age. We not only have technology in our lives—it's now smart technology. The cell phone changed our lives, but the smart phone transformed them. Our phones have been smart for years now. Our homes are now smart, where residents can communicate remotely to set alarms, lock doors and turn on or off lights. Our cars are smart. Soon, all our appliances and toys will be smart; then, our clothes will be smart, communicating with the washer when to use hot or cold water. It will be stunning. So much so, that I believe the critical element to differentiate people is their morals. Yep, I just said that. Our world will be so full of smart technology that we must be prepared ethically and morally for the technology that will be introduced so rapidly. We must harness it. It will be easier to merely be utilitarian instead of a "Good Samaritan."

In many ways, we're "building the bridge as we cross it." Every year, new realities are introduced and the older we are, the more challenging it is to climb out of our ruts and master new habits. In her book, *People and Places: A Book for Young Readers*, Mead wrote, "In the modern world we have invented ways of speeding up invention, and people's lives change so fast that a person is born into one kind of world, grows up in another, and by the time his children are growing up, lives in still a different world."[3]

Our problem, as Kevin Kelly writes, is that "we are morphing so fast that our ability to invent new things outpaces the rate we can civilize them. These days it takes us a decade after a technology appears to develop a social consensus on what it means and what etiquette we need to tame it."[4]

Wow. Talk about the need for new maps.

The Old Maps Don't Work Anymore

Before moving on, let's pause and examine two "case studies" (both from the education sector) for why we need new maps to teach our students and young adults.

Case Study One: The Public School System

Today, we are teaching the most educated generation in American history. Perhaps, in world history. More people have graduated high school and college than any generation we've seen. It sounds cliché to say: "College is the new high school" or "Grad school is the new college" but in many ways it's true. So many have achieved extensive diplomas and degrees, you must earn one more to differentiate yourself.

Today's public school system, however, was invented by a public servant named Horace Mann over a hundred years ago. In 1837, Horace Mann served as the first Secretary for our nation's first Board of Education. His passion was to take a deteriorating set of American schools and bring them up to a modern standard. He became the leading voice for education reform during his day. Mann created a set of basic tenants he felt public schools should embrace and called those schools, "Normal Schools" because they were established to prepare kids for the "norms" of society. As his reforms began to take root, he said,

> *"Building a person's character is just as important as reading, writing and arithmetic. By instilling values such as obedience to authority, promptness in attendance and organizing time according to bell ringing prepares students for future employment."*

If you read his words closely, you can see he was about preparing children for the world they were going to graduate into—a world dominated by the Industrial Revolution. His system became the foundation to prepare youth to work in factories during the latter half of the 19th century and the first half of the 20th century.

Can you see both the "timeless" and the "timely" in his words? He spoke of the development of character in children. He talked about traits such as showing up on time and understanding authority structures. I don't know about you, but those sound like timeless virtues to me.

Notice, however, he also was timely. He spoke about "organizing time according to bell ringing" as a way to prepare kids to work in factories as adults. At the time, most factories utilized a bell or a whistle to start the workday.

Does a "bell" sound strangely familiar to you?

We continue to use them today. There's nothing inherently wrong with a "bell," but I am illustrating the fact that our current school system continues to employ elements that were designed to prepare kids for life a century ago. Factory work. I have not met one student recently whose goal is to work on an assembly line. In fact, our current school system, established in the Industrial Revolution, still reflects these times:

- They start with bells or whistles...like a factory.
- They're all about mass production...like a factory.
- The communication is one-way, pushed from the top...like a factory.

- The content is automated, identical and done in bulk…like a factory.
- The daily goal for the constituent is compliance…like a factory.
- The outcomes (products) are intended to all look alike…like a factory.

Please understand, I am not suggesting all classes or schools are like this. Nor am I suggesting that factories haven't changed in over a century. But when we stand back to look at the product we're creating, we're losing ground, compared to past generations or other systems around the world. I am also not implying any one person is at fault for this. It's the system. Administrators, staff and faculty are all victims of the current system that needs updating.

Decades later, in 1914 an educator named Frederick J. Kelly was enlisted to design a system with which our government could screen immigrants coming to America. Do you remember what was happening in 1914? World War I was ramping up in Europe.

Boatloads of immigrants were docking at Ellis Island in New York, seeking a new place to live. So many of them that Mr. Kelly was needed to help our nation quickly determine where they belonged—in school, in factories, on farms, you name it. He created an evaluation system called: The Multiple Choice Test. Ever heard of it?

From the beginning, however, Kelly acknowledged that his "test" was not a helpful method for evaluating whether someone had actually learned something. It was simply a method for quickly screening applicants to see what they'd experienced. He wrote from the start, "This is a test of lower order thinking for the lower orders."

Kelly believed, as I do, that asking students to simply circle a letter on a list doesn't reveal much about how well they have mastered a subject. On the other hand, asking them to demonstrate a behavior or a skill reveals much more about what they know. Mr. Kelly could see the truth about the test he created:

- It doesn't evaluate learning well.
- It moves toward the lowest common denominator.
- It is built off of students' fear over scores.
- It pushes for conformity among students.
- It is an information dump, favoring memorization.
- It is fast becoming obsolete.

As you well know, we continue to use the "multiple choice test" today. Years after its creation, when Kelly was a university president, he begged educators to stop using it in class to evaluate learning. But, alas, the test had been embedded into our system. It was easy to grade and teachers loved it. He was fired and both schools and universities continued perpetuating a system that was sub-optimal.

Today, our students are demanding a new map. At "Growing Leaders," we talk to thousands of college students, high school students and middle school students every year. Our student focus groups continue to reveal that kids don't think schools are relevant enough to teach or prepare them for what they want to do.

TRAVEL GUIDE:

Do you see examples of an antiquated system where you are?

Case Study Two: Colleges and Universities
In addition to our K-12 school needs, university enrollment numbers have dropped for four years in a row, from 2011 to 2015.[5] I expect numbers to continue to drop, unless we update both our subjects and our pedagogy. One student put it this way, "When a student says they don't like math or science, what they're really saying is they don't like math class or science class."

Hmmm. Well said.

Why do I believe universities need new maps as well? First, they have become cost prohibitive for many students. When I entered college in 1978, it was possible to work a summer job and pay for the fall semester's tuition. At some schools, a summer job could cover the entire year's tuition. Today, that's rare indeed. According to *Trends in Higher Education*, costs have averaged double-digit increase each year over the last three decades, much higher than the rate of inflation.[6] About seven out of ten students graduate with student debt and the average debt is $37,172 per student in 2016, up six percent from the year before. Americans owe nearly $1.3 trillion in student loan debt, now more than even our national credit card debt.[7] Millions of students are strapped after graduation. We just can't sustain this trend.

Second, traditional classes are using old maps far too often. In the summer of 2011, Harvard professor, Clayton Christensen, met with several dozen higher education leaders, faculty and entrepreneurs to discuss the future of colleges. Dr. Christensen has become well known for his theory of "disruptive innovation" and he concluded that higher education was primed for change—even reinvention. The demographics of post-secondary students are changing measurably, as is the view of adult learning. It's moving away from the notion of everyone needing to attend a four-year institution, to a pragmatic life-long learning model where adults continue re-inventing themselves as they proceed through each life station. Christensen said, "Higher education is the last major sector of the economy to be disrupted. Within ten to fifteen years, the bottom fourth of the market will either go out of business or merge."[8]

Third, career readiness has become a hot button among institutions—mainly because employers say that schools are not preparing graduates for jobs. In a 2015 survey, over twice as many students felt they were prepared for careers than what employers reported on that same survey. In fact only 29 percent of employers felt that school developed the soft skills needed for a job.[9] In another report, *Bridge That Gap: Analyzing the Student Skill Index*," only half of college students said they felt very or completely prepared for a job in their field of study. But even fewer employers—39 percent of those surveyed—said the same about the recent graduates they interviewed in the past two years.[10] In summary, even when a graduate possesses some hard skills (math, science, technology), the soft skills that enable them to collaborate with a team and compete in their industry are lacking.

Simultaneous to all of this, America is enduring a "graying" of its faculty, with Baby Boomer professors remaining in the classroom into their sixties and seventies. When they refuse to rethink their pedagogy, this can be a problem for 21st century students. The gap between the professor and the student is greater today because of the dynamics of this fast-changing world, in which our kids grew up. This year, I spoke to a student who told me she wished her instructor would utilize social media apps and on-line learning, but her professor actually still used—an overhead projector. The world and mind of the Baby Boomer professor is vastly different than his or her student today.

So what does this 21st century student look like?

Perhaps John Tyler Hammons serves as a picture of this emerging generation. John served as the 47th Mayor of Muskogee, Oklahoma, a city of nearly 40,000. He gained national attention when he was elected in 2008 at the ripe age of 19. He was a teenager. As a college student who wasn't old enough to buy a beer, Hammons served as the leader of that city for four years before enrolling at the University of Oklahoma School of Law. The picture becomes even more vivid when you realize he won 70 percent of the popular vote, running against a 70-year old man in the election. They were from two totally different generations and paradigms. John Hammons was among the youngest mayors in U.S. history, and certainly of a city that size. When asked why he ran, while still a college student, he simply replied that he felt he had some ideas that would make the city better. (That's what I find in most students I meet.)

This is what school is supposed to be about: equipping an emerging generation to take their place in history; to improve their world; to solve problems and to serve people. Horace Mann would agree. A commencement speech Mann gave two months before his death served as a clarion call for students to embrace his worldview: "I beseech you to treasure up in your hearts these my parting words: Be ashamed to die until you have won some victory for humanity."

Beginning with the End in Mind

This mindset sets the stage for the rest of the book. The path of the pioneer requires we be adaptable yet steady. Pioneers must be principled, yet entrepreneurial. Before we meet the natives in this new territory in the next chapter, and prepare to lead them, I want to ask you a question. What if we took Stephen Covey's advice and began with the end in mind? What if we started with a clean slate and asked ourselves:

Travel Guide:

If we were to start over and create a new educational system today, what would we do?

Would we launch new methods or simply repeat what we've always done?

If Horace Mann were alive today to do what he did in the 19th century—to revamp a failing school system—what kinds of changes would he make? What do you suppose he would create to prepare kids for the norms of society today? In short what would that educational pioneer do if he were guiding us today? I think that maybe, just maybe, Horace Mann would look around our educational culture and balk. Let's imagine for a moment what a pioneer like him might do. I wonder if maybe, just maybe, he'd suggest the following ideas:

1. **Experience instead of test scores as a gauge.**
   Instead of merely asking students to take a written test, I think he'd have them demonstrate behaviorally that they've mastered the subject. Experience would be the gauge, not just circling a letter on an exam.

2. **Homework during the day—not at night.**
   I think Mann would jump on board with the "flipped classroom" movement. He'd likely leverage students' predisposition to watch YouTube and put the content online. Then class time would be experiential, doing homework assignments.

3. **Open book, open notes all the time, instead of lecture—drill—test.**
   Because our world affords us the ability to look up anything online, he'd teach that skill, allowing students to use accessible content, but learn to synthesize it and offer practical, researched-based solutions.

4. **The use of images to help retention.**
   I believe Mann would readily observe how visual this new generation is and would leverage the power of images and icons to help kids retain ideas. He would agree that images are, indeed, the language of the 21st century.

5. **Creativity would be fostered over compliance.**
   Seeing that innovation is the crying need of a world full of problems and bigger than ever, he would encourage creativity in the classroom—not merely asking students to "color in the lines" and to regurgitate the lectures.

6. **Transformation of your role from "informer" to "interpreter."**
   In today's world full of information that's accessible all the time, he would see the teacher's role as a "Sherpa Guide", helping students

scale new mountains with the information they've dug up. He'd give context to all the content.

When former hockey Hall of Famer Wayne Gretsky was asked why he was so successful on the hockey rink, he replied with a phrase that's been repeated time and time again: "I don't skate to where the puck is. I skate to where the puck is going."

This is something I hope we can say as we survey the needs of our young. Can you see where the puck is going? Are you willing to look outward and move toward those needs in the future? Will you make the adjustments necessary?

- What if I told you students today are not lazy after all, they're just disengaged with the way adults teach them?
- What if I told you our kids are more ready to address the world's problems in a relevant way, but simply get stuck with our current methodology?
- What if I told you teens actually want to do something that matters, but we've only offered them virtual pastimes to occupy their days?
- What if I told you students would be less anxious and stressed out if we gave them more control of their day?

When Alexander the Great marched his men right off the map—it was new territory. It may have been land and terrain unlike any they'd seen before. You can bet, however, they looked for water in that new place. Everyone needs water, wherever they live. I am sure they looked for something edible in those new places, too. It may have been something they'd never eaten before, but they definitely needed food. The fact of the matter is, they were looking for both the foreign and the familiar; they hunted for the exciting and the essential; they sought out what was new and what was necessary.

Do you see my point? The "necessary" must always link up with the "new." This is what good pioneers always do.

Prepare yourself. We are about to formally meet the natives in the new territory.

CHAPTER 3

WHO ARE TODAY'S NEW NATIVES?

The learning characteristics of Generation Z and what we must do to connect.

The greatest gifts we can give our children are the roots of responsibility and the wings of independence.

—Denis Waitley

I wish you could meet Dylan. He is a former boyfriend of Zoe, whom we met in chapter one. He remains a family friend. Dylan's a typical teen who furnishes us with yet another picture of what's coming in the future. I'm not so sure we're ready for it.

I met Dylan last year. At 15 years old, he's a case study of a new generation, born since the turn of the century. He entered his freshman year of high school a bit nervous, but he developed a style that was scrappy and independent. He plans to "hack" his way through adolescence. He games for 3-5 hours a day, and Googles for even more hours. He is a "screen-ager," claiming his friends rarely sleep and "they game a hundred hours a week." Almost weekly, he'll binge watch a season of shows on Netflix. When I asked him what he imagined doing for a career, he told me he wants to continue his hobbies and get paid for it. After high school, he plans to do his education on-line so he can stay close to home. Maybe even at home.

When I inquired if he had a girlfriend, he said he did—but added that they haven't met in person. They met on-line. They text, Instagram and Snapchat a lot, but they attend different schools. In fact, he met most of his friends on screens, playing games or interacting on social media. Like his girlfriend, he's not met many of them face to face. Several are global friendships. When I asked why—he said he feels safer in a relationship that he can start or stop on a screen. He can walk away at any moment. Part of Dylan's uncertainty is his own identity. He's still figuring out what gender he prefers, both for himself and his companions. He's got options.

While Dylan's life is drastically different than mine at 15 years old, he's found a way to make it work—so far. But Dylan is not alone. He's part of a new generation of kids who think and feel just like him. Here are some telling statements we gathered from focus group conversations with middle school and high school students:

> *"I have a sister who went to college, and now has tons of debt and no job. I don't want to get into the situation she did. I think people lied to her about her career."*

> *"My personal life is OK, but the world is screwed up. Every time I watch the news it gets into my head. I try to block it out, but it stresses me out."*

> *"For me, life is about beating the system. And I think the system is rigged. Everything seems to be against me getting what I want."*
> *"My dad is gone; my mom is always on Facebook, from the time I get home from school until I go to bed. She has no idea what I am doing at night."*

Dylan represents a new type of person you'll need to understand if you plan to reach and teach kids in our world today. In fact, I believe Dylan and his peers are digital natives—the new natives—in our culture. In the land of tomorrow, you're the immigrant. They're the natives. They seem to intuitively understand where the world is heading, as our world deals with:

- **Ubiquitous technology**—we use it everywhere.
- **Pluralistic ideology**—we buy into almost anything.
- **Addictive pathology**—we can't cope without something.
- **Superficial theology**—we believe in nearly everything.
- **Artificial methodology**—we seek virtual answers from anywhere.

According to the Pew Research Center, students today put technology in the same category as "air and water." In short, they believe: "I must have it to survive." The same report reveals that college students would rather give up their "pinky finger" than their cell phone.[1] Wow. That's quite a trade-off, don't you think? What's more, teens interact with romantic partners "mostly digitally" and 31 percent have been the recipient of a boyfriend/girlfriend "breaking up with them in a text."[2]

A recent study conducted by Common Sense Media found that 50 percent of teens believe they are addicted to their phones, and 60 percent of surveyed parents agreed.[3] For years, we've known that students sleep with their phones. Recently, I began hearing—they're showering with their phones. Yep. They put it in a small plastic bag and place it on the soap dish, just in case they need to respond to a message.

How about ideology and theology? According to NPR, a higher number of Americans are religiously unaffiliated than at any time in recent U.S. history—and those under 30 especially seem to be drifting from organized religion. A third of young Americans say they don't belong to any religion.[4] I've found, however, they've traded in one God for many gods. They want to "feel" spiritual, so they've created a buffet—seeking something to satisfy their soul. I often hear students say, "I don't believe in religion, but I want to be a spiritual person." Today—pluralism is expanding across the landscape. It's easier to say "no" to one and enjoy a mixture of many.

Lets' talk about other addictions, which are America's most neglected diseases.[5] Addictive behavior is practically rampant. According to a Columbia University study, "Forty million young Americans over age 12 meet the clinical criteria for addiction involving nicotine, alcohol or other drugs."[6] More than 60 percent of high school students report having easy access to drugs and alcohol at school.[7] One in ten teens suffer from addictions, and a higher number experience addictive behavior. Sadly, only 1 in 20 of these addicted teens gets treatment.[8]

It's overwhelming. It's enough to put us in survival mode. We are coping with life, not conquering it or connecting with it. While our heads are often spinning, wondering where the good old days have gone, our kids lack quality leaders who understand how to be both timely and timeless. We've got to get this right.

Believe it or not, I remain optimistic about the future, and about our youngest population of emerging adults. They're savvy and social, and they represent our hope for tomorrow. But their "race of life" is full of hurdles that society has created.

If I were to summarize the hurdles, it would be with these three "A" words:

- **Anxiety**—a world full of messaging and expectations requires margins.
- **Addiction**—a world full of stimulants and options requires self-regulation.
- **Amoralism**—a world full of pluralism and tolerance requires convictions.

I'll talk at length about these issues in the chapters ahead. We will examine anxiety and amoralism in the chapter, "Storms on the Horizon" where I will offer research and suggestions on how we can respond as leaders. We're living in new territory.

New Kids on the Block

The numbers are just coming in, from studies of younger teens. Sociologists debate over what to call them as a population. Many suggest the term *iGeneration*, since they grew up in the "i" world. (For years, I've used the *iY Generation* for the same reason). Others call these kids *Homelanders*, since their generation launched about the same time as the Department of Homeland Security. They're part of a population (1) who grew up post-911, where terrorism is a huge part of the landscape, (2) who are living in the midst of a sour economy—it's all they remember, (3) who are facing the resurgence of racial unrest and (4) where uncertainty defines our culture.

For our purposes, let's call them *Generation Z* (following *Generation X* and *Y*). Many compare these kids to the *Silent Generation*, born between the *Seniors* and *Baby Boomers*. Like the *Silent Generation* who grew up during the Great Depression, war and a tough economy will likely shape them into adults marked by pragmatism and caution.

Want a summary?

According to a report from the marketing research firm Sparks and Honey, these young teens are from a smaller population who's more about coping with reality than about virtual reality, which marked the *Millennials*. For instance:

- Their movies are *Hunger Games* and *Divergent*, where youth are being slaughtered and kids no longer feel as central to the world.

- They multi-task on five screens, not one or two. They experience FOMO: Fear Of Missing Out. They try to consume it all at once.

- They have strong filters inside. Teen attention spans have gone from 12 seconds in 2000, to 6 seconds today. We'd better be engaging if we want their attention.

- They plan to get educated and start working earlier, but they will be "school hackers," and will not necessarily attend a traditional liberal arts college.

- They tend to feel "overwhelmed." They can be full of angst, living in a broken world they never unplug from—receiving 1,000 messages a day.[9]

Natives in Their Own Words

So, let's take a moment and listen to their heart. At Growing Leaders, we hosted several focus groups of students, from *Generation Z* (the *Homelanders.*) We targeted middle school and young high school students, and launched provocative conversations to see if we could catch a glimpse of what makes them tick and what motivates them to act. I thought you'd benefit from the following statements from these students, and the conclusions we drew after interviewing them:

1. I worry a lot about my future and the future of the world.

"It's hard, but I try to keep myself thinking about the positive as much as possible." —*6th grade male*

"Our generation cares about the world; not just for ourselves, but for generations to come. We don't know what could happen in the future if we don't. We want to make sure future generations have everything they need to survive." —*9th grade male*

"I'm glad we have ISIS, because without them we would be living our lives as a lie, thinking that everything else is OK when really nothing is OK." —*6th grade female*

2. I love the Internet, but I don't trust it.

"I like social media that disappears because people can stalk your pictures. It's really creepy. My brother had someone hack his Instagram account." —6th grade female

"Being careful about what you say on social media is being drilled into us all the time. We think about that a lot." —8th grade male

"I don't let people follow me online unless I know them. I get more requests from people I don't know than from people that I do know, so I keep my account private." —9th grade female

"Having your parents ask you for your password is one of the scariest things ever. My parents have no idea what's going on in my life, so when they go through my phone and see things they didn't know about, I can't handle it." —6th grade female

3. My parents are oblivious to the issues I face and what's going on in my life.

"I'm scared that one day my mom will figure out how I hid all of my social media accounts on her iPad." —6th grade female

"My mom is busy all the time, messaging her friends on Facebook and my dad's on his phone every day, catching up on the news." —10th grade male

"I got Snapchat so I could post things that my parents wouldn't be able to see. Plus, I want to keep my Snapchat streak going." —7th grade male

"My parents are mostly clueless to the stuff that's going on in my life. When they take my phone away, I just get on-line with my iPad." —9th grade female

4. I build my social status through social media. I'm addicted to my phone.

"When I get grounded, and my phone is taken away, I always give my username and password to my friends so they can login and keep up with everything going on." —9th grade male

"For five years I've slept with my phone at night. I hate to admit it, but now I shower with my phone every day." —10th grade female
"My friends and I use code names on social media to talk about our crushes in a public space. I don't think I could live without my phone." —9th grade female

"If my friends post something on-line and it doesn't get enough "likes" they take it down fast. It's our social report card." —10th grade male and female

---

TRAVEL GUIDE:

How will you reach Generation Z?

REALITIES THAT SHAPED THEM AS KIDS

1. Terrorism
Memories are post-9/11 and terrorism has always been a central issue.

2. Recession
Their memories surround a sour economy and unemployment.

3. Racial Unrest
Riots and demonstrations are common, declaring minorities matter.

4. Global Competition
Due to today's global economy they battle internationals for jobs.

5. Social Media
Information is ubiquitous. This is the first generation that doesn't need adults to get it.

6. Complexity and Uncertainty
Simplicity is replaced with clutter, noise and activity.

7. Social and Ideological Pluralism
Relationships and beliefs are mixed and blended.

Contrasting Generation Y and Generation Z

Do you remember Matt, Zoe and Savannah from chapter one? Matt is from Generation Y. Zoe and Savannah, although different, are both from Generation Z. While they're all growing up in the same home, with the same parents, they're not the same nor do they see life the same way. Generation Z possesses some unique characteristics.

In many ways, we need to stop assuming they'll simply be extensions of Generation Y (or the Millennials). They're the younger counterparts and are growing up with new realities that make them different.

While Generation Y grew up with computers and iPods, Generation Z is growing up with touch-screens and social media. Their phones have always been "smart." Bill Clinton is a president from history, and Madonna is an aged veteran…like Elton John or Michael Jackson. Transgender is a growing reality. And a business tycoon and reality TV star like Donald Trump can become president. We live in a new day. Based on research from Growing Leaders and Sparks & Honey, here is the contrast:

The shifts this new generation will bring…

- While Generation Y grew up with a strong economy and self-esteem, Generation Z grows up in a time of recession, terrorism, racial violence, volatility, and complexity.

- While Generation Y subscribed to everything social, Generation Z doesn't want to be tracked, preferring Snapchat or Whisper to send a message that evaporates.

- While Generation Y watched YouTube, Hulu, and Netflix, Generation Z wants to co-create, live stream and help to make up the activity as they participate.

- While Generation Y loves sports and adventure, Gen Z sees sports as a tool or a trade, not for play. Their games are inside, not outside. Teen obesity has tripled since 1970.[10]

- While Generation Y initiated text messages as a norm, Generation Z initiated communication through images, icons and symbols, even instant messaging.

- While Generation Y worried about their growing social status and their "likes" on social media, Generation Z worries about the economy and world ecology.

TERMS THAT SUMMARIZE THEM

- **Instant Access**
  They have a Google reflex, and can find answers now. No waiting.)

- **New Normal**
  They grew up with terrorism, recession, and other common hardships.

- **On Demand**
  They expect entertainment when they want it and they can't stand boredom.

- **Multi-Cultural**
  They're a mix of ethnic races; 50 percent increase in this identity since 2000.[11]

- **Immediate Feedback**
  They insist on responses from social media, games or friends.

- **Constant Contact**
  They're always connected, with few margins for solitude or silence.

- **Blended Family**
  They are used to new definitions of family, identity and sexuality.

- **Anything Goes**
  They grew up at a time when traditional morals are in question.

THE EVOLUTION ON THE HORIZON

We clearly live in a time of transition. It may just be we'll feel this way our entire lives. Certainly, our children will. One the next page is the evolution I see coming as I study demographics and culture. Based on reports by the *Monthly Labor Review*, *The Futurist* and *World Population Prospects*, 2012 U.N. edition, Generation Z will display a move from today's to tomorrow's reality[12]:

Millennials or Gen Y (1983-2000)	Homelanders or Gen Z (2001-2018)
1. Use technology for entertainment	1. Will use technology to learn
2. Competes with 80 million for jobs	2. Will compete with 172 million for jobs
3. Have 2-4 siblings	3. Will likely have 0-2 siblings
4. Share the planet with 7.5 billion	4. Will share the planet with 11 billion
5. Largest population is peers	5. Largest population will be older
6. Growing problem with obesity	6. Gigantic problem with obesity
7. Communicates with text	7. Communicates with images
8. Shares things	8. Creates things
9. Multi-tasks with two screens	9. Multi-tasks with five screens
10. Confident and self-absorbed	10. Cautious and self-directed
11. Focuses on today	11. Focuses on the future
12. Optimists	12. Realists

> For a helpful list of paradoxes Generation Z is facing, consult your Travel Guide.

I spoke to Dylan recently—and one reality came to light immediately. Due to his preference for screens when interacting with others, and the overwhelming amount of emotionally charged information he's exposed to as a teen, he's not developed the interpersonal skills to dialogue face to face with others, especially when the topic is controversial. Dylan told me he had just "blocked" several of his "friends" from messaging him after a heated argument over a recent decision by President Trump. He wasn't emotionally intelligent enough to discuss or debate the topic in a civil manner. And may I add—neither are millions of others.

One of the hottest issues for educators today is "civic readiness." When you combine a student population who's not been conditioned to host conversations in person, with a culture that's divided over police brutality, gender equality issues, illegal immigration, same-sex attraction, transgender bathrooms and a presidential election that split a nation more than any in recent memory—you have a recipe for social disaster. Minimally we have a challenge on our hands when it comes to educating our young to be civic ready. I am not sure we were ready for this.

TRAVEL GUIDE:

How are you equipping the young to navigate these changes?

SEVEN MAJOR SHIFTS AS GENERATION Y BECOMES GENERATION Z

At this point, let me summarize much of the information I've offered in this chapter. It appears at this junction in history, there are at least seven significant shifts taking place among our youth. Get ready. We'll soon be reading more and more about this next generation of kids emerging from among the American population. Our work with them demonstrates a "morphing" among the population, shifting away from old realities and into new ones. Here's what we've found:

1. **Confidence is morphing into caution.**
   A kid who grew up between 1990 and 2000 had a very different experience than a kid who grew up between 2005 and 2015. In the 1990s, America's economy was expanding, the Dot.com era was birthed, clean-cut boy bands hit the pop charts, and soccer mom's became a voting demographic. In contrast, the last ten years offered an economic recession, daily terrorism headlines, racial unrest, an increase in gender confusion, healthcare headaches, unemployment and the debt soared. The average student has a different reality today.

2. **Idealism is morphing into pragmatism.**
   Ten years ago, Generation Y reported it was very common for them to get anything they wanted—the new iPhone, Abercrombie and Fitch jeans, a tablet, a tattoo or piercing. Today, money is a bit tighter and there's been an increase in multi-generational households[13]; people having to share space and resources. Slowly, millions of adolescents

have shifted into a world that is not about them. Many are forced to think practically and to think ahead. Optimism can become cynicism.

3. **Attacking an education is morphing into hacking one.**

As Generation Y graduated from high school, it was the norm to apply to multiple universities in hot pursuit of a liberal arts education. Parents told them: "If you're going to be successful, you have to go to college." Today, more and more grads don't assume this to be true. They will "hack" their way through their preparation for a career, mixing free Ivy League school classes with on-line certificates and real world experience. Kids see their older siblings paralyzed by debt and they don't want it.

4. **Spending money is morphing into saving money.**

According to a report from marketing firm, Sparks and Honey, these younger teens are not spending money as quickly as their twenty-something brother or sister. While the average Gen Z kid has $16.90 a week to spend, they often don't spend it right way.[14] While Generation Y spent money boldly and with few boundaries, 57 percent of Generation Z prefers saving money to spending it.[15] Once again, they're reality forces them to think ahead and prepare. This could be a good thing.

5. **Consuming media is morphing into creating media.**

Generation Y popularized the practice of spending hours watching YouTube videos, television shows on Hulu or movies on Netflix. While young teens still do that, they prefer to create or "curate" the media, not just consume it. They desire interactive experiences where they participate in the video's outcome. They love making the content. Three out of four wish their current hobby could become their full-time job.[16] That's far more than Millennials reported when asked about it.

6. **Viral messages on social media are morphing into vanishing messages.**

The scorecard is slowly changing for kids today. As social media tools like Twitter, Facebook and Instagram launched, students kept score on

"Likes," "Shares," and "Views." Younger kids have seen the downside of being tracked on social media by future employers, parents and teachers, and now prefer messaging that evaporates, like Snapchat, Whisper, and Secret. (At least it seems to evaporate). The digital footprint is seen as a potential danger that can be used against you.

7. **Text messaging is morphing into iconic messaging.**
As our world becomes more complex and uncertain, Generation Z intuitively wants to simplify communication. Instead of sending text messages, their messages are morphing into images, symbols and icons. Many now send emojis instead of words. They have strong filters and want content to be shared and understood rapidly. While Generation Y grew up with slightly longer attention spans, Generation Z has an attention span of 6-8 seconds. Approximately 11 percent have ADHD.[17]

Travel Guide:

How can we help them step out, take risks and show bravery?

How can we help them see the bright side of things and stay hopeful?

How can we aid them to sort out goals and find the right educational path?

How can we affirm the idea of saving money and planning ahead?

How can we foster their creative gifts and monetize them in their career?

How can we help them see the power of sending constructive messages?

How can we utilize metaphors and images to communicate with them?

Connecting with These New Natives

I'd like to take the remainder of this chapter and talk about how we should lead these future adults. In the following chapters, we'll continue to unpack who they are and the world they'll lead as time marches on. For now, however, I am sure you're pondering just how to make a connection with them since they're growing up in a different world than we did. Let's start with some researched-based ideas.

To connect with Generation Z, we should:

1. **Keep it short.**

   Remember, they have strong filters and short attention spans. They can binge watch Netflix for hours, so they can pay attention to a long stint of content. The key is to engage them within six seconds. That's how much time we have for them to make up their minds about engaging with us.

2. **Make it visual.**

   They are visual learners. Images are the language of the 21st century. Among teens, Instagram is the fastest growing social media tool. In short, pictures beat words. This means we'd do well to anchor our big idea with a metaphor, or better yet, with an actual image or visual on a screen.

3. **Feed curiosity.**

   Whet their appetites. They want to discover new content and pass it on. Build a hunger for interesting facts, and relay why some are important to know. The numbers tell us they're naturally curious, consuming Buzzfeed and all sorts of daily data. Feed it and channel it in a positive direction.

4. **Give them ownership.**

   Students support what they help create. Help them own the message. Don't do the work of learning for them. Once they're curious, let them dig and find. They'll value something they've discovered more than what's given to them without effort. Push them to be creators, not consumers.

5. Make it interactive.

They love connecting socially. Place them in small communities to talk. They are an "upload" generation who wants to talk, create and offer their opinion. So let them. While it takes longer to teach something with interaction, it sticks longer as well. If you want retention, foster interaction.

6. Gamify your content.

Make your message an interactive game with quests, points and badges. A huge percentage of Generation Z is gaming in some way. Try utilizing points, competition and achieving badges (with or without technology) to position them in their natural habitat. Learning has gone from Gutenberg to games.

7. Offer a cause.

Most kids want to do something very important and almost impossible. This has always been true for adolescents. They have a natural bent for risks as their teen brain (the frontal lobe) develops. Why not use this for redemptive purposes? Give them something meaningful, not hypothetical, to pursue.

Can we learn to speak their language? The Latin root word for "educate" is "ducere" which means to "push out." We've seen learning as something we do to students, not something they do for themselves. The key is—learning is not something done "to" someone. It is something they choose to do. We should not put students in a passive mode as we teach. We must be inspirers of learning. We must help pull ambition out of them, not push information into them.

Think "pull" not "push."

Get ready. This is only the beginning. Generation Z makes up the youngest kids getting measured today. Sixty-six percent of 6-11 year olds list "gaming" as their top source of entertainment, and fifty-one percent of male teens say it is their number one source of entertainment.[18] In fact, among our youngest generation in the U.S. they often see outside sports as a health tool, not as something you do for play. More of them are inside, not outside, and they are multi-tasking on five screens.

I believe video game scholarships will pop up all over the world soon. Schools will find ways to use them for educational and redemptive purposes. I know, I know. It seems so unreal. But this is the emerging world our kids live in and embrace. What they need are "pioneers" like us who'll march off the map and leverage all of this to equip them for life. It will be key for educators (and other caring adults) to capitalize on today's realities in order to teach our students.

Allow me to illustrate.

If you were to drive by Conner Middle School in Cincinnati, you'd see a picture of what I'm talking about. If you happened to look up as you passed by, you might just see students…on the roof of the school. Yep, you read that right.

In 2016, seventh graders began tending to homemade beehives, as a project-based-learning assignment that year. Why, you ask? It all began when teacher Julia Hansel recognized she needed to engage her students differently than the traditional methods most schools use. So, she launched into a project called "A Plea for Bees." She began by showing her students all kinds of foods that honey bees pollinate, amounting to about a third of what we eat. She then unveiled the fact that bees were suffering from CCD (Colony Collapse Disorder). This prevented them from playing their role in nature. Hansel said bees are a critical link in U.S. agriculture.

In response, the students first decided they would write letters to their community informing them of this problem and disclosing what they planned to do to help solve it. They then measured the rooftop, recorded temperatures, noted locations of sunshine and shade, and built scale models of a new hive for the bees.

The beauty of the project is—it utilized multiple subjects, including math, science, engineering, art, writing, social studies and more. Like real life, the project-based learning didn't segregate these subjects, but integrated them.

The project is just the beginning, however. The students also created picture books telling the story of the bee problem and how everyone can do something to help. They're now sharing them with elementary school students. Julia Hansel has created a win/win/win situation: the students win, the bees win and the community at large wins. She concluded, "It's gratifying to see what the students can do. To see them work together, be creative, ask questions. Empowering the student is my favorite thing."[19]

As it should be.

TRAVEL GUIDE:

How do you pioneer new territory by engaging students in real problems?

EIGHT SHIFTS WE MUST MAKE TO LEAD THEM WELL

May I talk straight? We have to change our minds about how to lead these kids. In my book, *12 Huge Mistakes Parents Can Avoid*, I offer a list of shifts adults must make to lead kids well. Let me suggest some of those shifts here:

1. **Don't think CONTROL, think CONNECT.**

   Too often, our ambition as a parent, professional or teacher is to seize control. We want to govern every action and direct each step kids take. Studies show that parents who over-program their child's schedule often breed kids who rebel as teens. Why? They never got to truly be a child. Let me remind you: control is a myth. None of us are actually "in control." Instead, good leaders work to connect with the next generation. Why? Because once we connect, we build a bridge of relationship that can bear the weight of truth. We earn our right to genuinely influence them.

2. **Don't think INFORM, think INTERPRET.**

   May I remind you—today's young people are the first generation that don't need adults to get information. It's coming at them twenty-four hours a day. What they need from us is interpretation. Their knowledge has no context. Adults must help them make sense of all they know; to help them interpret experiences, relationships, work and faith via a wise, balanced lens. Discuss together what's behind movie plots, books, and technology. Teach them how to think.

3. **Don't think WHAT, think WHY.**

   Students today have been told what to do, by all the adults in their lives since day one. Authors Art Levine and Diane Dean say they've become addicted to an adult checklist. We told them what to do 24/7. I believe the need of the hour is to tell them "why" something is important to do. When we explain why, we get engagement at a deeper level. We grab their hearts not just their heads or hands because now they have motivation for doing the "what."

4. Don't think "DO IT FOR THEM," think "HELP THEM DO IT."

Adults have been committed to giving kids a strong self-esteem for thirty years now. We wrongly assumed, however, it would come from simply telling them they're special and awesome. According to the American Psychological Association, healthy and robust self-esteem actually comes from achievement, not merely affirmation. In our attempt to protect them, we've actually created a new "at risk" child: middle class and affluent kids who are depressed because they didn't really do anything to earn the trophy. Sure it's quicker to do it yourself—but it's better to transfer a skill.

5. Don't think IMPOSE, think EXPOSE.

When adults become scared their kids are falling behind, we tend to impose a rule or a behavior on them. While mandatory conduct is part of life, it carries negative baggage with it. When students feel forced to do it, they often don't take ownership of it; it's your idea, not theirs. Why not think "expose" instead of "impose." Give them an opportunity they can't pass up. Make it enticing. They then participate because they want to, not because they have to. It feels like motivation, not manipulation.

6. Don't think PRESCRIPTIVE, think DESCRIPTIVE.

So many kids today have had everything mapped out for them by an adult. Recitals, practices, playground time, lessons, phone games and the list could go on and on. Even Lego sets now have diagrams of what to build and how to build it. We're removing the need for kids to use their own imagination and creativity. Instead of prescribing what they should do next, try "describing." Describe an outcome or goal, and let them figure out how to reach it with their own ingenuity.

7. Don't think COOL, think REAL.

So many adults—from parents, to teachers, to youth pastors—try so hard to be "hip" and emulate what kids are doing. They think that if they can just be like the kids, they will be "liked" by the kids. In reality, grown adults can rarely pull this off without being laughable. No doubt we want to be relevant with our style, but students do not look to us to be cool. They need us to be authentic. Learn to laugh at yourself. Be self-aware. Genuinely listen. Speak in a conversational tone that's believable. The only thing worse than being un-cool is being unreal.

8. **Don't think LECTURE, think LAB.**

When our young people do wrong, the first thing we usually want to do is lecture them. It's the quickest way to transmit an idea, but it's not the best way to transform a life. Just like science class, kids need a lecture AND a lab to learn. We must create environments and experiences from which we can process ideas. There are life lessons to be found everywhere—trips, meals with influential people, service projects. The lab is where head knowledge is transformed into understanding. More on this in chapter 7.

WE GOTTA BELIEVE…

In the end, it is easy to draw the wrong conclusions about the potential of kids like Matt, Zoe, Savannah and Dylan. Since they're so different, we don't understand them. Since we don't understand them, we tend to assume the worst. Today's kids need adults to believe in them. For over a decade now, we've been whining about what a lazy bunch of entitled slackers they are. These naïve "screen-agers" are unready for life and work, and will likely "boomerang" home just like their older brother did.

But what if we believed in them?

Thomas Edison told the story of how he became such an incredible inventor. It's a powerful illustration of belief and a bit emotional for me to retell his story.

When young Tom returned home from school one day, his mother noticed he had a piece of paper in his hand. He told her it was a note from his teacher and she was the only one who was supposed to read it. When she did, she grew tearful. When the boy asked what it said, his mom replied, "Your son is a genius. This school is too small for him and doesn't have enough good teachers to train him. Please teach him yourself."

From then on, Edison's mom removed him from school and he was self-taught. She allowed him to curiously pursue what interested him and to devour it. Years later, after his mom died, Edison was rummaging through her belongings, and came across that note from his teacher. When he read it, he was stunned. It read, "Your son is addled (mentally ill). We won't let him come to school anymore. We don't have the teachers to handle him. You'll have to teach him yourself."

Edison wept and wept for hours, and since that time, gave his mother credit for cultivating his genius as an inventor. She saw something others didn't in her boy. What she read and what that note said ultimately led to the same result—Tom Edison had to learn at home. But what was behind it meant everything to that kid. Someone had believed in him.

Who knows? There may just be another Thomas Edison near you.

CHAPTER 4

WHAT ARE THE LANDMARKS ON THE NEW MAP?

Six shifts in today's culture and ideas we must leverage to make progress.

Do not confuse motion with progress. A rocking horse keeps moving but does not make any progress.

—Alfred A. Montapert

Have you ever seen a police detective movie, where a cop is standing behind a wall, at the corner of a building with a gun? As he ponders his next move, he pulls out a mirror he can hold out at arms' length in order to see what's around the corner. With this mirror, he can spot the offender he's chasing or any other dangers that may be lurking. That little mirror always plays a role in the detective apprehending his man.

This is a picture of what I'd like to do for you in this chapter.

On the heels of the first few chapters, I hope to share with you a "mirror" that will enable you to see what's around the corner. I want to help you spot some realities before we turn the corner and face them. I'll do my best to allow you to recognize the landmarks in this new territory we're about to tread upon. I'd like us to peer into the future. As one might expect, marching into new terrain means we'll spot new landmarks— new rivers, hills, valleys, lakes and plains. We'll want to get acquainted with this new land, since we'll be spending our future there.

TOMORROWLAND

Walt Disney and his team opened Disneyland in 1955. One import-ant territory in his theme park is "Tomorrowland." You've likely visited it. Inside, Walt attempted to enable guests to peer into the future and wonder with him what life might look like fifty to a hundred years from now. At the risk of sounding pithy, you and I are walking into a very real Tomorrowland . . . today. It feels strange, at least to us. In fact, it feels like we're marching off the known maps we created. We don't seem to "get" what's coming. Case in point. In 2006, CNN listed Mark Zuckerberg on the list of *10 People Who Don't Matter*. In 2004, Bill Gates said: "Two years from now, spam will be solved." And in 1997, Nathan Myhrvold, former Microsoft CTO, said: "Apple is already dead." Twenty years earlier, Ken Olsen, the founder of Digital Equipment Corporation said, "There's no reason anyone would want a computer in their home."

Yep. We are immigrants just getting acquainted with this new world.

What makes this task extra challenging is—millions of us are aging. Measurably. About three in ten Americans working today are Baby Boomers. Another third of workers are from Generation X.[1] As Millennials and Generation Z (the ones I call Generation iY) continue to make up the majority of the workforce, the leaders feel a gap. It's not just a generation gap, but a communication gap and a motivation gap. In their book, *Generation on a Tightrope*, Art Levine and Diane Dean tell us "50 percent of college professors are uncomfortable with their students."[2]

Why? We're different ages, we speak differently and are motivated differently. Consequently, the mirror is reflecting big adjustments that we need to make if we're serious about reaching this new generation.

Are you ready?

The young people we met early in this book—Matt, Zoe, Savannah and Dylan—will all become adults in a very, very different world than the one I entered as a young adult. In 2015, 72 percent of adults in America owned a smartphone, a thing that didn't even exist 10 years ago.[3] This is like 1960's science fiction.

Most unskilled, repetitive labor, as much as 47 percent of all current employment, will be almost completely automated.[4] This would include drivers, factory workers, food prep, custodians, and the like. Think Tesla, think Smart devices. So our kids may have jobs that look nothing like the ones we did as we entered our careers.

Artificial General Intelligence, as I suggested earlier, will be the norm. Computers that think and learn at the human level and sometimes beyond the human brain will be the norm. They can be programed to compute and problem solve ethically. So our kids may need to develop skills that no artificially intelligent computer can do.

Completely artificial brain maps and cognitive function of simpler organisms, possibly up to the level of mice can be uploaded into auto-mated, mechanical avatars. This opens up a scary, even immoral world that outsources human acts, including sex robots. So, our kids must adopt a moral compass to determine what's amoral and what's immoral.

My friend Chris Arias says, "Strangely, the world seems to be growing both more charitable and more selfish at the same time. I have a lot of faith that our children's generation has the potential rise to the unimaginable challenges that lie ahead. But at this fascinating crossroads in human history there's also a sense that a traditional worldview and ethic will come under increasing assault in the western world."

Once again, I ask: are we preparing our kids for this new world? As time marches on, *Generation iY* is reaching adulthood, and the youth from Generation Z are emerging with their own identity and are taking the spotlight.

Some social scientists who've chosen to study this new population of kids suggest that Generation Z began in 1995. Fortunately, this doesn't produce a significantly different sampling of results than those of us who believe Generation Z began around the turn of the 21st century. The reasons I choose 2001 as the beginning point for this emerging generation are the tangible markers from that period:

- We had entered a new century and millennium.
- We experienced the largest terrorist attack on our soil.
- We began hearing of corporate scandals: Enron, Tyco, Worldcom, etc.
- The economy began to shift downward, in both business and real estate.
- Trust in government had waned measurably after two presidential scandals.
- A war in the Persian Gulf began that has continued their entire lives.
- Social media began playing a role in shaping our very persona and identity.
- TSA and the Department of Homeland Security nudged us to focus on safety.

Down through the last century, each new generation began with tangible cultural shifts. For instance, the Builder Generation started with the Great Depression. The Baby Boomers launched with post-World War II expansion. The Gen Xers began in tandem with the birth control era. You get the idea. There are usually markers that signal a new paradigm, a new population and, hence, a new generation. Each one grows up with shared tragedies, music, TV shows, heroes, celebrities, fashions, technology, memories, etc. I believe the markers I've listed above signal a new paradigm in our society; fear plays a larger role in our decisions and perhaps has even led parents to choose having careers over having kids. The population of Generation Z is down. So, let's find out just why these kids think the way they do, based on today's culture.

DEFINING CHARACTERISTICS OF TODAY'S KIDS

They grew up in a day where not only the World Wide Web prevails, but social media does as well. Their country has been at war their entire lives. They've only seen two presidents in office the first sixteen years of their generation. They grew up in the shadows of the Columbine High School massacre, the September 11th terrorist attacks, the Dot.com bubble bursting and the economy crashing. The world is a scary place—almost every day and almost anywhere you go. They've seen movie cinema shootings, Boston Marathon bombings and school massacres. It's just life.

To date, they've yet to witness a thriving economy, so most don't have a naïve worldview on how easy life should be—as their Millennial siblings did. When they started driving, they likely never used a printed map, but a GPS on their smart phone. In fact, most don't remember a day without a smart phone. Norms around marriage and society are changing. They'll be the first adults to grow up in a truly diverse culture in America where, as adults, there will be a more equal blend of ethnicities in their communities and work places.

So just what kind of child is today's society producing? How do we summarize the characteristics that make up the bump part of the bell curve on these young people?

Here are some characteristics of Generation Z:

Realistic

While the students I meet are fairly happy and well-adjusted, they're not giddy like so many were in the 90's. They tend to be more realistic than idealistic. They've become jaded from the tough economy, terrorism and complexities of life. Some observe them as cynical. Can you blame them? They're over the "everyone gets a participation trophy." One study showed they are the least likely generation to believe in the American Dream, and over 80 percent of Generation Z students are concerned about both the cost of living and the cost of college.[5]

Private

For them, Snapchat and Whispr have taken over Facebook. While Millennials loved all things social, Generation Z watched their older siblings get in trouble from posting controversial content on social media sites, and now they don't want to be tracked. Can you blame them? Apps with disappearing content (like Whispr or Snapchat) have seen explosive growth, while Facebook lost 25 percent of this demographic since 2011.[6] Despite their random posts on social media, many are secretly guarding themselves from trackers, hackers and stalkers. Parents have warned them to not give out their information to anyone they don't know.

Entrepreneurial

Current statistics reveal that 72 percent of current high school students want to start a business.[7] They may just be hackers not slackers. Do it yourself. Be your own boss. Maybe try several gigs. This is the first generation of kids who can get noticed without an agent and/or launch a business cheaply without a sponsor. We've gone from blue-collar and white-collar workforces—to a no-collar workforce. They may just start a company or invent an electronic game, wearing a t-shirt at home. Instead of worrying about a publisher liking their manuscript or a record label liking their music—they can simply post a blog or a song on YouTube and watch others recognize their talent. No middleman. No coat and tie. No business cards.

Multi-tasking

More than one study reveals that Generation Z prefers to multi-task with five screens, not two.[8] This is up from the results of Millennial generation studies. As I've mentioned, they experience FOMO (Fear Of Missing Out). In fact, according to Seemiller and Grace, "interactivity is replacing physical activity."[9] Consider Generation Z's access to the web. One survey found that 100 percent of all Gen Z students indicate being on-line at least one hour per day, and nearly three-quarters within one hour of waking up. They rapidly move from one attraction to another.[10]

Open-minded

Consider what's been in the news as they've matured: transgender issues, child poverty, and hate crimes in various places. Open-mindedness is the ability to consider new perspectives and ideas, and it's a reoccurring theme in this generation. Research from Corey Seemiller and Meghan Grace, shows that 70 percent of Generation Z students in the study see themselves as "open-minded". Further, 73 percent describe themselves as compassionate. Given they're from the most diverse generation in history and have access to all kinds of social media viewpoints, it makes sense.[11]

Hyper-aware

These students are constantly racing through their newsfeeds on mobile devices, while juggling emoji-filled conversations and writing tomorrow's English paper. They are hyper-aware of what's on their screens; some call it 4-D Thinking. It's more than three-dimensional. They are used to diversions—but can keep a conversation going while simultaneously tending to four other tasks. If you think they're not good at creating, just watch as they do all their curating. They can synthesize images and content quickly, not realizing that if the task is for school, we'd call it plagiarism.

Overwhelmed

According to Dr. Michael Leahy, "Today's typical high school student endures the same anxiety levels as a psychiatric patient did in the early 1950s." In any given year, about one in five will experience an anxiety attack.[12] Why? Their world is overwhelming, cluttered with information coming at them at the rate of a thousand messages a day. I believe they are overwhelmed because they are over-connected. In addition, however, they feel the pressure to make the grade, make the team, make the cut, and eventually make the money. Even a multi-tasker is maxed out. They're savvy on so many issues because no one wants to be a loser or miss out.

Technology reliant

I noted this in chapter 2, but it bears repeating. The Pew Research Center reports, "Students put technology in the same category as air and water." Their phone or tablet acts as a lifeline to the world around them. They have a tough time imagining a world without this technological umbilical cord. In 2011, 38 percent of children under 8-years old had ever used a mobile device. By 2013, that number had climbed to 72 percent, according to Common Sense Media (just 28 percent never used one). That's a measurable jump. Today, 9 of 10 preschoolers have been on-line.[13]

Upon reviewing the characteristics we've gathered from research, it's easy to see that these defining qualities are a trade-off. Some good, some not so good. If these statistics are accurate, we're safe to describe the bulk of this new generation as:

- Down-to-earth
- Distracted
- Distressed
- Discerning
- Determined

We definitely have a new kind of adolescent to prepare for adulthood.

How Will They Look as They Enter Adulthood?

Whenever I write on the topic of the emerging generation, (I've now seen four in my career), I like to include a chart. In it, I attempt to help people see how the newest population of kids compares and contrasts with past generations. We are living at a time in modern history when there are six distinct sociological generations living at the same time. Because people are living longer and we're still giving birth to babies, we can see six varying mindsets—or paradigms—as each generation launched their careers.

Five of these generations are influencing the world today, and I've included them in the chart on the next page. Observe the categories (the issues) down the left-hand column and notice how each new generation reacts to the previous generation, upon entering adulthood and their career:

	Builders Silent Generation	Boomers Pig in Python Gen
Birth years	1929-1945	1946-1964
Life paradigm	Be grateful you have a job	You owe me
Attitude to authority	Endure them	Replace them
Role of relationships	Significant	Limited; useful
Value systems	Conservative	Self-based
Role of career	Means for living	Central focus
Schedules	Mellow	Frantic
Technology	Hope to outlive it	Master it
Market	Goods	Services
View of future	Seek to stabilize	Create it!

| Busters | Millennials | Centennials |
Generation X	Generation Y	Generation Z
1965-1982	1983-2000	2001-2018
Relate to me	Life is a cafeteria	I'm coping and hoping
Ignore them	Choose them	Do it yourself
Central; caring	Global	Utilitarian
Media	Shop around	Pragmatic
Irritant	Place to serve	It's my hobby
Aimless	Volatile	Multi-tasking on 5 screens
Employ it	Enjoy it	Hacker
Experiences	Transformations	Reinvent me
Skeptical	YOLO	FOMO

I'd like you to notice something intriguing.

In the chart on the previous page, can you see a pendulum swinging back and forth, as each generation becomes adults? The Builders, (marked by the Great Depression) were more cautious than the preceding generation. After them, the pendulum swung back with the Baby Boomers, born post-World War II. It was a confident generation again. Generation X followed the Boomers. Their alias was "Baby Buster," because their population launched with the birth control pill. Instead of a "boom" it was a "bust." It was another cautious generation. Then came the Millennials (or Generation Y following X), who were large and in charge—yet another confident generation. Today, Generation Z (Centennials) is once again more cautious and savvy to a world that's broken and complex.

Consultant Don Tapscott is a Gen Z optimist. His 2008 book, *Grown Up Digital*, features a study of 11,000 kids who were asked whether they'd rather be smarter or better looking: 69 percent chose "smarter."[14] Social researcher Mark McCrindle, of Sydney-based McCrindle Research is also an optimist. He's been looking at Gen Z for seven years. "They are the most connected, educated and sophisticated generation in history," he says. "They don't just represent the future, they are creating it."[15]

TRAVEL GUIDE:

How can you leverage these realities to equip the young for life?

PYRAMIDS AND RECTANGLES

Let's step back for a moment, and peer at the big picture. You are likely reading this book because you care about kids—as students, as athletes, as employees and even more, as your own children or grandchildren.

While few adolescents take the time to read and care about demographics in their society, they are always affected by them, if only indirectly. Each of us grew up in a world that due to the sheer size of our contemporaries, affected how we interacted with that world. If you are part of a larger generation, for instance, you might feel a bit more confident, as you and your cohorts received more attention from vendors, marketers, and product designers. If you're part of a smaller population, you tend to be more aware of a world that's larger than you; that you're not the center of it all.

So, let's talk about our population as pyramids and rectangles.

Down through history, a nation's population usually looks like a pyramid. With the young at the bottom, the size of the children's population is larger than the adult population because people start dying in mid-life, then in their 50's, then 60's, then 70's and so forth. You get the idea. The populations looked like this:

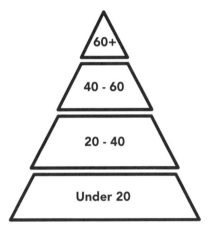

Today, with people living longer and fewer having babies, our population now looks more like a rectangle than a pyramid. In fact, when we look more closely, we appear to be an hourglass. Larger at the bottom (Millennials are about 80 million strong), smaller in the middle (Generation X is about 47 million strong), then larger at the top, as the Baby Boomers become the seasoned elders (with 76 million strong) and about 10,000 retiring every day. The current population looks more like the chart on the next page:

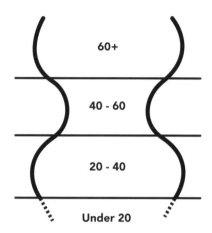

Paul Taylor, from the Pew Research Center, writes, "In every society since the start of history, whenever you broke down any population this way, you'd always get a pyramid. But from 1960 to 2060, our pyramid will turn into a rectangle. We'll have almost as many Americans over age 85 as under age 5. This is the result of longer life spans and lower birthrates. It's uncharted territory, not just for us, but for all of humanity. And while it's certainly good news over the long haul for the sustainability of the earth's resources, it will create political and economic stress in the shorter term, as smaller cohorts of working age adults will be hard-pressed to finance the retirements of larger cohorts of older ones."[16]

Let's look even more closely.

Two Hills and Two Valleys

Over the last couple of years, I have illustrated our opportunities and challenges in America, as "Two Hills and Two Valleys." By this I mean, if you look at the various generations horizontally, you find a large "hill" among the Baby Boomer population, since they number about 76 million people. Then, you find a "valley," as Generation X represented a smaller population, about 46-47 million. Next, the Millennials came along, as another "hill." They're the largest generation in U.S. history, at 80 million strong. Finally, Generation Z symbolizes another "valley," at about 59 million.

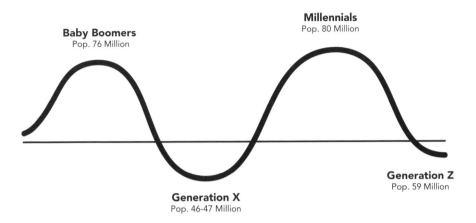

Baby Boomers
Pop. 76 Million

Millennials
Pop. 80 Million

Generation Z
Pop. 59 Million

Generation X
Pop. 46-47 Million

Pause and reflect for a moment. This has ramifications on social security and retirement. As I've mentioned, thousands of Baby Boomers retire each day in America. They will leave leadership positions needing to be filled. Even if everyone in Generation X were a brilliant leader, there would not be enough of them to fill the vacancies left by the Boomers. The young adults among the Millennial generation will be needed for leadership, ready or not. I say, let's get them ready.

In addition, millions of these Baby Boomers are expecting a social security check and too many are unprepared for retirement without the help of government checks. While the Millennials are beginning to work, too many are unemployed or underemployed, and, at least for now, cannot contribute enough to the system. Following them, Generation Z is much smaller—and cannot sustain the economic needs that the Boomers, Xers and Millennials will expect as they retire.

The future is something we need to help them think about and prepare for. Our kids will be required to ponder and plan for the future far better than the Millennials have been able to do so far. While the information coming at them every second screams at them to pay attention in the moment—we will need to help them plan for a future we can only imagine. Perhaps cultural anthropologist Margaret Mead said it best:

"We are now at a point where we must educate our children in what no one knew yesterday, and prepare our schools for what no one knows yet."

My questions are—Can we talk to students about the future in a way that's hopeful and doesn't overwhelm them? Can we help them out without stressing them out? Can we coach them, but not constrain them? Can we obsess over preparing them and not just protecting them? Can we equip them to do what we neglected to do ourselves?

Again, Paul Taylor adds, "Today's Millennials—well-educated, tech savvy, and underemployed—are at risk of becoming the first generation in American history to have a lower standard of living than their parents. Meanwhile, about 10,000 Baby Boomers are retiring every single day, many of them not as well-prepared financially as they'd hoped. The graying of our population will put stresses on our social safety net and present our elected leaders with a daunting challenge: how to keep faith with the old without bankrupting the young."[17]

My concern is that we're not mixing well as generations. We, adults, are more comfortable with our peers, and students have never been so present with each other. Multi-generations don't connect well, nor do we have natural places to connect as former adult and adolescent generations did. Our changing demographic has produced an America in which young and old don't look, think or vote alike. We have one party that leans older, whiter, more religious and more conservative and the other that trends younger, more non-white, more liberal and more secular. As author Paul Taylor adds, "There's more animosity between partisans now than at any time in modern history. Some of it spills beyond politics into everyday life, influencing where people live, whom they befriend and how they search for news."[18]

Younger generations are leaving "membership" in political parties, local churches or religious affiliations, ethnicities (more are mixing) and even genders. Old traditions are giving way to newer trends. Instead of asking how past tradition informs us, we're asking—what's trending on social media? While they say they value loyalty, the young actually value opportunity, wherever it may lift its head. Can you blame them? Life seems like a system that's rigged. It's every man for himself. How do we respond?

THREE BIG BALANCING ACTS

I'd like to get very practical at this point. In each chapter, I try to furnish ideas for you to apply the data we've examined. My goal, in fact, is to turn research into reality. As I mentioned earlier, my objective is to be "pracademic," offering academic research, but leaving audiences with practical, actionable items.

Let's begin with some balancing acts.

Most of us don't get to choose the students we lead and serve. They're like family—we inherit them. If you're a leader, your job can be compared to performing a "balancing act." (For example, employers must constantly balance the organization's goals with the personal welfare of their team members. Parents must balance both the house rules with their relationship to their children.) It's important to remember we must lead each young person while balancing two paradoxical realities or needs in the process.

I have noticed high school and college students are pushing back on the kind of unhealthy leadership we educators, employers and parents have offered up until now.

In response, may I suggest three balancing acts effective leaders must perform to connect with and guide today's students into a healthy future. We Must Balance:

1. **Being organized with being organic.**

    Today's emerging population is extremely savvy. Having been exposed to on-line information since pre-school, they can spot a "fake" from a mile away. They despise inauthenticity. They withdraw from anyone who seems disingenuous. So, how do we offer programming that doesn't feel, well . . . programmed?

    Few doubt we can make any progress unless we organize our efforts with students. Planning and organization are a must. At the same time, our work with students must feel organic; it can't be too packaged, but must come across as being real and authentic. Too often, Millennials and Generation Z avoid our plans because we have over-programmed or over-produced them. And it's often about meetings and mere words. Blah. Blah. Blah. We must work to balance organizing our projects while remaining serendipitous in the moment.

    Question: The next time you plan an event or program for students, how could you involve them in the process to keep the program relevant? How could you ensure the execution comes across simple, interactive and real?

2. **Embracing the real and the ideal.**

Educators and youth-staff often mourn the issues kids face today—suicide, mental health problems, addictions, gender confusion, etc. Many live in a broken world. Our job as leaders is to continue to hold up the "ideal" for what they can become, never losing sight of their potential. Simultaneously, however, we must embrace the messy reality they face today. The key is to be able to look at their current performance (albeit less than stellar) and not lose sight of their future potential. Then, we must turn potential into performance. The key is to "be" real, yet "see" the ideal.

We must envision the ideal while looking at the real and embracing it. We cannot live in denial, but we must live with determination. Some kids will push you to abandon the ideal. Some adults will push you to ignore the real.

Question: When you communicate with your students, how can you relay that you are aware of the difficult realities they face (that your head is not in the sand), but remember to relay the noble ideals you believe they are capable of growing into as adults? We must juggle the real and the ideal.

3. **Celebrating both diversity and harmony.**

As we create resources and events for students, I'm reminded of the diversity of ideology and backgrounds kids possess today. They experience ethnic diversity, cultural diversity, values, philosophy, and passion diversity. We must somehow allow for these differences, yet foster harmony on what we all have in common. In the midst of the wide array of what kids offer, we must enable them to see the value of collaboration on something bigger than any one of them.

Former Navy Captain, Michael Abrashoff, once said, "The military tells us we must offer diversity training, but it seems to me what our sailors most need is unity training. How can we mesh our differences into a single unit and get results?"[19] Well said. Both are important, but in the end, diverse groups must work together.

Question: How can you communicate that you welcome the uniqueness of each student, while at the same time call them to work in collaboration and harmony toward a common goal?

TODAY'S CULTURAL SCENE

In the revised book called, *Generation iY*, I offer a diagram to illustrate the world our students are growing up in today. I include it here because it continues to be one of the most helpful gauges to assess what we must do to lead our kids into healthy adulthood and leadership. It enables us to see how today's cultural SCENE has produced an unintended paradigm in millions of adolescents.

How today's SCENE hinders development:

Our world is full of:	Consequently, students can assume:
S—Speed	Slow is bad.
C—Convenience	Hard is bad.
E—Entertainment	Boring is bad.
N—Nurture	Risk is bad.
E—Entitlement	Labor is bad.

It's easy to see how the five words that spell "SCENE" describe our 21st century world. But note the list on the right. Too often, these are conclusions teens draw; they're the unintended consequences of today's scene. Reflect for a moment on the products or services that are hot right now; the ones that blow up fast and are popular overnight. Are they not items that are quick, easy, amusing, safe and comfortable and most of all, free. (Think apps and video content).

Now, pause and consider something else.

It seems to me that the ideas of slow, hard, boring, risk and labor are the very realities that enable me to mature into a good adult, a leader, a husband and father. I am suggesting that our world of speed and convenience actually hinder the natural development of virtues we need to become strong adults. When things come quick and easy, I fail to develop the emotional muscles I need and require intentional exercises to fully mature.

I remember exactly when and where I learned the life skill of conflict resolution. I learned it playing outside with a dozen or so friends in a big field in back of our house. After we did our homework, we'd grab our baseball bats and mitts and play ball. Unsupervised. We'd choose sides and umpire our own games. In the process, I learned interpersonal skills and conflict resolution.

I often joke that today kids get less and less time outside to do such things. When they do, there are often four mothers outside doing the conflict resolution for them.

The Formula

The fact is, we must become more intentional about student development in certain areas, especially as fewer life skills are cultivated naturally. In short:

The less natural life skills are cultivated during childhood, the more intentional we must be as we lead them in adolescence and young adulthood.

A Prescription

So—before we know what to prescribe for student development today, we must ask two simple but profound "travel guide" questions as we observe them:

TRAVEL GUIDE:

What social or emotional muscles seem to be weak?

What practices can we introduce to them to develop those muscles?

Just like a fitness center enables us to develop physical muscles, specific social and emotional activities enable us to grow internally:

- It is in waiting that I build patience.
- It is in face-to-face collaboration that I build interpersonal skills.
- It is in attempting risky ventures that I build courage.
- It is in struggling that I build perseverance.

- It is in boredom that I have margins to imagine and think creatively.
- It is in challenging labor that I build an appreciation for a strong work ethic.

Basil Maturin believed, "Discontent is the first step in progress. No one knows what is in him till he tries, and many would never try if they were not forced to." I am convinced this statement can be applied to both the teacher and the student.

THE SIX TRADE-OFFS NOT WORTH MAKING

I'd like to examine a case study for how to better lead our young. As 2015 came to a close, an unbelievable story resurfaced in the news. Do you remember hearing about Ethan Couch, the Texas kid who got crazy drunk and drove his nice pick-up truck off the road, killing four people in the process? To make matters worse, he then ran from the accident to avoid the consequences. While this is appalling enough, the story went viral when we heard his attorney's defense for his conduct: "affluenza."

Affluenza is a term (used tongue-in-cheek) by some psychologists to describe the inability for adolescents to even know what's appropriate because they grew up with privileges and money. It blinds them from seeing right from wrong. Life is pretty much about them. In short, affluence clouds clear judgment. Ethan was caught, but due to his affluenza, got no prison time, only probation. A few months later, we found out the story wasn't over.

Ethan's mother, Tonya, actually helped him escape his Texas probation to flee to Mexico. Yes, she sure did. Mama felt his light sentence (no prison, just probation) was too much for her boy to handle, and she wanted to free him from the clutches of the law. In fact, before escaping to Mexico, she actually threw him a "going away party."

Enabling Young People

Psychologists have used a term for decades now to describe what this mom is doing. They call it: enabling. It's when a leader actually fosters unhealthy behavior. It usually happens due to conflicted motives—we want what's best but feel sympathy for the other person and somehow feel we should lighten their emotional burden. In this case, because Tonya felt sorry for Ethan, she overlooked the obvious negative consequences to her actions and eased the pain he feels today. Equally sad is that Ethan is now no longer a minor; he's 18 years old. But when adults lead kids like this, they can be 18 and still not be adults.

An enlightening study was released out of the UK. The research shows that people don't see age in terms of years, but in terms of major life events. Further, most don't feel like adulthood really begins until 29 years old.[20] That's incredible to me. Although our young adults are rich in potential—we don't really expect them to perform responsible acts until a full decade later than we expected a century ago. I believe it's detrimental both for our kids and our society. In many states, we give them the rights to adulthood at 18 or 21, like smoking, drinking or voting. We don't, however, expect the responsibilities that accompany those rights. It's unhealthy. Their rights and responsibilities should always go together. While this story is preposterous, it is a picture of so many adults today. We enable our kids and prevent them from maturing into healthy leaders. Be very careful as you lead teens and twenty-somethings that you don't make trade-offs that feel right in the moment, but end up harming them in the end. May I suggest a few?

The six bad trade-offs to avoid:

1. **Unwittingly teach them to dodge responsibility to avoid pain.**
   No matter what the circumstance, we enable our kids when we help them run from duty. We can certainly debate what duties are suitable, but we must always teach them to never dodge responsibility in the name of personal comfort.

2. **Put their happiness today above their discipline.**
   When adults incessantly talk about just wanting our kids "to be happy," we send the message that personal happiness is a higher priority than discipline. I have found I am most happy when I have built self-discipline into my life. It breeds self-respect.

3. **Condition them to escape risks simply to guarantee safety.**
   Our obsession with safety has actually damaged kids emotionally. They may be safer physically, but they are growing up risk-averse. An unhealthy pursuit of safety tells students to avoid risk. Our nation was built on risk, with no guarantees.

4. **Enable them to feel entitled to perks by helping them take shortcuts.**

   Pleasure is a high priority in our culture today. Many live for weekends and suffer from FOMO (Fear Of Missing Out) and YOLO (You Only Live Once). This hinders them from thinking long-term; they can feel entitled to perks and often can't delay gratification.

5. **Foster narcissism in them by putting their own desires above the law.**

   Ethan Couch was unwittingly taught to think of himself before others. He killed four people and ran from his consequences—twice. How can we expect our kids to see the bigger picture of their community if we've conditioned them to put "me first?" Too often we condition kids to expect playing time, special treatment and perks.

6. **Prioritize today at the expense of tomorrow.**

   Our kids will not mature into healthy adults in 20 years if we've conditioned them to think only about today. They often feel entitled to everything now. Tonya Couch's lack of healthy leadership blinded her son. The further out we can see, the better the decisions we make for our young.

I believe a wise word to live by goes like this: "Never give up what you want most for what you want now."

In the end, Tonya didn't help her son, Ethan, at all. Bail was set for a million dollars. Both faced prison time for years. The lesson for us? Enabling actually costs us all in the end. In the words of Margaret Mead, "The solution to adult problems tomorrow depends on large measure upon how our children grow up today."

It's time we get this right.

Over the next several chapters, we'll begin to unpack how to lead, teach, parent and manage these kids. For now, however, let's start with the immediate need. Just how do we communicate with this emerging generation? How should we attempt to connect with a new population who describes themselves as follows:

- I spend the equivalent of a full-time job on several screens each day.
- I met my best friends through Tumblr and Instagram.
- I binge watch YouTube and Netflix.
- I am not totally sure about my identity.
- I don't identify with an ethnic race, but with the human race.
- I don't remember a world before social media.

I believe we must adapt our messaging. It's likely we don't need to change "what" our message is, but "how" we deliver it. It's not the principle that is antiquated (discipline and honesty will always be relevant), but our pedagogy. We've got to use new means to relay our message.

Matt, Zoe, Savannah and Dylan, and yes even Ethan, all need the adults in their life to adjust but not appease. They need us to adapt but not adopt the new trends in Tomorrowland.

Are you willing to keep your principles, but trade in your pedagogy?

CHAPTER 5

WILL YOU SAIL OR SURRENDER?

Five ways to adjust our sails today instead of surrender to the winds of culture.

> *When the winds of change blow, some people build walls, while others build windmills.*
>
> —Chinese Proverb

I want to introduce you to another member of the emerging generation. My niece, Lauren, has been sailing since she was in elementary school. Her father, Brad, took her out on a boat off the coast in Orange County, California and Lauren soon fell in love with the sport. She started taking lessons at nine years old and has been sailing on a regular basis ever since. In fact, she sailed competitively at the intercollegiate level while attending U.C. Long Beach. She's quite amazing.

Now, let me share something that may sound so obvious it's ridiculous.

While competing, Lauren did not have the luxury to choose the weather. During certain periods of the season, she might be sailing against significant winds or in turbulent waters. At times, the water current was quite intimidating. The contests did not take place on a quiet lake. That would be more my speed.

The only times I've been out on a sailboat was with Lauren, my brother in law, Brad, or some other experienced sailor. (I'm a passenger, not a sailor.) Watching them, you get the idea, they're quite at home on the water—constantly sizing up the weather, the wind and the waves they're facing at any moment. It's what good sailors do. Not once have I seen them shake their fist at the wind, resentful that it didn't cooperate with their plans. Neither have I seen them sit down and surrender to the wind, deciding that since it wouldn't cooperate, it was useless to sail. Nope. In every case, I would watch them evaluate the wind's direction and somehow leverage it to take the boat exactly where they wanted it to go. There are a few lessons in those scenarios for us.

In my book, *Generation iY*, I suggest that in many ways, today's culture is like the wind. It's always moving, ever volatile, constantly changing. Too often, instructors, coaches, and administrators get angry or give up, believing it's impossible to make progress within the current conditions. Students' attention spans are just too short. They are disrespectful. They don't want to sit in a classroom. Their parents are over-bearing. They don't want to work hard. And, they're glued to their cell phones.

Full of technology, video on demand, social media and screens everywhere, today's culture is sweeping through our lives, affecting almost everything and everyone in it's path. Some might claim it's a hurricane, out of control. When it comes to today's students, I see too many adults shake their fist in frustration, upset at the culture and what its done to create today's "lazy, entitled kids." They're upset over how these young "screenagers" just don't get it; how they're apathetic, not empathic; and how they have low emotional intelligence and almost no work ethic.

Then, there's another group of adults who look out upon the horizon of culture and just give up. They conclude there's nothing they can do about it, so they might as well just surrender to the winds of culture. Their budget is too small, and they've lost all hope of restoring any timeless virtues that have been lost. After all, this is the 21st century; it's a new day. It's impossible to rebuild in any measurable way. An increasing number of instructors and coaches are just giving up.

I just read a report that shocked me. After surveying the faculty in my home state, the Department of Education realized they must have hit a nerve. Approximately 70 percent of the 53,000 faculty surveyed said they are "unlikely" or "very unlikely" to encourage graduates to enter the profession and become teachers.[1] In other words: Hey, I've experienced this job and I don't suggest you follow me. Only a trifling 2.7 percent said they'd encourage graduates to become teachers.[2]

Every year, thousands of young and enthusiastic instructors start their first day of work. "Within five years, between 40 and 50 percent have either left the profession or are considering doing so," according to Richard Ingersoll, a University of Pennsylvania professor and a scholar on our national teacher workforce.[3]

In California, the drop is occurring from the start. In 2001, 77,700 graduates were enrolled in teaching programs in California. By 2012, that number had dropped to 19,933. Even for students, it's easy to see that the classroom is a tough place to serve and, often, isn't working very well.[4]

According to one UK report, the problem is global. More than half of all instructors are considering leaving the profession in the next two years due to workload and low morale. It follows an earlier analysis of government figures by the Association of Teachers and Lecturers, revealing that almost four in 10 instructors quit the profession within a year of qualifying.[5] Here at home, roughly half of U.S. teachers report feeling "under great stress" several days a week; job satisfaction is at a 25-year low,[6] and almost a third of teachers say they are likely to leave the profession within the next five years.[7] What's more, most parents apparently believe the system is not working, either. According to a Phi Delta Kappa/Gallup poll, approximately 80 percent of Americans give grades of "C," "D," or "F" to our nation's schools. What a sad commentary on the current state of affairs.[8] Too many of these folks began yelling at the wind, and then gave up.

I believe we need to think like sailors.

Instead of these two reactions—frustration or surrender—what if we sized up the winds around us, then leveraged them for our purposes? What if we actually used what's trending in culture to take the kids where they need to go? A good sailor can take even contrary winds and use them. That's precisely what we must do. Staying current on the culture, and making constant adjustments, prevents the need for drastic turnarounds. Change can help us reach our goal efficiently.

So, we have three choices today:

1. **Yell at the wind**—Become angry, withdraw, complain and just survive.

2. **Surrender to the wind**—Lose our resolve and give in to the culture's whims.

3. **Adjust the sails**—Use the current and wind to take students where they must go.

THE SHIFTS WE'VE SEEN IN TODAY'S CULTURE

Even since I entered my career, our world has experienced seismic shifts in how we live, communicate, connect and do a workday. Lots of cultural wind and waves.

As I observe today's realities, I notice people have the same needs we did fifty years ago, but we've found new ways to meet them. Some good, some…well, not so good. At times we actually drift into a "new normal" without noticing. For instance…

1. **Workouts…are the new work.**
   Generations ago, no one needed to go to a gym to lift weights or run. Many worked manual labor jobs on a farm or a factory. Now, we need gym memberships to stay fit.

2. **Movies…are the new books.**
   While I know books still sell, many from the emerging generation would rather wait for the movie to come out. They watch 35 movies for every one book they read.

3. **Musicians…are the new philosophers.**
   In times past, men like Socrates, Plato or Augustine gave us our worldview. Today, it's Katy Perry, Justin Bieber or Kanye West. Hmmm … I'm not sure they're qualified.

4. **Athletes…are the new heroes.**
   Instead of statesmen or military generals, we choose celebrities from a playing field or basketball court … you know, people who throw a ball really well. Makes sense.

5. **Starbucks…is the new front porch.**
   My friend, Len Sweet, said it first. We used to gather on a neighbor's porch to enjoy community and drink lemonade. Today, we meet at a coffee house for a latte.

6. **Texts…are the new letter or phone call.**
   We used to take time to write a letter or even make a phone call. Today, we don't have time for that kind of labor. We text or tweet. It's short and sweet.

7. **Facebook and Instagram…are the new social hook up.**
   There was a time you had to go to a school dance or a church social to meet a special friend. Today, we do it virtually from the solitude of our own bedrooms.

8. **Netflix…is the new Blockbuster.**
   Today, you don't have to drive to a store to rent a video. In fact, you're antiquated if you do. Just get the movie On-Demand, on your TV or device . . . and don't leave the couch.

9. **Smartphones…are the new Rolodex.**
   I remember using that little contact cardholder to look up numbers and network with people. Today, you have all those names and more on a portable device.

10. **Twitter…is the new headline news source.**
    We once read newspapers for the latest updates. Today, many don't even visit websites. They use social media; watching for tweets to fill them in.

Our Task is to Adapt Not Adopt

The key to good leadership is catching the wind and capitalizing on it to take you where you need to go. And, perhaps more importantly, to take the students under your care where they need to go. Our job is not merely to adopt what's trending in our culture. Leaders don't just fit in. Our goal is to adapt, not adopt. There's a huge difference. We adapt to the realities of our day, leveraging current methods to say what must be said to our young. Once again, we are timely in our methods, but timeless in our mission. We are timely in our communication style, but timeless in our content. We are timely in our pedagogy, but timeless in our purpose.

Adapting communicates to those in the emerging generation that we're lifelong learners; that we are still teachable and that we're privy to current events and trends in culture. It does not mean we give in and act like we're young again.

When I worked on staff with Dr. John C. Maxwell, we discussed a story that dated back to the volatile decade of the 1960s. Apparently, a small college endured a student demonstration on campus one semester. Many coeds were up in arms about an academic policy, and found the administration unwilling to even talk about it. So, what did the students do? They decided to walk out of class. Hundreds of students just left the classroom. During this period, the faculty wasn't sure how to deal with such a walkout, so they did nothing. Essentially, they sat on their hands. At semester's end, the students received no grade for the classes in which they missed several days of school. When they inquired about it, administrators replied that they weren't sure how to report their grades. They were unready. After all, they'd never experienced something like that in the past. In effect, the students basically responded: We know we were acting like immature students when we walked away. We just didn't expect you to do the same.

It's a great statement, declaring what those students needed. They didn't need the adults to "adopt" what they were doing. They needed them to "adapt" to the current problems and respond to them. They needed leaders, not imitators. They wanted them to lead, not languish. Those students desperately needed participation, not passivity from their leaders. Whether they were right or wrong—those students sent a message every adult needs to hear from the younger generation:

We may act like kids, because we are. Please don't do the same. We need you to lead us. This means we adjust the sails, and take our boats where they must go. Fixed on the right destination, we must constantly assess the weather, observe the waves and tug on the ropes to ensure we are heading in the right direction.

TRAVEL GUIDE:

What are some areas you can "adapt" but not "adopt?"

From Barbarians to Bureaucrats

The fact is, when we merely "adopt" what's happening, we tend to drift. Cultures do this; schools do this, and families do this as well. Years ago, Lawrence Miller wrote about this topic in Barbarians to Bureaucrats. He observes that companies, organizations and schools "evolve" over time, but actually the evolution usually becomes a "drift" away from the very premise it was built upon.

The process starts with the "prophets." They're the people with a vision for something new. They're idea people. But they're usually threatening to the existing order and are often ignored, criticized, frustrated or otherwise rejected.

Eventually, however, people recognize the need for change. That's when the "barbarians" step in. They're the ones with the influence to knock heads together, and gain the power to implement the changes the prophets suggested earlier. They are often people like Steve Jobs, Ted Turner, or Oprah Winfrey. They conquer territory that some assumed could never be conquered and foster change.

Following the "barbarians" come the "builders" and the "explorers." These people take the empire the "barbarians" conquered and begin to build bridges, chart courses and develop systems that enable the empire to grow and prosper.

Next, come the "administrators." This type of person almost always follows, because the "builders" and "explorers" get bored and need someone who enjoys managing a system. They add no new ideas or wealth, but simply keep things running smoothly.

Eventually, the "administrators" give way to the "bureaucrats." These folks not only add no new ideas, but they actually suppress innovation and focus their effort on maintaining control of the empire. Change is too messy or expensive. To keep money flowing, "bureaucrats" tend to concentrate on cost-cutting and re-organizing, milking what's left of the old ideas. It's important to note—one of the chief goals of the bureaucrat is to suppress the rise of any new order of prophets.

The final phase of this downward spiral is the shift from "bureaucrats" to "aristocrats." They're the ones who've inherited the wealth of the previous generation and occupy themselves with consuming the last benefits from the old ideas. Fortunately, they don't last very long in a competitive climate because they get bumped off by new "barbarians" who promote the ideas of outside prophets from other places. In short, change will either happen to us, or because of us.

Adapting means we shift. Adopting means we drift.

TRAVEL GUIDE:

Are we moving in a good direction or an unhealthy one?

Can you think of any other shifts that have taken place?

How must we adapt to our day; to "adjust the sails," and still move forward, building timeless skills into our students?

GAME CHANGERS

So far, I've tried to make the case that change is in the wind. And we must embrace it. We are in new territory with or without a new map. Generation Z may just assume that adults are an ocean away, drifting with the wind. Instead, we must utilize that wind to push us toward our goal: to develop a healthy, thriving population of adults from our current generation of kids.

When we master this art, we can make adjustments that become "game changers." You know what a game changer is, don't you? In the game of football, it can happen when the defense intercepts a pass in the second half. In baseball, it can be a stolen base or a homer at just the right time. In life, a game changer can alter the very way people approach an issue. It occurs when a leader chooses to adjust the sails, and finds the adjustment so fundamentally better, that others get on board. These improvements often create "paradigm shifts" for people. May I remind you of the importance of paradigms?

Much has been written on paradigms or paradigm shifts, so I'll simply summarize its meaning here. A paradigm is a set of rules that define boundaries and tells you how to succeed within those boundaries. It is a lens with which we look at life, approach life and evaluate it. A shift occurs when those rules change. Paradigms ultimately become a pair of glasses by which we see or don't see reality.

Let me illustrate. Take a second and read this simple phrase out loud:

Paris in the
the Spring.

If you looked closely and consciously, you noticed that the word "the" appeared twice in the phrase. If you simply relied on your established paradigm, you assumed you knew what I meant to say and read it incorrectly. You left out one of the words.

We do this all the time. In fact, our paradigms are necessary because they help us see things without giving much conscious thought to them. We need them or we would become overwhelmed with all the information we consume each day. Sadly, our paradigms also prevent us from seeing things—because they are boundaries or blinders, keeping us from realities that are actually present.

Case in point. Do you remember when Blockbuster video stores were at the center of our personal entertainment? We would rent DVDs and watch movies we'd picked up at a store. Sadly, Netflix founder Reed Hastings approached Blockbuster with the idea of selling DVDs on the Internet, and later streaming video on our television sets, but Blockbuster thought the idea was ludicrous. Now, Blockbuster's been replaced by Netflix. They didn't adapt.

In the fall of 2016, BlackBerry announced their plan to stop making smart phones. When I remember their beginnings, it's hard to believe. BlackBerry led the way almost 20 years ago, with their iconic mobile device, its QWERTY keypad and its sophisticated software. At one point, they owned 50 percent of the market. In the end, that shrank to 1 percent. Sadly, when BlackBerry failed to anticipate primary changes in the market, iPhones and Androids took over. They failed to adapt.

The good news is—we can be intentional about change. Even game changers and paradigm shifts. The purpose of this book is to equip you to create those game changers. Our world needs them. Our 21st century culture needs them. Our children need them. So, let's review a handful of past "game changers," and see what we can apply to our leadership today.

LESSONS FROM FIVE GAME CHANGERS:

Game Changer #1: Dick Fosbury and the High Jump (1968)
Dick Fosbury was an Oregon State University student-athlete who knew there had to be a more effective way for jumping the high bar in track and field events. So, in the late 1960's, Dick began attempting new methods for the high jump. He studied the various iterations of the high jump over the last century—including the *Scissors*, developed in Scotland during the 19th century; the *Eastern Cut-Off*, created by Mike Sweeney as the 20th century dawned; the *Western Roll*, invented by George Horine, in 1912; or the *Straddle*, developed by Russian-American jumpers in the 1940s. Each of these techniques didn't leverage the human body as much as he felt was possible. So, he kept working on new approaches. Folks saw the fruit of his labor in the 1968 Olympic games in Mexico City. It was called the *Fosbury Flop*. At first, the crowds laughed at his face-up, head-first technique—it just looked awkward. He wore two different shoes, and leaped differently than each of his competitors. In the end, however, Dick was the last one laughing. He won the gold medal. Today, the *Fosbury Flop* is the standard for high jumpers.[9]

Question: What's your high bar? Can you get over it in a new way?

Game Changer #2: Roger Bannister and the Four-minute Mile (1954)
Roger Bannister did what most assumed was unattainable for a human being at the time: he ran a mile in under four minutes. Public opinion believed no one could do it and the media put that in print. In fact, in 1939, the current record holder, Glen Cunningham had even claimed it was biologically impossible. But Roger was both a medical school student and an athlete, and his research led him to believe he could do it, despite the naysayers. He trained with two pacesetters Chris Brasher and Chris Chataway who ran a half-mile each alongside of Roger and it paid off. In 1954, fifteen years after Cunningham said it could never be done, Roger Bannister crossed the finish line in just under four minutes. It stunned

sports fans and ushered in a paradigm shift for runners everywhere. Since breaking this record, more than 950 others have accomplished the feat. It was a game-changer.[10]

Question: What's an impossible goal that, if you reached it, could change life for many?

Game Changer #3: Pop Warner and the Forward Pass (1907)
In 1905, college football was a slow, grinding, low-scoring game, because it was all about running. A running back would take a handoff and struggle for a few yards on a good run. And it was excessively violent. President Roosevelt even wondered if the U.S. should end the game after eighteen deaths and his own son's injury to the head. After a meeting with Ivy League schools, a decision was made. In 1906, the forward pass was introduced to make the game safer. It met, however, with great resistance. It was seen as a "sissy" play, and it felt awkward and unfamiliar.

Consequently, no NCAA team adopted the forward pass into their offensive plan. That is, except for St. Louis University, who quickly realize how it offered a new way to reach the end zone. So they put it in their game plan. By year's end, they'd outscored opponents 402-11. This raised eyebrows. But it wasn't until 1907 that the pass drew national attention, when Coach "Pop" Warner, at Carlisle Indian Industrial School, PA mastered it. His players were smaller and couldn't compete with bigger teams—so they had to rely on it. Passing became one of their surprise weapons enabling them to win game after game, against stronger teams. Needless to say, the forward pass caught on. It was a game changer.[11]

Question: What's a new opportunity or strategy that you could capitalize on?

Game Changer #4: James Q. Wilson and the Broken Windows Theory (1982)
Social scientist James Q. Wilson developed his "broken windows theory" in 1982. He believed that human behavior—particularly crime—could be impacted by simply making small changes in an environment, like repairing broken windows. In a high crime area, broken windows signal, "no one cares." If one is broken, soon all the windows get broken. George Kelling, a criminologist confirmed its truth, but when he proposed that New York fix the windows to clean up crime, they laughed.

When crime soared in the 1980s, however, William Bratton was ready to act. Rudy Guliani asked Bratton to take over the NYC police. He then insisted they fix the broken windows in a high crime neighborhood and see what happens. Crime dropped measurably. During the 1990s, New York City violent crime declined by more than 56 percent. Property crimes tumbled by about 65 percent. The idea spread. Minor, seemingly insignificant quality-of-life crimes were tipping points for violent crimes. Window repair jobs, however, were also tipping points to drive criminal activity away.[12]

Question: What's your broken window to fix that could lead to a dramatic impact?

Game Changer #5: David and Goliath: Infantry vs. Artillery (1040 BC)

You probably remember this legendary story of the boy, David, who met a giant on the battlefield, when ancient Israel fought the Philistine army in 1040 BC. Man to man combat was actually common in those days—one army would send out a single infantry soldier to challenge a man from their enemy. It was winner take all. Instead of both nations losing thousands of men, one man would die and the rest could live. The story of David and Goliath is often taught as a picture of great faith. No doubt it is.

Malcolm Gladwell reminds us, however, it was also a story of strategy. Every army possessed three types of warriors: cavalry, infantry and artillery. It was a little like rock, paper and scissors. Each had an advantage and a disadvantage. Goliath was the strongest Philistine infantry, standing taller than anyone else on the field. Israel assumed they had to send infantry out to meet him. But when none of Israel's infantry wanted to take on the giant, David saw the situation as an advantage. Goliath was big but he was slow. With a sling, David was artillery and possessed the advantage of speed and distance. What he lacked in size and strength, he made up for with his smaller size and speed. Artillery beat infantry just like rocks beat scissors. Israel's infantry saw Goliath as too big to hit. David saw him as too big to miss. What everyone else saw as a disadvantage . . . David saw as an advantage.

Question: What's your disadvantage that you could leverage as an advantage?

Evaluation: What We Learn from These Game Changers
Let's push the pause button and evaluate what we can learn from each of these game changers in history. I chose each one because they represent various paradigm shifts we can make; a diverse list of changes we can apply when it comes to reaching kids today. Let's take a brief look.

What We Learn from These Game Changers:

- Dick Fosbury teaches us there are times when **tweaking** is not enough.
- Roger Bannister teaches us to do our **homework** before we assume too much.
- Pop Warner teaches us to capitalize on **opportunities** when they arise.
- James Q. Wilson teaches us **small but visual** changes can transform a culture.
- King David teaches us to perceive a **disadvantage** as a potential **advantage**.

Alvin Toffler put it this way, "The illiterate of the future will not be those who cannot read or write. The illiterate of the future will be people who cannot learn, unlearn and relearn. The question for us is, 'What have we learned that we need to unlearn?'"

How can we take the wind and waves we face, and transform them into a tool we can employ...rather than a trial we must endure, or a tragedy we must avoid?

TRAVEL GUIDE:

Which of the "game changers" above are most relevant to you and why?

When Change Happens Within a Generation

Allow me to remind you of the obvious. Those of us who lead must not only keep up with today's changes, but lead those essential changes over the next 20-30 years. As I've stated before, the winds are already blowing. The big question is—can we guide our young, so they can orchestrate the right adjustments as they lead the way into the future? I have referenced anthropologist Margaret Mead already in this book. She has helped me consider how change takes place in history—and how we can thrive in an era of rapid progress. Mead notes that when change occurs quickly and shapes us within a single generation, one or all of four realities exist.

When change happens within a generation, look for these realities:

1. **The recognition of an imminent threat.**
   Contemporaries identify dangers that could damage or destroy what we enjoy. If we feel we are about to lose something precious, we are more apt to adjust to new realties, better ways or to invent solutions. This has led to the discovery of insulin, penicillin, and other medications or vaccines in the field of healthcare.

2. **The abandonment of an old practice.**
   When people naturally migrate to a superior method for making progress, we tend to shift within a single generation. For centuries, humans used horses for transportation, but it took cars only a generation to replace them. At first, cars were called "horseless carriages" because we only saw them as replacements.

3. **The introduction of new technology.**
   This one's easy. As new technology is created, people can change within a single generation when they see it offers a better way to reach a goal. There was a time we didn't know we needed a smart device in our hands to make progress and connect with people. Now we can't imagine life without them.

4. **The presence of rarely gifted leaders.**
   The final shaper of fast change is the introduction of persuasive and brilliant leaders who influence us to do what we might not have done otherwise. I think of Winston Churchill, or Susan B. Anthony, Martin Luther King, Jr. or Steve Jobs as such leaders who made us think differently, quickly. They had rare gifts.

My question for you is: can you help the people around you with any of these four realities above? Do your colleagues and friends recognize an imminent threat to healthy living? Are they ready to abandon an old, irrelevant practice? Do they experience enough new technology that enables them to achieve their goals in a superior fashion? Are there any leaders they'd listen to that would help them "adjust their sails"?

TRAVEL GUIDE:

Which of the four items above are you experiencing?

THE BIT MARKET

Let's close this chapter by evaluating the best way to approach change. I'd like us to consider one of our *Habitudes®*. (*Habitudes* are images that form leadership habits and attitudes.) The image is: "The Bit Market."

A new president took over a drill company that was known for manufacturing popular drill bits for electric drills. The executive took time to meet every employee on his first day, and to close the day, hosted a meeting to talk about the future. Before he spoke, each of the vice presidents took time at the podium to boast about how great the company was. They elaborated on the fact that they'd sold 60 percent of the drill bits sold in the U.S. that previous year. They were sure their future was bright. They were proud of their success.

When they'd finished, however, the president took a moment to remind them of an important reality. He thanked them for their speeches, but then said: "We're just forgetting one very important truth. There is no market for drill bits."

And after a palpable pause, he continued. "The market is for holes."

Everyone sat stunned, staring, waiting for further insight. He then smiled and said, "People buy our little drill bits not because they love pieces of metal. They buy them because they want to make a hole in some wood. The moment someone comes up with a better way to make a hole, these drill bits will be obsolete."

He was right.

The people in the room had fallen into the trap so many fall into. We become enamored by the product or the service we currently offer, and forget its not an end in itself. It's only a means to an end. When we fail to see this, we become blinded to seeing new opportunities—new paradigms—that would allow us to create a shift. Imagine for a moment.

What if a company, down the street, developed a laser method for making a hole in a piece of wood, at a very affordable price? We would stop buying the old-fashioned drill bit immediately, wouldn't we? What's important is an easy, quick way to drill a hole, not the device that does it. No one I know still uses an Eight-Track Tape player to listen to music. Nor do they use cassette tapes. In fact, very few even use compact discs. These are all old drill bits. We now download or stream our music onto our portable device. The tapes, the vinyl and the discs are all methods to get our music. Methods come and go; the mission stays the same. Programs and products come and go; the purpose stays the same. Leaders know the difference and with their eye on the goal, will trade out old "drill bits" to reach that goal most efficiently.

Effective leaders focus on three actions:

1. **They keep their eye on the hole, not the drill bit.**
   While their team is tending to the current drill bits, they are keeping watch on the big picture, making sure it's the best way to reach the objective.

2. **They are always looking for new ways to make holes.**
   They attend conferences, read books and meet with mentors to discover new trends and updated methods to achieve their goal in the most effective way.

3. **They sell the hole to the stakeholders, not the drill bit.**
   They know that they must focus on the outcomes, not the inputs, of their strategy. People care most about reaching the goal, not how you did it.

Someone once said, "If the locomotive train industry had realized they were really in the transportation business—they might have been the first to jump into the airline industry." Good leaders know what to hold tightly to, and what to change. They understand what is timeless and what is timely.

What was timeless for Dick Fosbury was getting over the high bar in the best way possible. He simply traded in the current "drill bit" for a new one. Pop Warner knew the goal was finding the most efficient way to get into the end zone, not finding the best runners. Running was only a method for scoring, but passing the ball became an even more effective way to do so. He didn't just improve his current "drill bits." He found a whole new one to use.

TRAVEL GUIDE:

What is the "hole" you're trying to drill?

Is it time to trade out some old drill bits for new ones?

Jack Welch, taught me something years ago. Shortly after he took over General Electric as Chairman and CEO in 1981, he met with his executives for an exercise. They listed all the products they sold—from blenders and toaster ovens, to stoves and refrigerators—and then they discussed their value to the company and customers. As they talked about each product, they asked themselves:

- Does this need a facelift? (It's good, but it just needs an update.)
- Does this need an overhaul? (It's purpose is good, but now it must be altered.)
- Does this need a funeral? (It once was good, but no longer is relevant.)

General Electric decided they would only keep the products that could be number one or number two in the industry. Otherwise—change was in the wind. Did it work? You tell me. Under Jack Welch, G.E.'s value increased by 4,000 percent.[13]

I believe every school, every company, every athletic team and every family should walk through this exercise as they determine how to lead the emerging generation. In fact, I want to challenge you to make your own list and have the same conversation regarding your methods for reaching and teaching students or young professionals. What would you change? What would you terminate?

We've had this discussion at our organization, Growing Leaders, more than once. As we consider what new events and resources to offer schools and organizations, we've typically created books and enlisted speakers. While both are still effective in many places, we could see change was in the wind a few years ago.

We had to adjust our sails.

Our *Habitudes*® books are our most popular resource but students prefer digital content today. Fewer are reading books and more are using a tablet or a phone. When possible, they're on a big screen playing a video game. So, we re-purposed the *Habitudes* images, using a new medium. You might say, we changed out our drill bit. We positioned the lessons, still driven by images, in an on-line format.

The students get a password to engage in: "*Habitudes*Play." We have gamified the principles we teach using quests, videos, discussion questions, competition, collaboration and badges. They now learn life skills and leadership via a game-like platform. Meanwhile, the facilitators get a password to receive "*Habitudes*Online." Instead of printed copies of teacher's guides, power point slide decks, and DVD's, they get it on a screen.

We've found that change requires work, but it is worth it.

I suppose I'm merely learning the very habits my niece, Lauren, practices when she sails on a windy day. Lots of hard work; lots of pulling on ropes and turning cranks; and lots of discerning the direction of that wind. I'm learning to enjoy sailing more and more.

TRAVEL GUIDE:

What could you do, that if you did it, would be a game changer for your school?

CHAPTER 6

THE SECRET TO HEALTHY PROGRESS: SWING SETS & PLUMB LINES

There is value in looking back to find plumb lines in order make progress.

We all want progress, but if you're on the wrong road progress means doing an about turn and walking back to the right road. In that case, the man who turns back the soonest is the one who is most progressive.

—C. S. Lewis

If you're like me, you never appreciated hearing your dad reminisce about how he walked to school, fourteen miles, in the snow, without shoes, uphill…both ways. Few kids I know want to return to those "good, old days"—even in their memories.

On the other hand, I think we'd all agree we can learn from the past. Those "old days" included elements that embedded some timeless virtues in the people who lived during that time. The past is both horrible and wonderful.

Allow me to reflect on some of the biggest ways our world is different for students today—and how it may affect these future adults. Journalist Amber Dusick inspired me to do this when she wrote about being a mom in a world very different than the one she grew up in thirty years ago. So I sat down and had some fun reminiscing myself. Here is the shortlist of changes since my childhood days, fifty years ago.

1. Seat Belts

In my early years as a kid, cars didn't even have seat belts. I remember riding in the back of my grandpa's pickup on trips to Dairy Queen in Danville, IN. At least until the "Buckle Up, It's the Law" signs emerged. It's obviously a good law, but boy are we safety-obsessed now. My kids have never ridden in the bed of a pickup truck. It's far too scary.

2. Childproofing

Oh my gosh. Hazardous, dangerous cleaning products were all over the house—and often were left open. They had those scary skull stickers slapped onto them, however, so it was fine. My children? I say this tongue in check, but any product was stored very high and protected by a force field, lasers, electric eyes, locks and secret codes.

3. Helmets

I didn't even know what a bike helmet was when I was young. Helmets were for football players and soldiers. And we did crazy things. We'd climb huge trees, ride our bikes over a ravine, or pull skateboards or wagons at full speed down a hill. But . . . my kids today? No way. In the words of some parents, "Our kids wear helmets at the dinner table."

4. Screens

I liked screens when I was a kid. Except, the only screen I had was a black-and-white TV. And this screen was an auxiliary form of entertainment. Most of my time was spent making up stuff to do— games, sports competitions, imaginary scenarios, you name it. Lots of creativity and running around. Today—not so much. It's all prescribed.

5. Cell Phones

As a kid, I saw these in science-fiction movies. Are you kidding? Those were gadgets for the distant future. Now, every teen has them. Why? Two reasons: worrying and wandering. Parents worry where their kids are, so the device is a tether to keep them "on the line." Not a bad idea, except we became paranoid. In 2007, 30 percent of parents of college students said they communicated daily with their child.[1] Imagine what that figure is now.

6. Inside

This one's big. My entire life, until I was seventeen, we did stuff outside of the house. No adult "prescribed" our games either. Outside meant freedom. Risk. The unknown. Autonomy. We were explorers. My kids growing up? Yeah, right. Freedom to wander around at night? No way—at least not until they are older. Like thirty-five.

7. Trouble at School

If I got in trouble at school growing up, mom and dad would find out about it, and I'd get in trouble a second time. They supported the discipline of my teachers. Today—if a kid gets in trouble or makes a bad grade, mom and dad often march down to the classroom and confront the teacher. They side with their child believing them over an adult.

This list, of course, is simply about fun memories of a world that's gone. As I reflect on them, however, it seems there are some timeless elements we dare not let go of, even today. For instance, playing outside is not superior to playing inside, perhaps, but experiencing autonomy is an essential ingredient to growing up healthy. Helmets and seatbelts are not signs of a lesser world today, but they unwittingly relay the message that we must always "play it safe." That's actually more dangerous than going without a helmet. Cell phones and other portable devices are not evil; no one I know wants to be without them. But how do we nurture emotional intelligence in our young if we're all glued to our screens? There are valuable skills and qualities no civilization should be without. Each must determine how to sustain them in a world that changes so rapidly. How do we evaluate the moral and social implications of our evolving culture to prevent losing what actually sustains us as a society? My point is simple. We must make progress, without being guilty of regress as we equip our young for adulthood. While past times might have been archaic, the traits they birthed might be helpful to retain . . . or, even, recapture.

Here's the question we face today. Is it even possible to lead our young into a world where no one can clearly see what's coming? In a rapidly changing society, can elders in a culture actually lead them—or are we irrelevant in the eyes of our youth?

Allow me to illustrate the challenge with some numbers.

THE TOUCHSCREEN GENERATION

Get ready. Just when you thought you knew the touchscreen generation, they got younger on you. Not only are attention spans decreasing and multi-tasking increasing, children are intuitively using tablets and portable devices at one year old. Yes, that's right—one year old.

In a recent publication of the Journal, *Pediatrics*, researchers found "almost universal exposure" to tablets and the use of smart phones (mobile devices) among young children. A 2013 report said that "72 percent of children age 8 and under have used a mobile device for some type of media activity." A 2015 survey showed "nearly 97 percent of parents said their children used mobile devices of some sort."[2]

Here are the most surprising findings[3] in *Pediatrics*:

- Nearly 97 percent of parents said their children used mobile devices of some sort.
- At age 4, the survey found three-fourths of kids owned their own mobile device.
- Of those children, about half multi-tasked on more than one screen at a time.
- 20 percent of one year olds own a tablet computer.
- 28 percent of two year olds can navigate a mobile device with no help.
- 28 percent of parents use the device to put their kids to bed.

Most surprising to lead researcher, Matilde Irigoyen, was how quickly children as young as three years old use such devices on their own. It goes without saying—it's a new world today. As Len Sweet says, "Gutenberg has given way to Google."

What Does All This Mean?

Let me offer some ideas on how we can make sense of this emerging world, and continue to grow healthy, well-adjusted children who are at home with technology, but not addicted to the point that their emotional intelligence and relational skills are retarded in their growth.

Do you remember when we used to say, "Middle school is the new high school?" What we meant was that kids are being exposed to realities earlier than in past generations. It used to be that sex and illegal drugs were the hot topic for teens in high school. Now, kids get exposed to them in middle school. The same could be said for realities such as smart phones and video games, social media and YouTube. Instagram is the new Facebook. Snapchat is the new text message. Twitter is the new micro-blog. Are students ready for these realities in elementary school and pre-school? Adults will have to decide that. For now, let me offer some initial thoughts on how to best navigate technology with your kids:

- **Remember that children (in general) cannot comprehend an addictive behavior.**
  Adults must lead them into healthy moderation, where they both understand and enjoy technology, but utilize it as a "servant" rather

than become a slave to it as a "master." This fosters self-control and the ability to delay gratification.

- **Remember that children will choose ice cream over lima beans—and screens over healthy alternatives for play.**
  While there are some exceptions, adults must be the ones to lead them in their emotional development, and introduce behaviors and habits that produce maturity.

- **Remember that children are drawn to entertainment, whether or not they learn something from it.**
  This is the genius behind TV shows like Sesame Street, Blues Clues, Super Why, Cyber Chase, Animal Atlas and Design Squad Nation. Adults must leverage what they're magnetically drawn to and make it beneficial.

Since technology is not going away, I believe we must harness it for constructive purposes. We've got to do more than whine about kids being in front of screens all the time. We must redeem it by finding ways to use it to mature them and develop them as career-ready graduates and leaders.

As children mature, they enter adolescence. They progress into a time where their brains are pruning and re-circuiting themselves. In this period, they are prone to take more risks, as the portion of their brain that senses rewards for risky behavior (i.e. the "likes" they receive from friends) far outweighs their sense of consequences for poor decisions (i.e. "I can't believe I got caught"). Dramatic changes often take place during teenage years. They need a pioneer with a new map to help them navigate all of this.

As I mentioned in chapter two, Alexander the Great progressed into new terrain, but no doubt hunted for timeless elements like water to drink and food to eat. He embraced the new, but he retained the necessary, as well. He recognized what they would always need in any land, to survive and to thrive there. In the same way, we must recognize that expanding does not always equal progress. A flood is water expanding, but it usually causes damage. To simply introduce new technologies, for example, doesn't always result in improvement. Growth always means change, but change does not always equate to growth. Our action must be channeled so that we (and our young) become better for it. In a nutshell, I am saying:

Our movement must lead to improvement.

SWING SETS

I want you to think about a swing set. Did you or a neighbor have one growing up? We installed one in our Atlanta home, while our children were young. It provided hours of amusement for all of us, as we swung our kids back and forth. Back and forth.

I believe a swing set is a helpful image of what we must do to lead well in our day. Just like a good swing, you must swing backward very far, to swing forward very high. The more you swing the seat back, the more you can swing forward for the thrill. Do you remember your child smiling as they yelled, "Higher! Swing me higher, Mommy!"

Wise leaders utilize vision that can see both backward and forward. They look back and learn from the past. They glean from past mistakes in order to avoid repeating them. Additionally, they seek what was helpful and timeless so they can carry those elements forward. They swing backward so they can swing forward well.

That's the engaging part of the ride, the swing forward. Children peer outward ahead of them, to see how high and far they can go. Ponder how futile it would have been for Alexander the Great to march into new territory, but be preoccupied with Greece, his home country. Do you think he could have progressed well if all he could think about was superimposing the old maps onto the new terrain and wishing for the land he used to live in.

Far too often, leaders grab only one of these two components. They are only looking backward, feverishly attempting to grip the past, fearing they might lose everything they hold dear. Or, they only swing forward, lusting for progress so much, they care little about how it may affect people morally or socially.

- One is primarily about caution and conserving.
- One is primarily about progress and profit.

Neither are complete without the other.

How do You Apply This?

To implement this kind of leadership (in your home, your work, your teaching), you must push "pause" and reflect on both the past and the future. I recommend you take time each month, if not each week, and use this exercise to stay on top of life. Grab a pen and your Travel Guide and respond to the following questions.

Swinging Backward

Swinging back means we get in touch with our heritage—our roots. Who we are, and how we got here today. We identify our foundation, both positive and negative. As we do, it is helpful to ask ourselves questions like:

- What is our foundation and heritage?
- Why did we decide to pursue our mission?
- What value did we seek to add to our community?
- What were the destructive elements we tried to discard?
- Were there principles we felt are essential to sustain ourselves?

Swinging Forward

Swinging forward means we've not forgotten why we exist and won't lose our sense of mission as we progress into the future. We identify our new realities and translate our mission for today's culture. Helpful questions might be:

- Where do we want to go today?
- How is the landscape different than it was in the past?
- What are the greatest needs we see in front of us?
- What new methods or strategies do we need in the future?
- How do we stay relevant by renewing our pledge to our mission?

TRAVEL GUIDE:

How can we utilize the past to leverage the future?

Kris Hogan is a new friend of mine. He's an educator, a coach and an athletic director at a private high school in Grapevine, Texas. As an innovative leader, Kris is always looking for fresh ways to help everyone he influences to grow and make progress. He explores new ways to instill timeless virtues in his student athletes and their families. You might say he's great with a swing set.

A few years ago, his football team played Gainesville State School. It wasn't your typical high school team. All the players at Gainesville State were criminals. They played on the team at their juvenile detention center. So, on that Friday night, a faith-based school played teens who had violated the law, who'd committed misdemeanors or felonies.

Kris saw this as a prime opportunity for a win/win situation. He knew those teens from Gainesville State had no fans, no parents in the stands rooting for them. Their support systems were almost non-existent. In addition, Kris saw how easily his own students could get caught up in themselves, with such a robust support system. So, he implemented a plan that involved everyone.

He emailed the families of his players and asked some of them to sit in the stands on the opposing side, knowing it would likely be empty. He instructed his players to assemble gift bags to give to the opposing team after the game, no matter who won. He had some cheerleaders cheer for the home team, and some for the opposition. He explained his goal to the students and invited everyone to participate. He wanted to give them perspective—life is not about you. He also wanted to communicate to the Gainesville State team that if you make good choices, you can always recover from your past. He wanted to give them hope—your life can have a future. The outcome was stunning.

Before the game, his fans made a spirit line for Gainesville. Throughout the game, those same fans, cheered for the Gainesville teens, rooting for them by name. They also met them afterward and embraced them. His players then met them in a big huddle after the game and gave them their gift bags and wished them well.

How did the young inmates respond? Most could not believe it. They said for the first time they felt what it was like to have a family. To be loved. Some cried when they returned to their rooms in the incarceration facility. All of them said they felt what it was like "to win." Kris' plan worked. The Gainesville team experienced hope. And at the same time, his players served a peer group that typically would be viewed as the enemy. Kris rode the swing set.

He swung backwards, drilling timeless values into his own kids, and at the same time, he swung forward, brilliantly facing a situation he'd never faced before. He did something completely uncommon, especially in the football culture of Texas. He knew the best forward swing includes wise reflection on the past and fresh resolve to go take new land. We utilize both to make progress.

Why Is This So Essential?

I focus on this issue because the last five hundred years of history have changed humankind profoundly. Our definitions and expectations of childhood have evolved, sometimes without our consciousness. Let me explain what I mean more deeply than I have in past chapters.

Several centuries ago, the category of childhood did not even exist. Everyone, regardless of age, were merely humans. Some were young, but no one distinguished between stages and ages. In his book, *The Disappearance of Childhood*, Neil Postman writes that it was the invention of the printing press that introduced the idea of children and adults. Why? For the first time, people separated into two groups:

- Those who could read.
- Those who could not read.

Until then, both adults and children shared in the same conversations, all about local and relevant issues in their community. There was no "baby talk," and both kids and grown ups wore the same kind of clothes. Both had the same level of education. All ages participated in family chores and each did what they could for the whole. We were all simply people. The data shows this actually fostered maturity in children.

Before books occurred, the average person did not engage in higher-level thinking, philosophies, theologies and ideologies. With print media, understanding differed. Postman writes that childhood became a category. "Childhood became a description of a level of symbolic achievement."[4] In fact, adults who did not read were often referred to as intellectually "childish."

Ivy Pinchbeck and Margaret Hewitt express it this way:

"Whilst under the traditional system of apprenticeship, 'childhood' effectively ended at the age of seven . . . the effect of organized formal education was to prolong the period during which children were withheld from the demands and responsibilities of the adult world. Childhood was, in fact . . . emerging for the first time as a formative period of increasing significance."[5]

Once reading divided us into age groups, other categorizing took place. The way we dressed children, in knickers and hats; the way we talked to them; the way we then segregated them in schools; and the information they read was all tailored for them. I want you to see—this is both good news and bad news. It was a natural evolution, but we may not have recognized the unintended consequences. We began a slow regression of expecting less of the young than generations had earlier.

Consider life as recent as one hundred years ago:
- Four year olds performed age-appropriate chores around the house.
- Nine year olds had begun to work on the farm or property.
- Eleven year olds were leading that work on the property.
- Fourteen year olds were driving cars.
- Seventeen year olds were leading armies, in WW I.
- Nineteen year olds were getting married and having children.

I'm not suggesting we revert to this lifestyle. I'm simply saying—it is inherent in our kids to be so much more than people who get lost on social media. Generally speaking, many parents today don't expect their kids to have much genuine interaction with the real world. Much of their activity is virtual. After all, they're just kids. We don't want them to fail, fall or fear.

The term "adolescence" was only introduced and popularized a century ago. Seeing how teen brains and hormones develop, we created a system to allow for it. We set them apart, and soon gave them their own music, clothes, vocabulary and lifestyles. This segmenting of our culture certainly helped adults understand and relate better to our young—but it didn't always help our young develop into mature adults.

Here's my point in a summary:

A culture that offers the young increasing information and autonomy without requiring equal parts accountability and responsibility produces "unready" adults. In fact, we should expect arrogant, entitled brats to emerge as they enter adulthood.

The adolescent brain, typically, desires further risk and challenge. This is why a boy would work a job, or become an apprentice as a young teen a century ago. The thrill an adolescent craves was met with authentic challenges. It was time to stop doing so much "sitting," and start some "doing." The primary way adolescents learn is by actually applying the information they know. Today's problem is, we've so categorized childhood, we're afraid to allow them to interface with real issues and challenges that would engage their hearts and minds. So now, we simulate them. We offer a facsimile of the real thing. We give them virtual realities with video games. We offer them virtual relationships with social media. We give them virtual connections with the Internet. We offer virtual intimacy through pornography. We give them virtual thrills and excitement with roller coasters at theme parks. We want it all under control. Nothing real. It's monitored and safe—or so we think.

Sadly, too many teens experience virtual maturity.

Plumb Lines

I'd like to offer another metaphor, besides the swing set. It's a plumb line. They're pictures of what we need today. Do you know what a plumb line is? They are long strings that have a weight attached to the end of them. A plumb line was used in the past to measure depth and accuracy. Most often it was a cord weighted with lead that was used to plumb the depths of an ocean or lake. A fisherman could use it to check out how deep the water was. But another use for these plumb lines is to measure accuracy. For centuries, they were held next to a wall in a building to evaluate if vertical structures were true. While next to a wall, gravity pulled the cord straight down, making it easy to see if a wall was crooked.

Through the years, these plumb lines were used as symbols in literature. They represented a standard by which one could evaluate if something was off and did not meet a standard. Once again, it was about depth and accuracy.

Plumb lines are what we need in every industry, every school, every athletic team and in every home to help us measure how deep we are or if we've gotten crooked. Metaphorically speaking, they are timeless standards that we agree to be a healthy measuring stick for character and conduct. Historically, our U.S. judicial system used the Bill of Rights as a "plumb line" to check precedents and to examine if an activity had become "crooked." We even used to call criminals "crooks."

So what does this look like, as we lead and teach students today?

"Past Forward"

I call this "past forward." I see examples of it in many communities and down through various generations. Perhaps my favorite picture of this was John Wooden, former coach for the UCLA Bruin basketball team. He referred to himself as an educator more than a coach. He used the game of basketball to prepare his players for life. He established "plumb lines" that became standards of excellence, both on and off the court. In his drills at practice, he never studied the opposing team UCLA was about to play. Instead, he focused on the process of preparation. If they were excellent, the score would take care of itself. He loved his team and told them so—but if they failed to execute what he knew they were capable of in practice, he'd stop, turn off the lights and have them leave the gym. And his standards were ones his graduates kept with them.

Each year, Coach Wooden sat down with his players to talk about his "pyramid for success," which represented qualities to help them excel. He introduced habits for first-year players, from how to put on their socks (to avoid blisters) to why he wanted them to have no facial hair, (they could catch a cold easier after a shower following games or practice). Plus, Wooden wanted clean-shaven men wearing suits to represent UCLA off the court. It was simply a standard.

I'll never forget hearing about the time big Bill Walton arrived from Helix High School his freshman year at UCLA in 1971, with a big red beard. After Coach Wooden shared his rule on facial hair, Walton let his new coach know—he planned to keep his beard. Wooden looked up at his new star player saying, "You really feel strongly about that beard, don't you, Bill?" When Walton agreed, Wooden affirmed him, saying he admired people who feel strongly about what they believe. At that point, however, he concluded, saying, "We're going to miss you, Bill."

It was a standard.

Bill Walton shaved his beard, met the standard and won two NCAA championships. Later, the fiery redhead got thrown in jail for protesting on campus. Like a loving Dad, Wooden was the one who bailed him out. Later Walton relayed what happened:

> *"One of the saddest days for Coach Wooden was the day he came down and had to bail me out of jail after I got arrested in the anti-Vietnam protest. He said, 'Bill, I know you feel very strongly about this, but I just don't think that you getting arrested and taking part in this demonstration is what it's all about.'"*

Wooden then referred to his standards, explaining how his young player could live out his convictions and represent the team well. Years later Walton would say of his experience playing on Wooden's team: "We have become John Wooden ourselves." In one sense, they did, by embracing Wooden's standards and values, as their own. And they all became better for it. They just needed a plumb line.

TRAVEL GUIDE:

What if we agreed upon a plumb line and held it next to our homes, our schools, or our teams? Are we crooked? Are we shallow?

Eight Essential Life Skills Students Need

As I peer out into the future, I see what's needed in the new terrain. Over the last four years, I've taken time to swing backward and forward examining what skill sets are essential to thrive in the land of tomorrow. Our team has conducted surveys among educators, parents, coaches and employers. We have hosted focus groups that included both students and graduates. We have looked at data from a number of universities, from the Pew Research Center, the Gallup Organization, the Barna Group and the National Association of Colleges and Employers (NACE).

From this work, we've developed a list of eight skills we believe are "plumb lines" we can use to evaluate our work with the young. We must both model these skills ourselves and impart them to this emerging generation. Some of these skills have been somewhat important in past eras, but have become essential today. Others of these hard and soft skills are timeless ones that successful people have always leveraged in their lives. Regardless of the industry they enter, these fundamental "life skills" can equip graduates to successfully navigate a career, as well as marriage, family and friendships. You might say, I used a "swing set" (looking backward and forward) to create a list of "plumb lines" for the next generation. I offer them to you here.

1. Problem Solving Skills

The fastest way to earn leadership on a team is to solve problems. Our world's population is larger than ever. Consequently, it's filled with more complex problems than ever. Several employers say it's the number one skill they look for in new hires. Unfortunately, employer surveys continue to reveal that recent grads don't have these skills.[6] One nationwide survey found nearly half of employers said recent college graduates have poor problem-solving skills. Students' tests suggest the employers are right.[7] I believe we must equip graduates to solve problems and serve people. Those who do will not only be employable, they'll likely be the leaders.

TRAVEL GUIDE:

How are you building problem-solving skills in your students?

---

2. Critical Thinking

According to the American Association of Colleges and Universities, employers are more interested in discovering a graduate who can think critically rather than focusing on what their major was in college.[8] Critical thinking is evidence-based reasoning. It is the ability to use objective, logical analysis and evaluation of an issue in order to form a judgment. According to an analysis by Patricia Greenfield at UCLA, life skills such as critical thinking and perseverance have declined with the prevalence of technology.[9] We must teach our young not only what to think, but how to think. They'll face problems as adults we never had to face, so we must equip them to evaluate objectively.

3. Emotional Intelligence

Daniel Goleman popularized this subject in 1995. It has become a buzzword today among both educators and employers. Emotional Intelligence (what some call EQ) is the sum total of our self-awareness, our self-management, our social awareness, and our relationship management. Along with many others, I believe EQ is a greater predictor of success in life than IQ. I believe success in school is made up of 75 percent IQ and 25 percent EQ. Success after graduation is just the opposite. It's 25 percent IQ and 75 percent EQ. It's the ability to manage your emotions and relationships. It's the capacity to get along with colleagues and take correction. It's how aware you are of others' needs and how you come across to people. Whether we call them soft skills, business skills, employability or executive skills, we've got to build them into today's graduates.

4. Values and Ethics

Sadly, there have been eras in history when people expected others, even leaders, to be corrupt—to lie, to cheat and to deceive. During these times society always wanes in its progress. Today, we say we value ethics, but too often we fail to practice what we preach. Cheating no longer carries the stigma that it used to. Less social disapproval coupled with increased competition for admission into universities and graduate schools has made students more willing "to do whatever it takes" to get the A. According to Study.com, back in 1940, only 20 percent of college students admitted to cheating during their academic careers. Today, that number has increased to a range of 75 percent-98 percent.[10] Is this a characteristic we want in the people who'll be leading our companies in twenty years?

> TRAVEL GUIDE:
>
> How do you instill the practice of ethics and values in your students?

5. Resourcefulness and Resilience

I'm certainly not the first to say it, but I'm convinced resourcefulness and resilience are the two meta-competencies today. Because of society's rapid pace of change, memorization is no longer what students need most to succeed (that's only required in school). What they need is resourcefulness—the ability to search and find answers; the ability to use what they have to find solutions. Why? They'll likely have several jobs and they might work in a variety of industries. The ability to locate an answer is of greater value than memorizing data that may be antiquated in a year. Further, resilience is huge because a world of change likely means lots of trial and error. They'll need to possess the ability to bounce back and experiment until they finish a particular task.

> TRAVEL GUIDE:
>
> How do you incentivize resourcefulness and resilience in students?

6. Creative Processing

Due to the rapid rate of change each year, the ability to think and process creatively becomes enormously valuable. Creative processing is the ability to look at a problem with a fresh perspective and to combine two or more existing ideas to invent an entirely new solution. Orville and Wilbur Wright combined their knowledge of bikes and birds to create the first airplane. Johannes Gutenberg combined his knowledge of words and wine to create the first printing press. Jennifer Henderson reports, "The Partnership for 21st Century Skills" stresses the importance of creativity in its guide: 'Many of the fastest growing jobs and emerging industries rely on workers' creative capacity—the ability to think unconventionally, question the herd, imagine new scenarios, and produce astonishing work.'"[11]

7. Analytical Writing

Often, when students fall behind in school, it's not because they lack intelligence. Many fail because they lack the ability to construct arguments, build ideas, and distinguish essential information from non-essential information. Kids who learn analytic writing not only get better at writing, they get better at every subject, to the point that schools that teach it are now models for what some are calling the "Writing Revolution". The reason for this is analytic writing is a keystone skill. This ability to articulate ideas is the foundation on which other skills can be built—literally, inside the brain. It allows students to improve at math, science, and social studies because it supports those skills in the same way that a keystone supports a foundation.

8. Leadership Perspective

I'll admit, I have a leadership development bias. I suggest, however, that I am not speaking of attempting to prepare every student to hold a leadership position, like the CEO or president. I am suggesting we must prepare them with a perspective— not for a position. A student who thinks like a leader sees the big picture can develop an action plan, can collaborate with people well, and implement ideas. After surveying both private and public colleges, The Higher Education Research Institute, based at UCLA, published their findings. In it, they report that in today's world, every student will need leadership skills.[12] It is not merely for the student government officers or the resident advisors. Our world is too complex to simply graduate followers.

> TRAVEL GUIDE:
>
> How are you equipping all of your students to think like leaders?

In 2014, Inside Higher Ed did a survey of chief academic officers. Ninety-six percent said they were doing a good job in preparing students for a career—but they may have been grading on a curve.[13] The proof may just be in the pudding. In a new survey by Gallup measuring how business leaders and the American public view the state and value of higher education, just 14 percent of Americans—and only 11 percent of business leaders—strongly agreed that graduates have the necessary skills and competencies to succeed in the workplace.[14] In chapter nine, you'll find illustrations of these skills and meet educators who are cultivating them.

> TRAVEL GUIDE:
>
> Do you have intentional methods to impart these life skills in your students?

The Size of Home Plate

By 1996, college baseball coach, John Scolinos, had already become a legend. He was 78 years old that year, and agreed to speak to 4,000 coaches at an American Baseball Coaches Association convention in Nashville. It was unforgettable for everyone.

He shuffled up to the platform, looking strange. He wore a home plate, attached to a chain hung from his neck. Who does that? Only strange baseball coaches, I guess. He spoke for 25 minutes, not once mentioning that ornament he wore.

Finally, as he began to conclude, he cleared his throat.

"You're probably wondering why I'm wearing home plate around my neck. Or, maybe you think I escaped from Camarillo State Hospital," he said, as folks chuckled.

"No," he continued. "I may be old but I'm not crazy."

"The reason I stand before you today is to share with you baseball people what I've learned in my life; what I've learned about home plate in my 78 years."

He paused.

Several hands went up as Scolinos asked how many Little League coaches were in the room. He then asked, "Do you know how wide home plate is in Little League?"

Someone answered from the second row, "Seventeen inches."

"That's right," Scolinos replied. "How about Babe Ruth League?" After a pause, a reluctant coach guessed, "Seventeen inches?"

"That's right again," he said. "How many high school coaches here today?" Hundreds of hands went up. Again, Scolinos asked his question: "How big is your home plate?"

"Seventeen inches," several shouted, now more confident.

"Right again. Now, what about college baseball? Anyone know?"

"Seventeen inches," they answered in unison. Finally, Coach Scolinos asked, "How about professional baseball. How big is home plate? And, how about the major leagues? Anyone know how big home plate is?"

Scolinos answered his own question: "It's seventeen inches," he bellowed, his voice bouncing off the walls. He then repeated it, "Seventeen inches!" "And do you know what they do with a Big League pitcher who can't throw the ball over those seventeen inches?" He paused. "They send him to Pocatello!" he hollered, drawing raucous laughter. "Now—why don't they say, "Aw, that's OK, Jimmy. You can't hit a seventeen-inch target? We'll make it eighteen inches or nineteen inches. We'll make it twenty inches so you have a better chance of hitting it. And if you can't hit that, let us know so we can make it wider still, say, twenty-five inches."

A long pause. The coaches were silent.

"What do we do when our best player shows up late to practice? When our team rules forbid facial hair and a guy shows up unshaven? What if he gets caught drinking? Do we hold him accountable? Or, do we change the rules to fit him; do we widen our home plate?"

The chuckles gradually faded as everyone caught his point. The fog had lifted.

Scolinos turned the plate toward himself, and using a Sharpie, began to draw something on it. When he turned to the crowd, with home plate pointed up, a house was revealed, complete with freshly drawn windows and doors.

"This is the problem with our homes today. With our marriages, with the way we parent our kids, with our discipline. We don't teach accountability to our kids, and there is no consequence for failing to meet standards. We just widen home plate."

A long pause.

Then at the top of his home plate, he added an American flag. "This is often the problem with our schools today. The quality of our education has gone downhill and teachers have been stripped of the tools they need to be successful, and to educate and discipline our young people. We are allowing others to widen home plate. Where is that getting us?"

Silence again.

He then replaced the flag with a cross, and said, "And this is the problem in the Church, where powerful people in positions of authority have taken advantage of young children, only to have such an atrocity swept under the rug for years. Our spiritual leaders have widened home plate."

You could've heard a pin drop. Those coaches assumed they'd learn something about curve balls and bunting, but had gleaned a lesson in life.

Coach Scolinos concluded, "If you remember one thing from this old coach today, I hope it's this: if we fail to hold ourselves to a higher standard, a standard we know to be right; if we fail to hold our children to the same standards, if we are unwilling or unable to provide a consequence when they do not meet the standard; and if our schools and churches and our government fail to hold themselves accountable to those they serve, there is but one thing to look forward to." With that, he slowly turned home plate around, and revealed its dark, black backside.

And walked off the stage.

Keep yourself at seventeen inches. Sounds like a plumb line to me.

CHAPTER 7

HOW DO WE LEAD STUDENTS FROM APATHY TO PASSION?

The keys to the 21st century brain and how to help kids own their education.

Children have never been good at listening to their elders but they have never failed at imitating them.
—James A. Baldwin

I stumbled onto a significant discovery about teaching and learning accidentally. I was mentoring a learning community of university students years ago, when one of them sent me an email asking who was choosing the topic for the next week's session. I was teaching leadership strategies to this group, and up until then, I had taught each lesson in a traditional fashion. When I saw the inquiry, I grabbed my laptop and typed in my response: "I can do that." Or, at least that's what I meant to say.

Without knowing it, however, I had mistyped. The letter "i" on my keyboard is right next to the letter "u." Unwittingly, I sent the message back: "u can do that." And he believed me.

At our next meeting, the students showed up ready to go. Before I could interrupt them, they proceeded to facilitate the discussion, the experiments, the learning and the outcomes. They were brilliant. In fact, they didn't even need me. I had never felt such satisfaction than in that meeting when my "mentees" taught themselves. They felt empowered because I sent the message: "u can do that."

I never told them it was an accident on my part.

"U Can Do That"

What I learned was all about metacognition. Metacognition (or thinking about thinking) is the secret to and the driving motivation behind all effective learning. It's how these new "natives" learn best. If we want our students to learn as much as possible, then we'll want to maximize the amount of metacognition they're doing. It's a relatively simple equation for students:

The more they reflect on their learning, the more they learn. The better they engage in the subject and how to communicate it to others—the more they actually own it.

This is what every instructor dreams about for their students. Our problem is that most classrooms are set up to promote metacognition in the teachers, not the students. We are far more engaged than our students. Most students sit back and wait for their teacher to simplify the material and make it easy for them to digest it. Some kids want to be "spoon fed." When we teach this way, we are like a personal trainer in a gym who says, "I'm going to make sure you learn fitness, so stand back and watch, as I lift all the weights for you."

That's ridiculous. No one meets a fitness goal without doing the work for themselves. And so it is with teaching and learning. One reason Matt is still living at home; Zoe and Savanna are lacking clear focus and Dylan can't seem to get off the couch are that adults have not equipped them to practice metacognition. I have failed at this as well.

The Over-Functioning Teacher

You see, I was like most teachers. I put a lot of thought into how to make my classes accessible and engaging. I considered what I knew about the subject, and how I first learned it. I reflected on what my students knew and how to utilize that knowledge as a platform for my instruction. I worked to be so engaging that no matter what preoccupied their minds (a girlfriend, a ballgame, a video game or the upcoming weekend), my class would grip them and hold their attention. Still, however, some students' minds would wander. How could this happen? I was good, wasn't I? Working so hard on a lesson plan and still not reaching every student is frustrating. But I had no one to blame but myself. I was hoarding all the best learning in my class. I was the only one doing any metacognition.

My common assumptions and problems:

My Assumption	My Problem
1. I must work hard to know my subject.	1. Do I ask students to do so too?
2. I put creativity into my lesson plan.	2. Do I require any creativity of students?
3. I reflect on what I want them to gain.	3. Do I give time for students to do this?
4. I prepare for the class time.	4. Do my students prepare for class time?
5. I own the responsibility for teaching.	5. Do they take ownership to learn?

How Learning Really Works

In 2005, the National Academy of Sciences summarized everything we know about learning in a report called, "How Students Learn."[1] Their research culminates in a single term: "metacognition." The NAS identified this word as the key to effective learning. Quite literally, meta means "behind," and cognition means "the act of knowing." Our task is to increase the amount of metacognition students do.

People simply perform better when they're both physically and mentally active; when they do the work themselves. It fosters ownership. Every faculty member knows that teaching is hard work. You have to constantly engage in and be aware of your process, and how to improve it. Ironically, this is exactly what makes an expert learner. We need to share the wealth.

This was demonstrated vividly by Eric Mazur, a physics professor at Harvard. Eric was teaching some of the smartest college students anywhere, but soon discovered how little they really understood. It was startling to him. Dr. Mazur decided he must push his students to think more, so he began making them teach each other. The transformation was stunning. His experiment evolved into the "Flipped Classroom" movement we've all heard about. Research shows it consistently produces superior results compared to traditional classrooms. Of course it does—it's all about metacognition. Flipping the classroom makes students the teachers, shifting the metacognition onto the students' shoulders.

The first person I ever heard did this was a ninth grade algebra teacher named Karl Fish. Years ago, he realized his students just weren't connecting with algebra. Imagine that. So he decided to speak their native tongue—and in the process began enabling them to do metacognition. First, he put his math lectures on YouTube. He figured they're watching videos on the site anyway; why not make it productive? This freed up his classroom time for all kinds of experiential learning, actually turning them loose on their homework, giving out prizes as students engaged each other. In short, he flipped his class before the act ever became popular. He called it "The Fish Flop." It can be done by anyone who's willing to turn the learning experience upside down. In summary, you move traditional styles to transformational learning:

Traditional Pedagogy	Transformational Pedagogy
1. Students are consumers	1. Students are creators
2. Teachers are commanders	2. Teachers are consultants
3. Fosters complacency	3. Fosters contribution

Giving Students Ownership

I'll be honest with you. During the last four decades I have worked with and taught students, I have seen lots of apathy. There's something about being a teen and being apathetic that go together. In adolescence, our brains are pruning themselves at an alarming rate and hormones are raging. Change is happening and it's usually accompanied with a sense of distance between the teen and the adult. It's normal and natural. However, the one ingredient I've seen spark passion in them is metacognition. We must allow students to "own" what they do and what they learn.

Hunter Maats and Katie O'Brien write, "We want our students to do as much thinking as possible, and that's why the world's greatest teachers actively avoid teaching." It's an irony. In their book, *The Straight-A Conspiracy*, they write,

> *"We've seen this tactic succeed on a personal level. Ten years ago, when we started tutoring full time, we did everything we could to help our students. It was our job to make sure that they understood and succeeded. Pretty soon, we realized that our desire to help was*

exactly what was hurting our students the most. They knew we'd do everything we could, so they stopped doing things for themselves. Eventually, we turned our tutoring sessions around. When a student asked how something was done, we'd play dumb and say, 'I don't know. We should probably look it up.' The student would look it up, ask another question, and we'd say, 'Hmmm. That's interesting. How can we find that out?' Again, the student would go to the book. After enough of those sessions, our students stopped bothering to ask us for the answers—they already knew all the behaviors that would lead to understanding.

Curious whether this shift in our students was just a fluke, we began working our way through the scientific literature, and the picture quickly became clear. Today's students have incredible resources—and a troubling lack of resourcefulness. They have brand new textbooks that they never crack open. They have the collected knowledge of the world available at the click of a mouse, but they never use it to look up things they don't know. After years of classroom lectures, students everywhere—regardless of cultural or socioeconomic background—had internalized the idea that students are supposed to get answers from teachers. At its core, that translates to the idea that the person in charge of their learning is someone other than them. And that's a huge problem because, ultimately, no one else can be responsible for our learning."[2]

Regardless of how brilliant your lectures are, you can't force your students to pay attention. It's up to them. Unfortunately, we consistently fall victim to the notion that if a student isn't engaged, it must be due to a bad teacher. From a neuroscience point of view, that's just not true. Sadly, when we do too much for them, rush in to solve their problems or do their thinking for them, we reinforce this idea. We become irreplaceable. And we do them a disservice.

> *"A great education doesn't come from a teacher who thinks for you. It comes from a teacher who nudges you to think for yourself."*
> *—Hunter Maats and Katie O-Brien*

This is why so many brilliant inventors emerged a hundred years ago. It's why my grandparent's generation had so much common sense and naturally figured out life's struggles. It's at least partly because no one instructed them in a class—they had to learn it for themselves. While they represent a far-less formally educated population, they were far better students of life. Metacognition occurred naturally.

TRAVEL GUIDE:

How do you foster metacognition in your communication?

The Best Way to Ensure Your Students Are Learning
Whether he knew it or not, Sam Levin started a little movement when he was a freshman in high school. When he complained to his mom that he and his classmates hated school, she responded, "Why don't you just make your own school?"

So he did.

As a freshman, Sam took a small step. He launched a school-wide garden that was solely cared for by students. Some woke up early on Saturdays to work with the plants. The garden still exists, five years later and serves needy families in the community. As Sam watched his classmates laboring at something they created themselves, he became convinced that teens were capable of putting time and energy into their studies too . . . as long as they got to own it. This was the only way he figured they would care about their subjects.

At Monument Mountain Regional High School, in Massachusetts, a handful of students now enjoy what's called the high school's Independent Project.[3] It's an alternative program described as a "school within a school," founded and run by students. The students in the program are supervised by teachers, but they are more like coaches rather than lecturers at a podium. Each class has a mix of 10 students, some straight-A students and others who are at-risk academically. Three to four faculty advisers are available to guide the students and to provide advice, but for the most part, they remain on the sidelines.

And boy has it made a difference in student engagement.

The Missing Ingredients

One of the reasons this project works is that it's added elements missing in so many conventional classrooms in our school system. As others have made this discovery across our country, it's transformed both students and teachers alike. Why? Let me suggest a few reasons.

- **The students own how they reach the goal.**
  Rather than the subject originating with an adult, the students get to work on an issue or project of their choosing. Timeless skills are nurtured but students remain engaged because they got to choose the subject. The job of the instructor is more to "expose" than to "impose." They learn the skills every school requires them to learn, but in their own methodology. Students support what they help create.

- **The students are active and moving.**
  Did you know, according to one study, that climbing a tree and balancing on a beam can dramatically improve cognitive skills?[4] We know this intuitively, don't we? Students in every generation have learned better when allowed to practice or experiment firsthand. However, we live in a day where things are streamlined. Adults are better at relaying theories than permitting on-the-job training.

- **The verbal matches the visual.**
  Another study found that children who were encouraged to gesture while learning, retained more of what they had learned.[5] These successful, transformative courses are different in that the students are hearing, seeing and gesturing, which connects with every learning style—kinesthetic, visual or verbal. It's difficult in a traditional classroom period to reach various learning styles.

- **The students actually do the teaching.**
  According to a study, people learn better when they expect to teach the information to another person. We all know this is true, but in most classes adults continue to do most of the talking. I know a professor who let's his students do all the teaching when reviewing for mid-term and final examinations. And they always fair better.

Do you see a common thread?

It's all driven by corresponding movement. Decisions. Application. Experience. The research on this is compelling—but instructors often fail to utilize it due to the demands of system. While nearly all teachers believe "hands on" lessons serve kids best, the teachers we've surveyed say their school teaches for the test.

By taking responsibility and ownership for their learning, students at Monument (and others like it) are pushed to think creatively and leverage their own talents in order to achieve. The class framework is similar to what will be expected of them in college and in the workforce, when they have to make their own decisions.

I love how high school senior Matt Whalan commented on this process: "Some kids say, I hate science or I hate math, but what they are really saying is: I hate science class or I hate math class."

What if we changed our pedagogy and ensured that our students really learn?

Race to the Bottom

Now—please hear me. I recognize this pedagogy is fundamentally different than the one most teachers or parents have used with their young. Teachers feel the pressure to produce students who generate certain test scores, so they migrate unwittingly into a "teach for the test" style in the classroom. According to a 2015 Bayer Survey for Facts of Science Education, "Nearly all teachers believe 'hands on' science lessons serve kids best, but 4 out of 5 teachers say their school teaches for the test."[6] Initiatives like "No Child Left Behind" and "Race to the Top" were well-intended, but often cultivated schools that simply did whatever they needed to do to receive the funding they needed. Over the years, schools have rightly worked toward measurable outcomes. Sadly, unless teachers are intentional, they feel their task is teaching for the test. They're evaluated on grades, not actual student discovery and transformation. Although few disagree that students need to be active in order to learn, we've seized control and become the active ones.

What's more, students have been conditioned to be "spoon-fed," both at home and at school, as I mentioned earlier. They've been taught by adults to simply "get the answer right" so they've become as pragmatic as the adults who lead them. They ask questions like: "Is this going to be on the test?" They often don't want to work at learning. They focus on the "product" not the "process," which means they might even resort to cheating to get the correct answer. In our next chapter, I'll offer some research on how the majority of our wonderful American kids cheat in order to get the grade they want. Their world outside of education has taught them to locate the quickest, easiest solution. And it's usually a quick and easy search, thanks to Google, Bing, Yahoo! Search, Ask—and sites like Wikipedia and YouTube.

Ultimately, time is short and precious for everyone. We all seem to be in a hurry today.

Further, educators are told America has fallen behind smaller industrialized nations—like Finland and Singapore—in almost every subject. According to the Programme for International School Assessment, U.S. students performed near the middle of the pack in 2015. On average, sixteen other industrialized countries scored above the United States in science, and twenty-three scored above us in math.[7] A nation that once led the pack, is now "average." This affects both our attitudes and actions. We're not at our best when teachers feel like they've fallen behind; when parents feel like they're late and when coaches feel like they're losing. It makes the labor of enabling students to experience the learning process challenging. Few of us have the margins to let students practice meta-cognition in class . . . or, as we rush out the door late and discover our child's shoes are untied. In the end, adults have sighed and said, "Ugh. It's easier just to do it myself." So, where do we begin?

TRAVEL GUIDE:

Do your students "own" their education? Why or why not?

REACHING EPIC STUDENTS

Years ago, futurist Dr. Leonard Sweet first suggested that students today make up an EPIC generation. This idea has been embraced by thousands of educators, and we, at Growing Leaders, have leveraged this term, EPIC, to inform our student events. By this we mean the letters that spell EPIC remind us of who students are and how they best learn. Perhaps this can serve as a grid for your teaching style. Each time I train students, I run my lesson plan through the grid of EPIC:

E—Experiential

Students have always preferred an experience over a lecture. It's more true today than ever. Consider the world they grew up in as children: fast food restaurants are play land experiences; children's museums aren't simply about gazing at a painting but touching, smelling, looking, hearing and sometimes even tasting. (Have you ever visited the World of Coca Cola in Atlanta?) Students grew up in an experiential world and now they are not looking for a "sage on the stage" with a lecture. I believe they are looking for a "guide on the side" with an experience.

I love the story of High Tech High School in San Diego, California. In 1998, forty public and corporate partners, led by Gary Jacobs, began meeting to discuss the current state of education in San Diego. Faced with a shortage of workers for the locally strong high tech and biotech industries, the group wondered why the local school system was not better able to produce more qualified workers. These local entrepreneurs decided to open a new high school and christened it High Tech High.

The school was founded in September 2000 with 200 students and currently educates several hundred students. At the High Tech High School the method of teaching is based on "project-based learning," which means that students are given a project which involves working independently or in groups and doing research to complete it. Some classes have projects where grades from different subjects will be all part of the same project. Reports say that projects the students have worked on include designing a human-powered submarine, genetic manipulation, designing a water treatment plant, a book on the Harlem Renaissance, creating a sitcom and building a robot from old computer parts. All students complete internships in the junior year. These internships are currently a 3-week immersion experience, working full-time at various companies or organizations in the area.

Question: Is there a way you could create a learning environment that uses experiences, not just instruction, to catalyze students to engage better? Even if it were once a week, what if you offered an experience and turned students loose to learn an idea by working experientially—and then discussing what they learned?

P—Participatory

This element is vital to metacognition. Consider, once again, the world today's kids have grown up in: adults have asked their opinion on everything. They have been central to culture, to the marketplace and to their families. Many of these children have weighed in on where the family goes on vacation since they were five years old. As young adults, many assume they can vote on who stays on the reality TV show each week. They've gotten to participate, to vote, to share their views, to "Like," "Dislike" or "Unfriend" and to have a "say" on what they want in life. For them, life has been a cafeteria, picking and choosing what they want to consume.

Schools in Finland have been able to capitalize on this idea and engage students better than most countries. In fact, Finnish test scores have been superior to most other industrialized nations for years. When American educators visited a classroom in Finland, they soon discovered one reason why. The class was both experiential and participatory. Students "owned" the direction of the course. In one illustrative experiment, students paired up and walked outside the school to a nearby wooded area. One student from each pair was blindfolded, then the pair ventured into the woods to choose a tree that would be theirs. The blindfolded partner would then experience the tree—walking around it, hearing the leaves crunch under their shoes; smelling it, feeling the trunk and branches, even licking it. All the senses were engaged, except for sight. When the pairs returned as a group outside the forest, the blindfolded students all removed their blindfolds and walked back into the woods to see if they could locate their chosen tree. In nearly every case, they were able to find it. It's the power of experience and participation.

Question: How could you provide a sense of "ownership" by allowing your students to weigh in on what or how they learned? How could you let them put their fingerprints on the subject so that it would look slightly different this year than last year, because they were in it? Is there any way they can personalize the ideas?

I—Image Rich

This generation of students has grown up in a more visually rich world than I did. My parents grew up with radio. I grew up with TV, but my kids have grown up with MTV. Even the music is attached to imagery. While I love images, (as a former art student), kids have a difficult time imagining a world without them. Consider the world they grew up in, full of YouTube, Netflix, digital cameras, and now, their phones are cameras. By adolescence, they're not teenagers, but "screenagers." Not long ago, Instagram overtook Facebook as their top social media tool. Then it was Snapchat. Then Whispr. The evolution continues, but one item remains constant: their love of images. They are a visual generation. (More on this in the next chapter).

I love the fact that educators who understand this, capitalize on it to reach their goals with students. They use metaphors in the classroom: narratives, visual aids, video and icons to connect students to information. In fact, some years ago, we began to hear about Division One NCAA football coaches who used images on the sidelines to call plays, snap counts and formations. Chip Kelly was among the first to use these images, as head coach for the Oregon Ducks, and not surprisingly, was able to pull off a high-speed offense, because student athletes were able to relate to images faster than a long series of words or hand signals. It just works. Unless you have kept your head in the sand for a decade, you recognize that students not only love images, but they need them to remember. Because so much information is thrown at them each day to consume, the messages that include images, symbols, icons or something visual tend to get through the filter and stick.

Question: How could you capitalize on an image or metaphor to relay the big idea you're attempting to communicate? While you must enable students to grasp rigorous and didactic concepts, how could you furnish a handle for them by using an icon to help them visualize and remember the idea?

C—Connected

This is yet a fourth reality that has evolved over the years. I ask you again to consider the world these kids have grown up in: they have been connected socially and technologically for over a decade now. And this reality has evolved since the 1990s, when email became central in our communication. As a rule, today's student can't imagine a world where they are disconnected from each other. They can't imagine a world without technology, social media and portable devices that enable them to remain "in touch" with each other 24/7. By their young adult years, they spend the equivalent of a full-time job each week, connected to each other through social media.

My friends at Louisiana Tech have been able to leverage this for over a decade now. More than ten years ago, math, science and engineering professors discovered that their students were dropping out of the programs at a high rate after their freshman year. In fact, it was too high for their liking. So, they shifted how they taught. First, those three departments began collaborating. (This was miracle number one). They decided to ask their students to pair up and work on a project from day one. They were to build a "boe-bot." This small robotic machine was to be constructed by the young students, and would require what they learned together in the classroom. Professors' lectures would answer the questions they had for their projects. (This was miracle number two). When finished at the end of the year, the students were graded on the project they'd built. And then following this experience, they were asked to engage on their senior project, which could take their remaining years at Tech.

The students were basically asked to look around the world and find one problem they'd like to solve. Then, they were to invent something that would solve it. It's incredible. I watched a presentation of what one class of seniors accomplished and was brought to tears, as they pursued harnessing solar power for undeveloped nations in Africa and providing resources for underserved populations in the U.S. In each case, the students connected in communities and solved a problem together.

Question: How could you break down your larger class into smaller communities and allow them to connect with each other to solve a problem? When could you stop your lecture halfway through, and offer a well-crafted question to these small communities (a question that can't be answered with "yes" or "no.")?

What if you were to push "pause" on your current teaching style and answer this:

TRAVEL GUIDE:

How EPIC is your teaching style?

I believe the more EPIC we are, the better chances we have to enable students to learn.

TWELVE CONCLUSIONS I'VE DRAWN ABOUT LEARNING...

As we ponder "free range" teaching and metacognition, consider these facts:

1. **Students support what they help create.**
   Some athletic coaches are empowering students to decide how practice goes, what players do, how long and when they do it. They're getting surprising results.

   How can you give ownership of a subject by letting students direct the learning?

2. **Students learn better when they expect to teach what they learn.**
   My friend George is a college professor who now has his students prepare each other for final examinations. Grades have soared as they actually engage their peers.

   What portions of your topic or ideas can you assign students to teach to peers?

3. **Students are incentivized if they know why a topic is relevant before they learn.**
   Two math teachers did an experiment. One taught in a traditional style; the other took time to cover "why" each section was important. Predictably, grades went up.

How can you share the "why" behind the "what" before you teach your subject?

4. Students bond with an experience more than a lecture.
As I stated earlier, some colleges are now using "project-based" learning, where the class becomes an experience—not just an explanation—and students are loving it.

In what ways can you create an experience from which your students learn?

5. Students engage more holistically when music is connected to the subject.
One faculty member I know selects a pop song, addressing topics in her classroom. Her students love their history teacher, now calling her the "music" teacher.

When could you incorporate a popular or even new song into the learning?

6. Students retain more when they physically gesture what they learn.
My son took a sign language class for his foreign language and found that the gestures actually accelerated his learning. This is a proven fact for all subjects.
Where is a spot in the course where students could align gestures with big ideas?

7. Students absorb more when more than two senses are involved.
As in the example from Finland teachers, students grasp and retain more when they don't merely listen to lectures, but they touch, smell, taste, hear and see the topic in class.

How can you cultivate an environment that includes all five senses?

8. **Students understand a larger percentage when they must practice it.**
   Students learn on a "need to know" basis. They engage when they must apply or practice the subject in real life. As a rule, application accelerates learning.

   How can homework be expanded into enabling students to actually apply the topic?

9. **Students connect with a subject when allowed to connect with each other.**
   Decades ago, Russian psychologists taught that learning occurs best in community; that we learn better in circles than in rows. Life change requires "life exchange."

   When could you incorporate smaller discussion communities in your classroom?

10. **Students comprehend information when it's connected to a narrative.**
    The effectiveness of the use of "story" has become widely known in our generation, but it is one of the oldest forms of pedagogy, dating back to cultures in ancient times.

    Where could you tell a story that ties directly into the subject they must learn?

11. **Students grasp new subjects when teachers connect it to familiar subjects.**
    Educators have used the term "schema" for years, but we often fail to leverage the idea. The best teachers build frameworks by attaching new subjects to familiar ones.

    In what ways can you use "schemas" (files) and attach known concepts to old ones?

12. **Students remember data when an image is utilized in their learning.**

A picture is worth a thousand words. It's the reason we created *Habitudes®*. They are images that form leadership habits and attitudes. Pictures are handles for data.

How can you leverage a visual, metaphor or image to anchor your big idea?

TRAVEL GUIDE:

Which of these do you embrace and practice?

THE "FREE RANGE" TEACHER

The term "free range" was originally used with farm animals. Free-range chickens, pigs, and other animals are allowed to move around and feed naturally. This is considered by many to be a kinder and more humane method of farming than directive or intensive methods.

In the same way—it's a far better way to feed students as well. It's a sort of "hands off" teaching method that coaches at first, then later consults—but ultimately creates ownership in the student to learn for themselves. It's a term describing everything we've been discussing so far. In 2008, Lenore Skenazy launched "Free Range Kids." Her website contains her argument that empowering kids with freedom to walk home from school or even ride the subway at nine years old enables them to grow up and take on other responsibilities that help them mature. The same works for teachers and parents. We need to stop controlling so much if our kids are going to become their best.

No doubt, buying into this idea doesn't make life better immediately. Pushing students to think for themselves creates disequilibrium inside. It can initially be frustrating and uncomfortable. I have said for years, however, that if we don't allow children to struggle in their learning process, they won't develop the life skills they'll need to succeed as adults. This means we need to change our pedagogy. The Latin term for "educate" is taken from two roots. One means "to push." The other means "to lead." At first, we assumed instructors must push information outward to our listeners. I no longer think this is the most effective method. I think we need to lead. And this means creating an environment where students become inspired and thirsty to learn; then we get out of the way. As teachers, we must become more sophisticated in our methods, drawing out what's already inside of them, not pushing out what's inside us. Effective teachers don't say as much as possible. They actually say as little as needed—allowing students to get on with their learning. We must simply model the behaviors for how to figure something out.

Simple Ideas to Ignite Metacognition in Students Today

I recognize all teachers don't have the luxury of "flipping their class." We can take some simple steps, however, to move students toward metacognition. Here are some ideas you can practice immediately as you enable students to learn:

- Create problems without offering solutions. Ask, don't tell. Bring up a genuine dilemma in our world and suggest the students consider how to resolve it.

- At least once a day, refuse to answer a student's question. Instead, encourage everyone in the class to look up answers and see what they find.

- Create disequilibrium. This is that awkward period of silence between the time a problem is clear and the moment a solution arises. Allow for silence and discomfort.

- Instead of traditional grading of papers, tests or essays, communicate how many mistakes were made on their project and turn them loose to find each one.

- Choose a day and let students plan the entire lesson for the class period. In fact, let them record themselves teaching it, evaluating themselves afterward.

- In your next exam, write in the wrong answers on those blanks— the very ones students have given in class. Let students grade the test, finding the proper answers.

- Ask students to pick a topic they feel they've mastered, be it a video game, a sport or a social media app. Then, have them write down how they mastered it and discuss it.

TRAVEL GUIDE:
Which of these could you practice immediately with students?

LEVELS OF MOTIVATION IN STUDENTS

Apart from helping students practice metacognition, we must identify what actually motivates them. Let's close this chapter by discussing how to inspire our students.

Last year, I met a junior at Miami University in Ohio. He was like so many others I meet: full of potential, but lacking clear ambition about a career. It's not so much because he lacks a vision. It's because he has twenty visions for his future. And it has paralyzed him from taking clear steps toward his future. Others, who act like him on the outside, lack motivation for other reasons. Carnegie Mellon University published the results of a study revealing why a disproportionate amount of college students today aren't as motivated as they need to be. The top reasons were:

- Students see little value in the course or its content.

- Students do not believe that their efforts will improve their performance.

- Students are demotivated by the structure and allocation of rewards.

- Students do not perceive the classroom climate as supportive.

- Students have other priorities that compete for their time and attention.

- Individual students may suffer from physical, mental, or other personal problems that affect motivation.

Sadly, the number of unmotivated students is rising. In a world of unprecedented opportunity and connection—wouldn't you think we'd have the most motivated generation of kids in the history of mankind? We've pushed them to succeed at every level: at school, in sports, and every other extracurricular activity.

But alas, many students are perceived as "unmotivated."

Student Achievement vs. Motivation

A series of papers from the Center on Education Policy (CEP) at George Washington University reveals that educators have focused far more on student achievement—i.e. getting test scores up—than on student motivation. Regrettably, this pushes schools to only measure test scores, and, hence, do whatever it takes to get those scores up, even if it's cheating. (Inflated scores have been posted countless times over the years in K-12 education). Let's face it—we're pragmatic. Our strategies to boost student achievement don't address the real problems of their disengagement. Upwards of 40 percent of high school students are chronically disengaged from school, according to a 2003 National Research Council report on motivation.[8]

The decline in motivation is a pressing and tangible problem.

Instead of student achievement, what if we targeted student motivation? When motivated they will naturally achieve. An inspired student, passionate about what he or she is learning is pushed from the inside out, not vice versa. Plus, I'm not sure teachers can compete with YouTube or Snapchat when it comes to engaging students. We don't have the budgets to compete with such sources of entertainment. We must dig deeper into the core of what drives people—especially young people—to take initiative.

Six Levels of Motivation in Students

Pause and think about the students you know who are motivated. I believe the following levels of motivation are in effect for those students.

1. I get to do something.
> The best learning doesn't take place while sitting in a classroom. Motivation rises in students when we enable them to get up and do something with their hands and minds. They must apply their knowledge. We truly learn what we do.

2. I get to do something interesting to me.
> Next, students engage more deeply when their "doing" intersects with an area of curiosity. I believe we can enable this curiosity when we teach well. Steve Jobs said, "The only way to do good work is to love what you do." Curiosity must be kindled.

3. I get to do something interesting, using my gifts.

The third level of motivation involves empowering students to utilize their specific strengths. Don Clifton wrote, "When we studied them, excellent performers were rarely well rounded. On the contrary, they were sharp."

4. I get to do something interesting, using my gifts with people I enjoy.

Because humans are social beings, learning can be accelerated by social integration. Growing in a community is deeply satisfying. In short, we tend to like people who like us and who are like us. We learn best when friends make us better.

5. I get to do something interesting, using my gifts with people I enjoy, and solve a problem.

The element of problem solving further engages and motives students. We are, in our best nature, problem solvers. It's what good leaders do; it's what engages people the most. It's even better when the problem is real, not hypothetical.

6. I get to do something interesting, using my gifts with people I enjoy, solving a problem regarding something that matters.

The ultimate engagement surfaces when the problem is important. The larger the challenge the higher the engagement. People are better when the stakes are high. For years I've believed that students want to do something that's very important and almost impossible.

Although our students are still maturing, adding any or all of these elements above naturally works to inspire them internally—rather than nag them externally. When we practice them well, author Donald Clifton reminds us we will see a signal in our students: They will anticipate it, and will be asking, "When can I do this again?"

Isn't this the dream of every educator?

Telling a Better Story

In my book, *12 Huge Mistakes Parents Can Avoid*, I relay the story of Donald Miller and his friend who complained to him about his teenage daughter, Brooke. The dad told Donald she was dating a "Goth" guy who wore black, did illegal drugs, had piercings all over his body and coerced her to withdraw from her friends. Dad didn't know what to do. Miller asked if he'd considered that Brooke was simply choosing a better "story" than the one he was creating as a father in his home.

When the man looked puzzled, Miller continued. Everyone wants to be part of a story that is interesting and compelling. They want their life to solve a problem. To do something that matters. This man's daughter had simply decided her life at home was boring—and her "Goth" boyfriend wasn't.

This got his friend to seriously think about what Miller had said. Over the next few months, he did some research and came up with an idea. Over dinner, this father shared about an orphanage in Mexico that desperately needed help. They needed a building, some supplies and some volunteers from the U.S. to accomplish their goals. Dad said that he planned to get involved, but didn't force his daughter or son to do so. In a matter of weeks, however, his kids were intrigued. This was a problem that needed solving. His son suggested they visit this orphanage in Mexico, and later, his daughter figured out a way to raise money for it online. Over the next year, this family's story became compelling. What's more—the kids owned it. Eventually, the teenage daughter informed her father she'd broken up with her boyfriend. She said she didn't know what attracted her to him in the first place. Needless to say, dad was elated.

I think I know what happened. The boring family became one that was compelling. Dad had invited the kids to do some metacognition in order to solve a problem that actually mattered. Come to think of it— isn't that what we all want?

Talk over these questions with your colleagues:

What makes fostering metacognition in the classroom difficult?

What are other ways teachers can spark metacognition in students?

Choose one subject and one specific lesson plan you've taught for years. Now, brainstorm ideas for inserting metacognition into that plan.

CHAPTER 8

STORY TIME: THE SCIENCE OF USING METAPHORS AND NARRATIVES

The old and new research behind the impact of utilizing stories and metaphors.

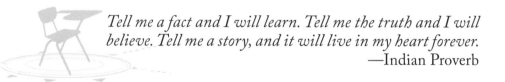

Tell me a fact and I will learn. Tell me the truth and I will believe. Tell me a story, and it will live in my heart forever.
—Indian Proverb

I will never forget hearing about a bet that was made between book publisher Bennett Cerf (co-founder of Random House) and Theodore Geisel, otherwise known as Dr. Seuss. It was serendipitous—but I'm so glad Dr. Seuss took the gamble.

The bet was made in 1960. It was for $50, not a huge sum even back then. Bennett wagered that Theodore could not write a children's book using fifty words or less. Bennett would give him $1 for each word. (As a writer myself, I'd say that's quite a challenge). Geisel took the bet and won.

The book was *Green Eggs and Ham.*

While Bennett Cerf never paid up, this book by Dr. Seuss went on to be his most popular book of all time, selling about 200 million copies worldwide over the years. (I assume Seuss felt he got his payback that way). Believe it or not, Geisel's first successful children's book was also written on a challenge. William Spaulding, (who worked for Houghton Mifflin), challenged Seuss to write a book using a limited number of 225 distinct words from a list of 348 words that were selected from a first grader's vocabulary list. While Dr. Seuss lost the bet (he used 348 words), his book, *The Cat in the Hat,* went on to sell a million copies.

These challenges were prompted when John Hersey, a Pulitzer Prize winning journalist, wrote an article in a May 25, 1954 issue of *Life* magazine titled, *Why Do Students Bog Down on the First R? A Local Committee Sheds Light on a National Problem: Reading.* The piece was extremely critical of school primers. At the time, kids were reading primers like *Fun with Dick and Jane,* which were anything but "fun" and didn't inspire kids to want to read outside of what was required. Additionally, TV was new and so much more appealing. *The Cat in the Hat* transformed children's books from that time on. The book's success allowed Theodore Geisel to exit the advertising business and enter the children's book business. He never turned back.

Challenges and Boundaries

Dr. Seuss' challenge was not just about money. It was about boundaries. How much could he accomplish with a limited set of words? Theodore Seuss Geisel was an artist; specifically a cartoonist. He later claimed that the bet forced him to ask hard questions about how to get through to the minds of young people. He decided it required eye-catching artwork, unique storytelling and a tone that didn't "talk down" at kids, patronizing them, but rather engaged them with life lessons.

These are timeless ingredients every generation of adults must utilize.

When I consider Dr. Seuss' books, written over a period of thirty-five years, I notice something interesting. He capitalized on the following elements:

- The power of simple. (They're easy to understand.)
- The power of short. (They could be digested quickly.)
- The power of sticky. (They're memorable for everyone.)
- The power of sharable. (They're transferable ideas for readers.)

These must be elements we utilize today.

TRAVEL GUIDE:

Is your communication simple? Short? Sticky? Sharable?

THE SCIENCE BEHIND THE STRENGTH OF A STORY

When I spoke individually to Matt, Zoe, Savannah and Dylan about this topic, they all lit up. Each one expressed how they wished their teachers would use stories and imagery more often in class. Why would they say this? My hunch is that images and narratives are the native language in the new world we are mapping.

In fact, people have always been enraptured by the power of a narrative. For thousands of years, since the first cave paintings were uncovered, we've known that civilizations passed on their cultural identity to children through the tool of images and stories. When visiting Phoenicia, Romania and Egypt, I saw first-hand the drawings that told the stories of past societies, etched on walls and pyramids. The earliest cave paintings were recently found on Sulawesi, an Indonesian island. Each painting has one element in common: people shared information with stories and pictures.

A walk through human history indicates almost every generation re-discovered this paramount truth—that people engage with and remember stories and pictures. But have you ever studied just why narratives are so intriguing, when compared to, let's say, didactic learning methods? In other words, why is an "illustration" so much more memorable than mere "information?" Why is it that when I tell a good story it doesn't require the typical lecture, drill, memorization and test model for my listeners to retain it? Why is it most of us enjoy a good novel, movie, TV show or a story a friend tells us?

Let's explore the answer to this question.

Part of the answer, at least, is because our brains become more active when hearing a story. Consider what it feels like to listen to a presentation, where the speaker uses boring power point slides with lists of bullet points. No doubt, it can engage certain parts of our brain. The visual aid helps, but the data listed on the screen is limited in how much it harnesses our minds. Scientists identify these parts of the brain as the "Broca" and the "Wernicke" areas. They are the language processing portions of our brain, where we decode words into meaning. They're important but limited.

When we hear a story, however, things dramatically shift inside us, according to researchers in Europe.[1] Not only are the language processing portions of our brain activated, but any other portion we'd use when experiencing the events of that story are as well. If we hear about the sweltering heat of a summer day, the preoptic area of the anterior hypothalamus portion of our brain lights up. If a person tells us how delicious their lasagna was last night, our sensory cortex lights up. When a friend describes how fast he was running on a track last week, our motor cortex is ignited. In other words, the better the storyteller, the more portions of the brain are engaged. It can be far superior to relaying mere facts. In many cases, the listeners actually feel as if they are experiencing the story itself. It is an experience.

Let me get specific. In the study I mentioned above, researchers in Spain used metaphors like "the singer had a velvet voice" and "He had leathery hands." They found that these descriptions roused the sensory cortex. When researchers spoke about "grasping an object" or "kicking a ball," the scans revealed activity in the motor cortex, which orchestrates body movements. The listener experienced what the speaker said.

Simply put, a story can put your whole brain to work.

Rather than failing to be academic or scholarly, as some educators fear, the use of stories is a superior way of engaging our brains, especially when compared to a didactic lecture. A story isn't less rigorous; it's actually more rigorous. It isn't less robust, but more. Sadly, while some educators assume stories are too elementary, and consequently, don't use them in a classroom, I believe the real reason we don't use them is that story telling is harder for us to master than lecturing. What a paradox. What seems simplistic is actually harder than what seems rigorous.

Now, don't get me wrong. I am aware of the need for critical thinking and rigorous academics. I simply have discovered that I can better enter that deep world through the doorway of a narrative and a metaphor. In fact, at "Growing Leaders," I have actually found I can tell stories that have transformed my way of life and my thinking—and transfer the identical impact on the students I teach. This fact has been confirmed by Princeton researcher Uri Hasson, who says that the person telling the story and the one listening to it actually synchronize their brains.[2] The storytellers had certain portions of their brain light up as they relayed the narrative and the scans demonstrated that the listeners had the same portions ignite as well, emotions as well as thoughts and volitions. The speakers' experience transferred to the listeners.

Why is this True?

The paramount question at this point is: Why is it that the sequence of a story has such a profound effect on listeners and their learning?

The simple answer is our brains are hardwired this way.

When dissected, a story is a connection of cause and effect. We think in narratives every day, regardless of what we do. At school, at the store, in our car or talking with a friend, our brains process life this way. The truth is, studies verify this. Jeremy Hsu explains: "Personal stories and gossip make up 65 percent of our conversations."[3]

When we hear a story, we naturally tend to relate it to our own experiences. This is also why metaphors work so effectively. Our brains search their filing cabinets, which activates our "insular lobe or insular cortex," enabling us to relate to a similar experience of disappointment, excitement, joy, disgust—you name it. Association is the natural and tenacious function of our minds.

John Bargh, from Yale University and Lawrence Williams of the University of Colorado demonstrated how the metaphor and a literal reality become linked when they performed an experiment:

> "Volunteers would meet one of the experimenters, believing that they would be starting the experiment shortly. In reality, the experiment began when the experimenter, seemingly struggling with an armful of folders, asks the volunteer to briefly hold their coffee. As the key experimental manipulation, the coffee was either hot or iced. Subjects then read a description of some individual, and those who had held the warmer cup tended to rate the individual as having a warmer personality, with no change in ratings of other attributes."[4]

The fact is our brains are always looking for patterns or links between cause and effect. They seek a relationship between what's said or what's seen and our previous experience. Pause and consider the ramifications of this on our communication with students. This means an educator can utilize a story to enable learners to come up with an idea, instead of merely suggesting the idea themselves.

That's what I call student engagement and ownership.

Once again, Uri Hasson, from Princeton, explains that a story is the only way to activate portions of the brain so that the listener turns the story into their own idea and experience. (It's why people so often will hear a story from someone and later tell the story as if it were their own). It appears that what psychologists have told us for years may be true after all: our brains don't distinguish between an imagined experience and a real experience. Both can be equally influential.

I have a question for you. Do you avoid using stories when you communicate or teach? How well do you utilize them? Have you learned to relay a good story? Jim Rohn once said, "Start where people are before you try to take them where you want them to go."

When we hide behind our need to impress listeners with complex thoughts and use complicated words, we fail to understand the proper hallway to enter the minds of the young. "Shooting above people's heads doesn't mean you have superior ammunition—it means you are a lousy shot," said Oscar Handlin. When we begin at the right starting point, we can take almost any student on the journey. We connect and we communicate. It was Sydney Harris who reminded us, "The two words information and communication are often used interchangeably, but they signify quite different things. Information is giving out; communication is getting through."

TRAVEL GUIDE:

How are you leveraging the power of a story when you communicate?

Have you mastered the art of using a story to teach or train?

THE POWER OF IMAGES

Let's shift gears, for a moment, and specifically examine visual learning. I'd like to focus now on the use of images as a tool to connect with students.

We live in a culture rich with images. We grew up with photographs, TV, movies, video, VH1, DVDs, Facebook and Instagram. We can't escape the power of the visual image—and most of us don't want to. We've grown accustomed to watching, not merely listening to, our music; radio gave way to TV, which gave birth to MTV. Even our music is inseparable from images. Our grandparents grew up listening to the radio for entertainment; kids today grow up watching YouTube. Not long ago our text messages contained merely words. Today, it's emojis. And the pace of this visual expansion continues to accelerate. As a child, I was among the first to mature with the television set—the "one-eyed babysitter." Today's adolescents are aptly called "screenagers," as their screen time is not limited to a television but has expanded to laptops, video games, tablets and smart phones.

I wonder, however, if most people recognize the history behind the use of images to communicate, pass on values, and teach the younger generation. How important have images been to mankind's communication? What role have they played as cultures talk to one another? And just how central will they be to our future, as information becomes ubiquitous yet ideas become more complex?

Consider this: As we make progress, there seems to be a regress to this simple, original pedagogy of pictures. As I've mentioned, the "new" isn't new at all; it is a return to something old. As we progress further into the 21st century we seem to be magnetically drawn to return to the use of pictures—to translate and transmit ideas to others. Our international road signs communicate to oncoming traffic with simple pictures. The visuals are, indeed, a universal language. Pictures are, indeed, a multi-generational language. Our human population, in many ways, is becoming iconic: information is passed along via a simple icon. Again, pictures are a timeless language, and effective leaders understand this. Best-selling author Tom Peters said, "The best leaders, almost without exception and at every level, are master users of stories and symbols." As you read further, I'd like to challenge you to reflect on the research and learn from our rapid migration back to this resource—images—for relaying thoughts. It is safe to say, the visual is going viral.

"The best leaders, almost without exception and at every level, are master users of stories and symbols." —Tom Peters

The Art of Human History

As I've said before, humans have a robust history of using icons, diagrams, symbols and pictures to communicate. From the cave walls of Mesopotamia to the pyramids of Egypt, people have used pictures to educate new generations about their past. Throughout time, images have been used in political, spiritual, cultural and military arenas to affect the schemas of that particular population. Spanning from pre-historic to modern times, images have impacted the way we think, process information, and engage the culture. Below are a few specific examples of how images have been used historically, as well as their impact on the memory process, the learning process, and the level of personal engagement they inspired during each time period. I believe we have something to learn from the past.

As one of the rare female pharaohs, Hatshepsut used images in Egypt from 1479-1458 B.C. As was common in Egyptian history, the buildings, statues, obelisks, and temples carried the images of that day. They influenced culture because they aligned with the learning process of the day. Some historians believe her effectiveness and place in history was due, at least in part, to her strategic use of images.

The primary purpose of using images, however, was to tell the story of a culture. Some common themes arose during the early pre-historic periods based on the images facilitated on pottery and cave drawings. Archaeologists have hypothesized the growth of abstract thinking in the images over time, which reflects how pre-historic people became engaged in new ideas and higher levels of learning. Over the centuries, artwork progressed as civilization did.

In the ancient Hebrew culture, parables and metaphors were employed to remind people of important truths. We see this not only in archaeological discoveries but in the evolution of language in their ancient writings. Over time, pictures were still used to teach, but they took on the form of tales and symbols. Instead of listing rules of conduct in a left-brained style of pedagogy (e.g. the Ten Commandments), Christ was known to have told parables as pictures of truth, enabling hearers to reflect on life lessons they could relate to through the characters in the story or the objects in the scenario. These visuals were a right-brained approach to learning.

In the Renaissance period, an array of communicative channels utilized images to enhance memory—helping people retain information longer than in the past. Books used visual metaphors; paintings and sculptures were central to education, and the stained-glass windows of the cathedrals contained pictures reminding people of what was most important. This has carried on for centuries, as teachers today find symbols and visuals to be very effective in helping students retain information. Despite our

Western preference for didactic teaching methods, educators in health and science are utilizing images to educate more effectively.

During the 18th century, as the United States of America was born, images played a central role in galvanizing patriots to the cause of freedom and revolution. We remember Benjamin Franklin's use of symbols and illustrations, especially the snake warning the British, "Don't Tread on Me." It was a sobering reminder—even to those who couldn't read—that revolution was imminent. Through the course of the Revolution, pictures of branches, eagles, trees and nooses, and the Liberty Bell were tools to call people to the cause. As chairman of the flag committee, Franklin chose stars and stripes in symbolic colors to remind Americans of their roots.

The fact is, history reminds us: the message that gets through is usually one that contains imagery. And today, we recognize this timeless truth again.

The message that gets through is usually one that contains imagery.

Picture Perfect Communication
Since the turn of the 21st century, significant progress has been made in our understanding of the human brain. Neuroscience now helps us recognize the role of the right and left hemisphere, how males develop more slowly than females in adolescence, the importance of the pre-frontal cortex, and what causes us to both remember and forget ideas. Some of the most profound discoveries inform us of the importance of imagery within our thoughts and actions. These insights we currently possess should stimulate leaders and educators toward the use of images and metaphors in their communication.

Why is teaching with images so effective?

1. The majority of people are visual learners.
65 percent of the human population learn visually.[5] That's two out of every three people you will communicate with today. An even greater percentage of people "think," using pictures. For example, if I were to say the word "elephant" to a crowd of listeners, most would picture a big gray animal, not the letters "E-L-E-P-H-A-N-T." Approximately nine out of ten brains work this way. This is a simple reminder that

people think using imagery. So if our message is to penetrate, this is how we must communicate. Teaching this way is organic. Aristotle said it best: "The soul does not think without a picture."

2. Pictures stick.

Reports from 3M confirm that visual aids in the classroom improve learning by 400 percent.[6] We like to see a picture, not just hear a word. We remember pictures long after words have left us. We retain the stories in speeches more than the mere words that were spoken. We remember scenarios. Faces. Colors. Why? They paint a picture in a crowded world of content. Post-modern society is a world saturated with data. People process approximately 1,000 messages a day, digitally and personally. The only hope we have that our message will stick is to ensure it contains pictures. This effect increases over time. One study found that after three days, a user retained only 10-20 percent of written or spoken information, but almost 65 percent of visual information.[7] Another study showed an illustrated text was 9 percent more effective than text alone when testing immediate comprehension, and it was 83 percent more effective when the test was delayed.[8]

3. Metaphors can provide a language for people.

When an image represents a truth or a principle, it can furnish taxonomy for understanding a topic or even how to approach a project, or a situation. The pictures make concepts memorable and employable. When someone views the image, they rapidly associate it with the principle. This enables imagery to play a primary role in creating culture in an organization because every culture speaks a language. A set of images can quite literally represent an entire value system or set of behaviors an organization desires team members to embrace.

4. Pictures can accelerate understanding.

As I've said before, when an instructor uses an image to represent a timeless principle, comprehension deepens and accelerates. There is significant impact in the learner when a visual aid is connected to a verbal explanation. It actually speeds up the learning process. According to the 3M corporation, the brain processes visual information 60,000 times faster than text.[9] People get the point in their head faster when they form a picture in their heart. The entire brain is engaged. This means images can accelerate both learning important concepts and applying them readily to life. When I teach, I try to offer a point for their head and a picture for their heart.

5. **Images engage our right brain and our emotions.**
In his book, *A Whole New Mind*, bestselling author Daniel Pink reminds us of our need for more right-brained communication.[10] The left hemisphere is didactic: it's about numbers, equations and facts. It's calculated and definitive. The right-brain is about creativity. It's innovative and dynamic. It gravitates toward images, which grip and educate the other portions of our mind. Certainly both hemispheres are necessary and work best in tandem with each other, but our world is increasingly driven by the right-brain ideas. My concern is, when budget cuts occur in public schools, the first items that tend to be eliminated are right-brain courses like art, music, and drama. While I realize current research tells us the two hemispheres blend more than we first suspected, we must find creative ways to engage the right-brain to connect with students.

6. **Pictures make us want to express and respond.**
It's been said so often, it has become a cliché: a picture is worth a thousand words. But the fact is, the statement is true. Images engage people and elicit response. It's why art galleries foster conversation as viewers gaze at the pictures. Visual literacy is the ability to encode (create a visual language) and decode (understand a visual language). Unwittingly, this begins to happen when people invest time with imagery. Jensen reveals that our eyes can register and process 36,000 visual messages per hour. Visuals are so engaging they make people want to talk.[11] Call me the master of the obvious, but in a classroom, I believe this equals student engagement.

7. **Visuals aid communicators in the persuasion process.**
A study released by the University of Minnesota reveals that using imagery actually aids the communicator to persuade an audience of their point.[12] According to the study, visuals aid listeners not only in grasping a concept, and understanding it more quickly, but it helps

them to remember the concept later and communicate it to others, as all as improve subsequent action on the part of the listeners as a result. The simple use of imagery enables the communicator to convince people of the ideas they are attempting to relay. My guess is, this is intuitive for all of us. A presentation using pictures (or something we can see) is superior to one that uses words alone. It not only involves more than one sense but it utilizes more memorable senses as well.

8. Visuals tell stories in our imagination.
A simple picture can spark a new thought each time you look at it. Why? Pictures tell stories. The poets and philosophers of our day are musicians and filmmakers, who paint pictures in our minds and inspire imaginations. They both use a screen. What's more, since 40 percent of all nerve fibers connected to our brain are linked to the retina, it's clear that what we see is intricately connected to how we think, feel, and learn.[13] Film director Martin Scorsese said, "If one wants to reach younger people at an earlier age to shape their minds in a critical way, you really need to know how ideas and emotions are expressed visually."

9. Pictures enable us to store huge volumes of information in our memories.
I know undergraduate students who memorize for their final examinations using images and diagrams. A single picture can contain vast amounts of data, which enables long-term memory. Visuals actually help us file information. In 2000, Hyerle informed us that 90 percent of the information that is retained in the brain is visual.[14] It appears obvious that images and visual aids should be the standard format for memorization and learning.

10. Images are the oldest form of messaging yet the preferred pedagogy today.
Research by Peter Houts, PhD, states that people in contemporary society prefer pictographs to words for instruction.[15] This is likely true for every generation, young or old, but certainly for today's emerging generation. Furthermore, his research showed that students who are twice as exceptional as others ("2e") are usually visual learners. So from the cave walls and pyramids of the

ancient world, to the classrooms of today, young people prefer to learn from images. Some of the best communicators in history taught using the power of the metaphor and image—from Jesus and His parables, to Dr. Martin Luther King Jr. and his famous speech about dreams during the Civil Rights movement. The cycle of history seems complete.

TRAVEL GUIDE:

What other reasons would you add to this list?

How do you capitalize on images when you communicate?

What Do Students Say?

I decided to take this hypothesis to the college campus. Over the course of two years, we asked more than 3,000 undergraduate students on 32 university campuses what enables them to learn and to remember. I recognized that effective educators and communicators use a handful of instruments to help listeners remember information. I wanted, however, to test their work, and see if their "end user" agreed. After assessing the results, three instruments emerged as most popular:

1. **MUSIC**
   The use of song and lyric to connect and remember information.

2. **EXPERIENCES**
   The use of hands-on activity and participation for learning purposes.

3. **IMAGES**
   The use of visuals and metaphors to engage and retain content.

I was then faced with a paramount question: why is it that so many faculty members refrain from using music or images? If it's true that students retain information and test better when instructors include one or more of the instruments above in their pedagogy, it would make sense that educators would employ them. So why don't professors use a learning process that actually works?

My primary conclusion is simple: The use of images (or the other items on the list) simply seems anecdotal. They don't feel scholarly. Over time, as higher education has become more sophisticated and rigorous, we have felt that anything which simplifies learning lacks rigor or depth. Images, for instance, don't appear academic. They're far too elementary. So many shun them.

But I would argue that images are not elementary at all. In fact, they prompt both thought and emotion. And they certainly don't lack rigor—in fact, they stimulate an entirely different hemisphere of the brain, often left untouched by educators. If the purpose of education is to help students learn, remember and apply truth, then it seems we have left out a very useful tool in the process. Images have been proven to stimulate creativity, retention and passion, all of which employers who receive graduates are begging for. I do not know of any employer who still asks about the GPA of a young prospect, but I do know they are asking about creativity, soft skills, and executive functioning.

And I believe images can help foster those needed skill sets.

Further, I am arguing that images become the entryway to left-brain learning. We may not end with images, but we certainly should consider starting the conversation with them. Once intrigue and engagement has been established, an educator, coach or parent can go deeper, progressing into left-hemisphere thinking.

Our Dilemma: Right-brained Students Must Attend Left-brained Schools

The columns below summarize how education has primarily taken place and why it fails to be effective. I recognize many schools have made an important shift from this traditional model, and perhaps this is over-simplified. But I believe these columns summarize why many students drop out of the educational process too soon:

Students Today…	Schools Today
1. Right-brained thinkers	1. Left-brained delivery
2. Learn by uploading, expressing self	2. Teach by downloading lectures
3. Experiential in nature	3. Passive in nature
4. Music and art enables retention	4. Music and art classes are first ones cut
5. Creativity drives them	5. Curriculum drives them
6. Desire to learn what's relevant to real life	6. Teach for the next test and to simply raise scores

Maya Angelou wrote,

"We are all creative, but by the time we are three or four years old, someone has knocked the creativity out of us. Some people shut up the kids who start to tell stories. Kids dance in their cribs, but someone will insist they sit still. By the time the creative people are ten or twelve, they want to be like everyone else."

In a 2013 Fast Company article, a team of social scientists at the University of Arkansas explained how they have drawn some of these same conclusions.

In 2013, *"they attempted to demonstrate the benefits of students' exposure to art. Their findings, published in the journals Education Next and Educational Researcher, are that students who are exposed to cultural institutions— like museums and performing arts centers—not only have higher levels of engagement through art, but they display greater tolerance toward others, historical empathy, better educational memory, and critical thinking skills. 'The changes were measurable and significant,' reported Jay P. Greene, professor of education reform and a researcher on the study. Just one museum tour was found to make 'a definite impression on students.' According to Greene, students on this tour retained what they'd learned 'even without an external reason for doing so, like a grade on a test.*

"Green's team was surprised by how much "academic" information the test group had learned and remembered through the art, when compared to a control group. Students were able to recall that one painting dealt with price supports during the Great Depression and another depicted abolitionists boycotting sugar. "These historical details were not standard in the curator's introduction," Greene explains. This signifies that the discussion-based format compelled the students to ask both important and relevant questions about the art. But something about the museum also enabled students to remember this information nearly a month later. That's remarkable, considering how quickly most kids forget knowledge learned for tests.

"Further, when it came to analyzing a new, unfamiliar painting, Greene reports there's "a big increase in how observant students were if they went to an art museum, as opposed to students in a control group who did not attend. They were much better at seeing details in new paintings than those who did not go." They were also better at relating the painting to their own experience, identifying subtext in the art and allowing multiple interpretations of the art. Finally, they were able to empathize with the people and scenes in a way the control group did not."[16]

Research clearly suggests that experiencing art (images) engages students better.

WE'RE ROLLING THE DICE

Because our organization, Growing Leaders, has observed the power of images time and again I knew we had to act. We didn't see schools or companies utilizing images, conversations or experiences to their full potential. In response, we were prompted to create the *Habitudes®* resources I mentioned earlier. (Once again, *Habitudes* are images that form leadership habits and attitudes.) After years of work in student development, we designed an instrument based upon images and social integration. Each chapter of these books provides a unique, memorable image that's coupled with stories, questions, a self-assessment and an exercise in which students can participate.

To get started infusing stories and images into your teaching and enabling students to practice the meta-cognition we discussed in the previous chapter, I suggest you try the following simple sequence. You might say, it will help you roll the DICE as you teach:

D—Begin with a Dilemma.
This is a real-life problem that incentivizes them. We begin with the "why" before progressing into the "what." This step should create urgency.

Question: How could you create intrigue with a dilemma?

I—Then you show an Image.
The next step is revealing the image, which represents a possible solution. Each of our more than one hundred images symbolizes principles to practice.

Question: How could you leverage images?

C – This sparks Conversations.
Next, allow them to process their application to the problem and principle in a small group. Interaction creates ownership of their learning.

Question: How could you foster conversation?

E – This should lead to an Experience.
Finally, we encourage all discussion to lead to an experience that can change their lives. We believe information without application is incomplete.

Question: How could you offer a platform for real experiences?

This four-phase sequence should always prompt deeper learning and discovery. It is simply a beginning that invites a student into growth and critical thinking.

TRAVEL GUIDE:

Where could you try rolling the "DICE" in your teaching?

I share a societal concern with sociologist Neil Postman. He writes that our world of electronic media and digital communication not only makes information available to anyone at any age, without discretion, it has dumbed down our thinking.[17] Kids now read less, and watch more. Social media pushes us to "stick to the surface" in our communication, remaining superficial and often emotional in nature.

When we watch a television show, for instance, we process visual information. We are not reading. The images often come at us at lightning speed giving us no time to think deeply about any of them. On the other hand, reading matures us because most of us cannot read, digest and critically think that quickly. Reading forces us to slow down and think. It pushes us to evaluate.

Consequently, if we don't utilize this predisposition to look at an image and leverage it to motivate them toward reading and critical thinking, we have missed the mark. We, as educators, have stopped short and are incomplete. In other words, as we roll the DICE above, we must mix reading and research into the conversations and experiences. We must engage both hemispheres of the brain.

In early 2016, a university science professor wrote our office (at Growing Leaders) and wanted to thank us for the *Habitudes*® images. He had read my book, *lifeGIVING Mentors*, and decided he should expand his approach to his students. At the time, his science class was not engaging the students as well as he wanted, and he knew he needed to spark some new conversations. The images enabled him to literally become a mentor to several of the young men and women in his classes, both undergraduate and graduate students. Because the images teach real-life principles, the students soon engaged in some vigorous conversations that he later shared had literally transformed some of their lives. Some engaged intellectually for the first time; others became engaged emotionally for the first time. And still for others, the conversations led to their own personal maturation.

It all happened when a college instructor chose to build more authentic relationships with his students. He decided to go deep. The images simply sparked the journey.

It is my undeserved privilege to read and hear stories like this all the time. The *Habitudes*® images are being used in all kinds of contexts—from elementary school classes all the way to learning communities in the White House, Pentagon, and Commerce Department. The images are being used in hundreds of NCAA Division One athletic programs across the country. They are used in hundreds of colleges to orient first-year students and to teach leadership to Resident Advisors. They're being used by professional baseball teams in the MLB, football teams in the NFL and basketball teams in the NBA. One coach wrote me saying he saw a difference in the attitude of his players in just two days, after discussing the *Habitudes* images. One middle school teacher said her students cheered when, at the end of the school year, she informed her class they'd be discussing book two of the series the next year. We even had a musician send us a rap song he'd written about the *Habitudes* images. It's so rewarding to see the emerging generation connect with ideas. They represent a map that residents of Tomorrowland actually understand. It's a familiar vocabulary in a new, unfamiliar territory.

Lara, a twenty-something living in Brazil, wrote me saying, "These images have transformed the way I live my life. It's as if my life is now marked, divided by the days before *Habitudes* and after *Habitudes*. It was through them that I met myself. I can remember each principle they stand for, and use them to reframe how I think. And so, it is the beginning of a new Lara, with these *Habitudes* inside me."

These are words every teacher loves to receive.

Much like Dr. Seuss, we've simply attempted to harness:

- **The power of simple**—they're easy to understand.
- **The power of short**—they can be digested quickly.
- **The power of sticky**—they're memorable for everyone.
- **The power of sharable**—they're transferable ideas for readers.

We believe we've found a way to inform this next generation on their journey into leadership and adulthood. May you find a way, too.

The role of images in vision is paramount. You cannot discover what you cannot imagine or see.

CHAPTER 9

MODERN DAY MAP MAKERS

Some ordinary leaders and educators who are paving the way for the rest of us.

If you think our future will require better schools, you're wrong. The future of education calls for entirely new learning environments. If you think we'll need better teachers, you're wrong. Tomorrow's learners will need guides who take on fundamentally different roles.
—Dr. Wayne Hammond

There is no better person to recognize the future than someone who is young. This chapter was appropriately written by my younger colleague, Andrew McPeak.

I met Rob Garcia a couple of years ago. You'll notice from his story that he is quite different from Matt, Zoe, Savannah, and Dylan. As I spoke with him over repeated conversations, I became more and more impressed. Gathering bits and pieces of this young man's story, I came to a major realization: someone had developed him as a leader, and they had done a really great job. Rob's story is one of success.

Rob is a product of Auburn University's aggressive Student Government Association and its leadership development process. As a freshman, Rob was among over a thousand students who applied for a prestigious position in Auburn's Freshman Forum, a leadership development program known as "Tiger Tuesdays" (an homage to Auburn's mascot). When Rob was in the program, those who were selected for the process were then organized into five groups of forty-five students. For an entire year, these forty-five students are in the midst of what can only be described as a "training ground" for future Auburn leadership positions. They were the first students called on to volunteer for events, but always felt like they were contributors to the execution of the SGA as a whole.

During his time on Freshman Forum, Rob came to believe that Auburn University gives more opportunity for student leaders to shift policy and to affect campus life than any other College or University in the country. What Rob was doing, he suddenly realized, would have a lasting impact on the school long after he was gone.

During his years at Auburn, Rob spent time transforming a number of on-campus initiatives. While serving on the "Traffic and Parking Committee," he helped to create a new parking and transit system that made traveling on campus 25 percent more efficient. He also helped reduce Auburn's parking costs, and he lowered the amount of tickets accrued by commuter students. Rob and his team introduced food trucks to campus when lines at the cafeteria got too long. They created a new "farm to table" initiative to promote healthy eating as well as to improve the local economy. They even oversaw the creation of a new fall break for students.

"What I loved about it most," he told me, "was that I was given absolute creative control. If I didn't have my ducks in a row, none of it would have happened. If I didn't do the research and wasn't presenting an accurate cost-benefit analysis, we wouldn't have gotten it done. Nothing makes you work so hard as knowing that without your effort, it won't get done." Sensing my next question, Rob told me, "This was so much more interesting to me than my academic performance."

Want to know what Rob is doing now? He is a project manager at a firm in Atlanta, just two years out of school. While he appreciates and recognizes the importance of his finance degree, it was his time on student government, he says, that best prepared him for his career.

Rob Garcia's development is a testament to the importance of leaders who see potential in the emerging generation and provide opportunities for them to take ownership over their personal development. Did Rob fail in living up to his leadership as a young student? At times, he likely did, but the potential benefits far outweigh the possible cost. The greater danger, as you've seen from previous chapters, is the fear of what might happen, which prevents other leadership programs from following in Auburn's footsteps. Too often, out of fear of what an 18-year-old leader might do, leaders choose to never develop their students at all.

Boomer Sooner

There is a precedent, set long ago in the United States, for being forward thinking and innovative. It's the same American spirit that birthed the concept of "Manifest Destiny" at the beginning of the great American experiment. It's an attitude that can reveal to us what it takes to move from a settler mindset to a pioneer mindset. It's mostly in the attitude, and a little in your willingness to upset your neighbor.

When President Abraham Lincoln signed "The Homestead Act" of 1862, it set off a fury of land grabbing across the United States. The law allowed for a settler and his family to stake claim to 160 acres of any land owned by the Unites States Government. They would receive a title to the land after five years of constant occupation and improvement of the land.[1] The Homestead Act led to a mass movement of pioneers; those who were unable to make a good life for themselves in the already settled territories on the eastern seaboard. As they sought fortune and prosperity on the American frontier, Lincoln's promise rang in their ears. As long as they could make it there first, the land was theirs.

In March of 1889, a section of the Indian Appropriations Act was amended, a section that would later be called the "sooner clause." It opened up the Oklahoma territory to settlement with one important caveat. No intended settler of the land could enter the territory before April 22, 1889. This created what would come to be called the "Land Run of 1889."[2]

As with all movements, there were a group of people who refused to wait until April 22nd. Part of their Manifest Destiny, they believed, included doing whatever they needed to do in order to ensure that they got the land they were meant to have. So, under cover of night, many early settlers snuck onto the land with their families and hid under brush or in ravines until April 22, when they would rush out to claim some land. Their sneaking around at night at first earned them the name "moonshiners" because they traveled by the light of the moon. Eventually, however, the name for this group of people became one that is now recognizable by Oklahoma sports fans all over the country: they were called "Sooners."[3]

At the time, the term "sooner" was derogatory—used to accuse early settlers of cheating, and leading to many court appeals and lawsuits. In 1908, however, Oklahoma University's football team adopted the name with pride, seeing themselves as a people who would do whatever they needed to in order to achieve their goal. Many who pioneer are seen as cheaters by their less aggressive peers, but it seems—especially in cases like these—history favors the early settlers who would risk their reputation for the sake of achieving their purpose.

It's hard to say what we can learn from a story like this. I am certainly not advocating that you act illegally to get ahead. At the same time, there is an important truth here about the character of people who are willing to do whatever is necessary. Look at it another way with me. Sooners weren't just illegal squatters, they were the few who were so desperate for a better life, they were willing to risk everything for the chance to grab it. Is this the attitude we have toward our work with students? Shouldn't it be? My worry is that, too often, we are okay with being late to make change—even though the need for immediate action is just as important today as it was in 1889.

What Makes a Map Maker?

In the second chapter of this book we talked about a profession that you might be tempted to believe is long passed: the mapmaker. After all, this is the 21st century. There are no more unexplored lands, unclimbed mountains, or uncharted depths. Right? If you believe this, I would argue that you would be wrong on two accounts. First, there are unexplored jungles and unfathomed depths still in our world. Some places, even today, are still hard to reach. Second, and perhaps more importantly, the job of a mapmaker has only partly to do with maps.

Map makers are formed by their disposition, rather than their profession. There are map making athletes, CEOs, educators, and people from many other professions at work today in our world. What unites this modern-day mapmaker with their more literal map-making cousins from history? As I've explored the personalities and stories of many of the world's leading agents of change, there are a number of characteristics, or dispositions, that have risen to the top.

Purpose and Aspiration

Having purpose and aspiration means having a foundational focus on a big goal, exterior to oneself. Almost every innovator worth noting has a strong sense of purpose that they can trace back to their formative years. Some moment of realization that led them to believe a problem they were facing could be overcome.

In seventh grade, a young 12-year-old heard about the problem of modern-day slavery. The shock of that realization, combined with the admiration he had for an anti-trafficking organization called the International Justice Mission, led a young Zach Hunter to create a student-led fundraising movement called, "Loose Change to Loosen Chains." Young people give pennies, dimes, and nickels to stop slavery and watch as their small coins add up. In just one year, Zach's movement raised $8,500 for IJM's work. College campuses all over the world have now joined Zach's LC2LC movement.

TRAVEL GUIDE:

What moment in your life would you point to as the genesis of the purpose and aspiration of your work?

Vision and Innovation

Vision is about seeing the world in a different way, and innovation is the ability to create systems and products to bring about the change you envision. Great map makers are only made when they can bring their ideas into reality. They must first see the problem, and then find a way to create the solution.

When, Scott Harrison, the founder of Charity: Water looked at the problems around the world, he became overwhelmed. Through some very innovative thought, however, he realized one single problem was a major contributor to many of the other injustices around the world: lack of access to clean water. The 663 million people around the world who live without clean water are beholden to a number of other issues like health problems, poverty, and inequality. Their daytime hours for useful work are reduced because of the amount of time it takes to walk to get water. There is a lack of access to education for girls who have to help their moms walk to find clean water. And there's gender inequality because women have no time to build lives for themselves. By digging one well, Charity:Water knew it could revolutionize an entire community.[4]

TRAVEL GUIDE:

What was your vision when you started your work as an educator?

Design and Preparation

The process of design and preparation is just like a lesson plan. You can't move forward if you haven't decided how it will be done. To envision the future is to see where you need to be in one or even five years. But to plan for it, is to know what you have to accomplish tomorrow, and the next day, and the next.

163

In 1952 Rev. Everett Swanson, an American missionary living in South Korea, came across thirty-five children who were orphaned by the Korean conflict. Realizing this was a need he should meet, Swanson decided to create a ministry for children living in poverty.[5] Today, this effort continues as Compassion International, and it serves millions of children all over the world. Compassion's business model is for individuals with means to "adopt" impoverished children, just as their founder did almost seventy years ago. This adoption requires just $38 a month, and provides the child with food and supplies for his or her family. This month-to-month strategy is now expertly executed to solve a problem in our world.

> TRAVEL GUIDE:
>
> How will you turn your greatest visions of the future into practical day-in and day-out plans?

Courage and Dedication

Finally, courage and dedication are required ingredients for modern-day map makers. The drive to complete what you start is essential—especially because there will be obstacles positioned to keep all innovators from succeeding. The courage to begin and the dedication to keep going are essential attitudes for even the world's best entrepreneurs, teachers, parents, and leaders.

Leroy Lamar moved into an "at-risk" neighborhood in south Atlanta where he quickly realized there was a disturbing problem. There was a large concentration of prostitutes working on his street corner. Seeking to understand the problem, Leroy began talking with his neighbors about the situation. And, eventually, he talked to the prostitutes themselves about why this street had so much late night activity. What he discovered was very depressing. He learned that when a prostitute gets too old to keep working, her pimp brings her to this street corner in Atlanta—and leaves her there. The corner Mr. Lamar moved to by chance, he discovered, is where prostitutes in Atlanta come to die. Moved to act, Leroy Lamar founded a nonprofit called Serenity's Steps, which aims to provide a path out of prostitution for the women that find themselves on his street corner. Over the years, Leroy and his wife have even invited young women to live with them, to rescue them from the streets.

Seven Modern Day Map Makers

The best way to illustrate the concept of a modern-day mapmaker is to introduce you to several that I've located. Let's meet some people who are forging new territory in the modern world. Leading the next generation can be tough, and no one knows it better than these seven leaders. It's the difficulty of change, however, and the need for it that makes the discovery of new territories possible. As you read their stories, consider how these ideas may apply to your own environment. What challenges did they face that you are facing now? What solutions did they come up with that you could use? How were they able to implement strategies that might work in an organization like yours?

1. Raleigh Werberger

Raleigh Werberger is Dean of Faculty and a history teacher at the Darrow School in New Lebanon, NY.[6] As the founder of the Darrow School's project-based learning initiatives, Werberger is the leader of some of the most innovative teaching practices at the Darrow School. It all started when he was working at a previous school and realized the struggles that his students were having with connecting the things they were learning with the real world. The other problem, of course, is that kids get bored.

Seeing an opportunity to expand the minds of his students with a school project about the world and how we get our food, Werberger came up with an idea for an assignment that he called the "Unhappy Meal." For this project, students would have to reverse engineer a McDonalds Happy Meal© from scratch. Students had to grow their own plants for tomatoes, lettuce, potatoes, wheat, and pickles. They also had to raise and slaughter their own livestock, and then assemble or bake all the ingredients together.

In an interview, Werberger said the intent was "to create a curriculum that would cross disciplines with science and social studies, provide opportunities for independent research, and teach students about the realities behind how the world feeds itself."[7] Werberger enjoyed the results of the project so much that he decided to share the idea with his fellow teachers in an online blog that became so popular it led him to write a book, *From Project-Based Learning to Artistic Thinking: Lessons Learned from Creating an Unhappy Meal.*[8] His book chronicles the one-year journey of this project and the lessons Werberger and the kids learned from this endeavor.

Today, Werberger is putting his latest class through another project. This time his students are working on "a project on processing food waste by having the teenagers research, design, build, and market to the public small vermi-composting bins, fueled by food-composting red wiggler worms."[9]

How is this all registering with the students? Pretty well I would say. "I thought it was a bit challenging because I've never done that before," said one freshman student, [but] "in actual life we're going to have to do something, not just write what we're going to do on paper. To learn to build is good for us in real life because sometimes we might need to fix something and need to understand how things work."[10]

2. Deirdre DeAngelis & The "Hochman" Program

In 2006, 82 percent of freshmen entered New Dorp High School in Staten Island, reading below grade level. "In the spring of 2007, when administrators calculated graduation rates, they found that four out of ten students who had started New Dorp as freshmen had dropped out, making it one of the 2,000 or so lowest-performing high schools in the nation."[11] Unsurprisingly, New Dorp was being looked at by the state education board for closure. There was little hope that they would be able to turn things around.

The educational crisis led principal Deirdre DeAngelis to investigate why New Dorp students were struggling so badly. The answer she found, after an exhaustive investigation, was a little surprising. Poor writing skills constituted most, if not all, of the problems they were facing. Students simply could not write in well thought-out and complete sentences. In the wake of this realization and the massive hurdle they were facing, DeAngelis made a bold move—she completely threw out the school's curriculum. New Dorp High School, she decided, was going to try something new.

"Seeking out ideas, DeAngelis took a handful of teachers to visit the Windward School, a small private school for first-through-ninth-graders located in a leafy section of White Plains, a suburb of New York City."[12] The school's writing instruction was made famous by their former head of school, Judith Hochman, who invented a now infamous teaching style that DeAngelis and her teachers sought to mirror. Under the Hochman program, students are trained to create complex sentences by combining smaller ones with the simple additives "but," "because," and "so." This methodology challenges students to consider why they are writing, not just what they are writing.

The adoption of this new analytical writing curriculum, dubbed "the Hochman Method," turned the school around in just two years. For the English Regents, test scores rose from "67 percent in June 2009 to 89 percent in 2011."[13] In the same time period, testing on the global history exam rose from 64 to 75 percent. These kinds of results, in such a short period of time, are almost unheard of in educational circles today.

The results are not just found in the numbers, but in the lives of young students now changed. "Before, I could read, sure. But it was like a sea of words," said one New Dorp student, but "the more writing instruction I got, the more I understood which words were important."[14] Writing an op-ed on both New Dorp School and the writing revolution surrounding it, Atlantic journalist, Peg Tyre, cautions the need for creativity as a part of this miraculous story as well:

> *"The secret weapon of our economy is that we foster creativity," says Kelly Gallagher, a high-school writing teacher who has written several books on adolescent literacy [...] "Formulaic instruction will cause some students to tune out," cautions Lucy Calkins, a professor at Columbia University's Teachers College. While she welcomes a bigger dose of expository writing in schools, she says lockstep instruction won't accelerate learning. "Kids need to see their work reach other readers [...] They need to have choices in the questions they write about, and a way to find their voice."[15]*

Both the Hochman method and the story of principal DeAngelis, who had the courage to turn her school around, only worked because they targeted the exact problem the school was facing. Students had no ability to express their opinions in any subject, and the method utilized at New Dorp High School was the perfect technique for overcoming their specific challenge. In the case of this struggling school—one that now serves as a model of transformation for others across the nation—the new maps they now use every day were just what was needed.

3. Sherri Coale

Sherri Coale has been the women's basketball coach at the University of Oklahoma for more than 20 years. When she first started in the 1996-97 season, the team had a 5-22 record. But things turned around pretty quickly because of Coale's attitude toward coaching and her innovative approach to helping her student-athletes succeed.

"We expect competitiveness everywhere," she told me when we spoke about her position. "Each of our players is a "tripod", [focusing on] athletics, the classroom, and the community [simultaneously]. It starts with the kinds of conversations that we have when we are recruiting. If [our players] can't be successful in multiple places, then [they] won't be successful at Oklahoma." The structure that this "tripod" rule has promoted within the women's basketball team teaches players that the attitude required of them on the court is the same one that will make them a success in the classroom, and in life. In the words of coach Coale, focusing on your whole person makes you into a player that understands the need for "humility, grace, and gratitude" in all things.

As you might imagine, this is not the normal approach to coaching in a competitive atmosphere like the NCAA, not to mention the BIG12, one of the most competitive basketball conferences. A more "typical" team would put basketball above all else, including grades and extracurricular activities. Coale's "tripod" approach shows her team and her school the core values they intend to live by, even if it hurts recruiting. Coale's team is frequently left off of ESPN's top recruiting classes because she makes it clear to potential players that they will be expected to participate in service projects during their time on the team, something many star high school athletes are unwilling to do.[16] Despite what many coaches would consider an "unorthodox approach", Coale's team has seen unbelievable success.

Starting in 2000, Oklahoma Women's Basketball began a string of NCAA tournament appearances that continues to this day. That's 17 years in a row. No small feat, but one that has been accomplished because of the unique approach by Coach Coale, not in spite of it. From the first recruiting conversation, to practice, to the film room, to team service projects, and exit interviews for every game, Coale's system is one that is committed to making her girls successful in life, not just on the court. Unsurprisingly, OU has found that the two go hand in hand.

4. George Siemens and Stephen Downes

Is there such a thing as a free education? In 2008 Dr. George Siemens, then professor at Athabasca University in Canada, along with researcher Stephen Downes, invented the first free online completely open course. This course led to a movement of free education of this kind, which included many of the world's most prestigious universities. A movement now called Massive Online Open Courses or MOOCs for short.

The emergence and rise of MOOCs have led some to believe that the greatest change coming to education, is the Internet. It seems inevitable that the internet would change the system of education, but never before the emergence of MOOCs had any education system been so clearly designed to fit with the nature and methodology of the internet. Namely, making courses completely free and accessible by anyone. The emergence of MOOCs, led by these two innovators, is a force that is now impossible to stop. Save for one problem.

In 2012, the New York Times declared this change in education to be so radical that they called it "The Year of the MOOC."[17] At that time, online open courses were growing faster than social media platforms, and the potential to reach people who were previously unreachable by education exploded. That is, until they measured one number that is a consistent predictor of effective educational institutions: graduation rates.

One study in 2013 found that student attrition was somewhere around 10 percent for these types of courses.[18] This means that even though a course may have 160,000 people in it, only 16,000 of those could be expected to finish the class over the next few months.

What's most interesting about this set back is that these lousy completion rates don't scare the founder of MOOCs at all. In a 2014 interview for University Affairs, Dr. Siemens talked about a still bright future for MOOCs. The failing completion rate "doesn't say anything about open learning or learning at scale," he pointed out. "It's making a huge impact in developing regions of the world. There are now [almost] 10 million students internationally who are able to access free, open, online education. That's the equivalent of opening 40, 50 or more large universities" across the globe.[19]

No matter how you feel about the idea of free education, the MOOC movement is allowing access to high level education for people—both young and old—who might not otherwise have access. This could be the world's best idea for solving the problem of educational access, a problem we have struggled with globally for the entire history of the human race.

5. Charlie Puttkammer and the Petey Greene Program

About an hour outside of Boston, MA you would find perhaps the least likely place in the country for educational innovation: a prison. Massachusetts Correctional Institution in Norfolk, Massachusetts is a medium security prison that houses about 1500 inmates and is home to one of the oldest prison education systems in the country. Spearheaded by Boston University, the program utilizes U.S. Pell grants to provide incarcerated young adults with a second chance at life.

After its launch in the 1970s, this program is the only one to have survived the "tough on crime" era of the 90s, in particular, the Violent Crime Control and Law Enforcement Act of 1994, which withdrew Pell Grant eligibility from people in prison. Boston University was the only program in the country to survive and continue to provide access to Bachelor's degrees for interested inmates.[20] This program provides a path toward reform and a leg to stand on, especially for young inmates looking to re-enter society with a chance at success. It has recently been reinforced with a new mentoring system.

Ralph Waldo "Petey" Greene, Jr. was a young drug addict who served a prison sentence for armed robbery. He found a new lease on life as a prison disk jockey. Greene went on to become a TV and radio personality in the Washington D.C. area. In his legacy, a friend and mentor named Charlie Puttkammer established "The Petey Greene Program," a mentorship and tutoring non-profit which supplements education in correctional institutions by preparing volunteers to help support the academic achievement of incarcerated people.[21]

Today the Petey Greene program operates in seven different states to help ensure the success of young incarcerated men. It's a program that sees potential in young men, despite their pasts, and helps them see how they can rise above their mistakes and still make a life for themselves.

6. John D'Eri

The D'Eri family is like many middle-class American families, they own a small business, they have two children, and they make ends meet with hard work. The one difference for the D'Eri's, and for many families all over the world, is that one of their sons, Andrew, is on the autism spectrum.

"Autism, or autism spectrum disorder, refers to a range of conditions characterized by challenges with social skills, repetitive behaviors, speech and nonverbal communication, as well as by unique strengths and differences." There are many types of autism, which can be "caused by different combinations of genetic and environmental influences."[22] Autism creates unique challenges for families, especially once autistic children age out of the education system, something that is often referred to by families with autistic members as "falling off the cliff". A term that takes on profound meaning when you learn that 90 percent of adults on the autism spectrum are unemployed.[23] Seeing this cliff coming, John and his older son Tom, decided to do something for Andrew. They wanted to give him a purpose.

John and Tom founded "Rising Tide Carwash", a small business that employs 43 people. Their competitive advantage, however, just might surprise you. 35 of their of their 43 employees are on the Autism spectrum. "Typically, people with autism are really good at structured tasks, following process, and attention to detail," Tom said in an interview. "So we saw that there were skills that people with autism have that make them some of the best employees you could have."[24] Many of their employees, including Andrew, come to them feeling lost, with very little hope for the future. The process of making customers happy and following a repeatable process, however, changes everything.

One dad's vision for helping his son has now become a sustainable business that is transforming the lives of many people. He's paving a new path for adults with Autism.

7. Linda Howe

As a professor of Nursing at the University of Central Florida, Linda Howe, Ph.D. discovered a problem. She recognized that students retain information better when they discover it for themselves rather than having it told to them in a lecture-style format. (Does this sound strangely like metacognition to you?) Howe developed a new method of teaching pharmacology called "The Village," which is now used by more than 70 schools across the nation.[25]

What Howe does is upload all the course content online for students to access at any time. Then, in the classroom, she removes the lecture in favor of group discussions, case studies, team-building exercises, and mini in-class projects. Students are given all the information for the class at their disposal at all times, and they are then told to use it in different types of real-world applications. This allows students to put their knowledge to use rather than memorizing it for a test or quiz. It also allows students to teach each other, filling in knowledge gaps or providing clarity on something they didn't understand. Experience, Dr. Howe has confirmed, is the best teacher.

"When I was a student, I hated just hearing [teachers] droning on and on and on," Howe said in a 2015 interview. "So I wanted to make it more interesting for the students. Whenever I go to a conference and someone stands up there and reads the slides to me, it's like, 'Oh my God, death by PowerPoint.' I just don't want my students to feel that way."[26] We can all rest assured that boredom is the last thing her students experienced in her classroom.

In May of 2016, Linda Howe, Ph.D. passed away at the age of 67. Her legacy as an innovative teacher lives on through her work. "In October 2015, Howe was honored for her innovative teaching strategies and inducted as a fellow into the National League for Nursing's Academy of Nursing Education."[27] Howe used the "flipped classroom model," and thereby encouraged students to take the ownership over their education into their own hands. This is something that I know all of her students will continue to do.

TRAVEL GUIDE:

Which of these case studies could best transform your work?

WHAT CAN WE LEARN FROM THESE MODERN-DAY MAP MAKERS?

You might have noticed common threads woven throughout these stories. Each of these modern-day map makers came to a problem, analyzed the issue, committed themselves to overcoming the obstacle, and invented or adapted a new method to solve the problem. It's a process that you might have seen in your own life, but if it's such a repeatable process, why don't more people do it?

My guess is you already know why we aren't all map makers. Leading change is difficult. The reality of a vision for the future is that only a few people see it, and even fewer are willing to take the risks associated with change. This, I believe, should not be a reason for us to fear becoming a map maker ourselves. The men and women whose stories are told above do not possess some special skill that you do not have. You are capable, and that's why I tell these stories. You are just like them.

As I read about and meet more and more map makers out in the world, however, I can't help but pick up a few lessons from these brave men and women. So, let's get practical. What can we learn from these modern-day map makers? Here are three important insights:

1. You won't tread new territory overnight.

When you set out to create change, you can't expect everything to happen overnight. Most of these folks spent their entire lives trying to figure out what the problems were and how the problems could be solved. Principal Deirdre DeAngelis had a school on the brink of closure before she could find the vision to provide direction and make a change. Coach Coale practiced her process through several losing seasons before she saw any of the results of her purposeful style. Creating change; rerouting a school or organization cannot happen overnight.

2. Innovation can come in small packages, yet leave a big impact.

Often the greatest innovations start very small, and roll out to a huge impact. Most of the best ideas only make sense at first in the smallest of contexts. The Petey Greene program started because one man had a transformative experience while in prison. Only later was a man able to take his story and turn it into a methodology. When Raleigh Werberger wanted to create a new way of learning for his students I am sure that at the beginning it was confusing for his students and upsetting for their parents. It was a small (and potentially boring) start to a now innovative and aspiring achievement.

3. **The greatest map makers are the ones who are focused on the needs of others.**

The pursuit of service to others is one of the only motivations that can keep you working toward your goal. The late Linda Howe was motivated by her passion for her students, and the knowledge that she could better prepare them only if they owned their own education. John D'Eri wanted to create a place for his son Andrew to work. In trying to meet this one need, he ended up helping lots of lost young men. George Siemens, the founder of MOOCs, knew that free courses would lose students more often than they would teach them, but he saw beyond poor finishing rates to realize the good that open courses can offer to the world. In the face of challenge and near failure, only our desire to serve others can motivate a move into new territory.

Your Legacy

I want to introduce you to one last map maker. Bobby R. Woodard is the Associate Provost and Vice President for Student Affairs at Auburn University. Although only starting in 2014, he has already taken on his role of empowering students seriously. Included in the more than 400 opportunities for leadership on Auburn's campus is the Student Government Association. That's right. Mr. Woodard oversaw SGA during Rob Garcia's last year at Auburn University.

"We must empower students to take what they learn in the classroom and apply it to the world around them," said Woodard, "preparing them to contribute to their communities and to be quality members of society."[28] From what I can see, Woodard and the leaders of Auburn University live up to their words. Rob Garcia is proof of that. Rob Garcia is part of Auburn's legacy.

You too have a legacy. It will have nothing to do with how many publications are next to your name on your resume, or how many peer-reviewed articles may quote your work. It has little to do with how many years you teach, or how respected the institution is where someone could find your office. Your true legacy lies in the line of young men and women who will enter the world with your words ringing in their ears. They are the real reason we march off the map. We are, each of us, paving a new way in the hope that those who come behind us might pick up the maps we draw and find their way to a better life.

CHAPTER 10

STORMS ON THE HORIZON

Adolescents today face a variety of challenges, but two are paramount to resolve.

The real voyage of discovery consists not in seeking new landscapes but in having new eyes.

—Marcel Proust

I've lived through a few storms in my day.

I experienced four earthquakes while living in Southern California. I felt the bitter cold of three blizzards while living in Ohio. I endured six tornadoes while living in Oklahoma. I encountered the tip of a hurricane while living in Atlanta, Georgia. And while living in Denver, I witnessed a day with 72-degree temperature, followed the next day by a snowstorm. In almost every place I've lived, in fact, locals would utter the phrase at some point: "If you don't like the weather here, just wait ten minutes."

Anyone who marches off the map should expect to encounter some turbulent weather. At higher altitudes, we know to expect colder temperatures. On locations closer to the equator, the climate is obviously warmer, and often has more rain. I bet Alexander the Great and his men experienced a variety of weather as they entered Egypt and marched across Persia. Or, consider the Lewis and Clarke Expedition. Meriwether Lewis and William Clarke must have known when they set out to pioneer new territory west of the Mississippi River they'd encounter very different and even inclement weather. The words later recorded about their journey went like this:

"In the predictable procession of wind, storm, and fog, the months ahead loomed as an endless round of rain-soaked days."

As they journeyed north, they encountered all kinds of precipitation, both rain and snow. In the journals from their team, we read:

- "We are all wet and disagreeable . . ."
- "It was a cold and a dreadful day . . ."
- . . . and most common of all was the phrase: "the rain continued as usual."

While the explorers huddled in their dank quarters and cursed the foul weather, the Indians went about their daily routine. Why? They were used to the weather and interpreted it as the spirits moving among them.

Two Weather Conditions Today

So, as we march off the map, trying out new territory and exploring new methods to reach our young today—shouldn't we expect some foul weather? New places always introduce both new terrain and new climates. It's natural and normal.

I believe we should anticipate all kinds of new patterns.

In fact, with change occurring more rapidly than ever, perhaps we can make the statement I mentioned earlier: "If you don't like the weather, just wait ten minutes."

When I survey the patterns of what's ahead, I'd like to focus on two tumultuous storms here. I mentioned these briefly in chapter 3, but I believe we need to explore further how we can navigate these "storms" I see on the horizon. In my view, if we care about the future, it is essential to determine how to equip our young to thrive as they mature amidst these challenges. Attempting the new pedagogies and subjects I recommend without addressing these "storms" would be tragic. The two I am speaking of are:

- Anxiety among students.
- Amorality among students.

Our young often experience these two downpours on a daily basis, and sometimes I wonder if we, adults, are unsure how to help kids overcome them. In the rest of this chapter, I'd like to explain why these tempests exist and what our students need from us as their leaders. Allow me to be your meteorologist.

Student Anxiety

In my book, *Generation iY*, I relayed the results of a 2007 study from the American College Health Association. The study included the largest random sampling of college students since its inception. The conclusions were sobering:

- 94 percent of students reported feeling "overwhelmed" by their lifestyles.
- 44 percent said they were so overwhelmed it was difficult to function.
- Almost 10 percent had considered suicide in the last year.[1]

A decade later, I wondered if the adolescent situation had improved. Had they learned to cope with a world filled with technology, materialism and demands on their time? I was hopeful, but alas, their reality has become more challenging.

In a report published in July of 2013 by *Elements Behavioral Health*, indicates that teen anxiety continues to rise. Symptoms like panic attacks, angst in social situations and obsessive-compulsive behavior are all indicators of the largest class of mental illnesses. These Anxiety Disorders are the most common of all mental illness among adolescents. They have been diagnosed in a full 25 percent of teens, and 30 percent of teenage females.[2] Many experts are seeing a rise in the level of anxiety and the incidence of anxiety disorders in both adults and teenagers. It's staggering.

Many educators wonder: do we really have more angst-filled students or are we simply diagnosing more of them—and they've always been around? Good question. My research tells me it's both. Certainly, there were anxious personalities a hundred years ago; no doubt, students got depressed. (I say this tongue in cheek, but had the medications been around, Tom Sawyer and Dennis the Menace would have likely needed Ritalin and Charlie Brown probably needed Prozac.) They just never got diagnosed. Mental health issues, however, are soaring says the American Psychological Association, and they are front and center on many university campuses. Ninety-five percent of college counseling center directors surveyed said the number of students with significant psychological problems is a growing concern in their centers on campus.[3]

The fact that a quarter of our teens will struggle with an anxiety disorder demands our attention. According to the report:

> *"This number has been steadily rising [...], for nearly a century. According to researchers who looked at mental health data for high school and college students from 1938 to 2007, more*

and more young people report symptoms of mental illness in general, and anxiety in particular.[4]

"Today, 85 percent of college students are classified above the average mental illness "score" of students in the 1930s and 1940s."[5]

"The study examined the surveys of over 60,000 young people self-reporting their emotions and symptoms. The researchers found that over the years, teens are describing themselves in changing terms. They are seeing more descriptions of feelings such as isolation, sensitivity, being misunderstood, narcissism, worry, sadness, low self-control and general dissatisfaction."[6]

TIME magazine felt this was such a vital issue in our culture, they ran a cover article in their November 7, 2016 issue. They documented this over-exposed generation of teens saying:

"Anxiety and depression in high school kids have been on the rise since 2012 after several years of stability. It's a phenomenon that cuts across all demographics—suburban, urban and rural; those who are college bound and those who aren't. A 2015 report from the Child Mind Institute found that only about 20 percent of young people with a diagnosable anxiety disorder get treatment."[7]

No matter how you look at it, angst is on the rise among teens.

The reasons for the rising anxiety vary. Dr. Jean Twenge, associate professor of psychology at San Diego State University, believes it's mostly due to the expansion of consumerism and materialism and the decline of quality relationships.[8] Pause and reflect. If a young person feels the need to possess more in order to measure up, he or she can feel pressure. Materialism is a terrifying master. My dad was born in 1930, at the front edge of the Great Depression. Those were different times. While folks did desire more clothes, cars, cash, crops and credit, most were content with "just enough." Life was more about "needs" than "wants." Today, Americans believe we need hundreds of gadgets and toys to survive. And if our neighbor owns them, we must own them as well. It's about keeping up with the Kardashians.

In addition, Dr. Twenge suggests diminishing quality relationships adds to our stress levels. If a student has less quality "face to face" time with family, because they're all busy, it heightens stress levels. As a kid, I believe debriefing the day at dinnertime with Mom and Dad helped me cope. Sadly, if role models at home (Mom or Dad) are stressed out as well from their work, kids not only fail to get processing time, but often emulate parents' behavior. It's normal. Our focus groups confirm Dr. Twenge's hypothesis. In short, it goes like this:

> ### *High materialistic pressure plus low quality relationships equals greater stress levels.*

I believe, however, there is yet another big reason for our anxiety.

The Impact of Social Media

Generation Z—the kids who've grown up in the 21st century—has never known a day without the ping of social media messaging: Facebook, Twitter, Snapchat, Whispr, Pinterest, Instagram, YouTube. . . you name it. What the personal computer was to the Millennials, social media is to Generation Z. Today kids are growing up with social media—all day, everyday. It's a whole new world.

Let's examine the unintended consequences of this world.

The first "social media" appearance was a website called *Six Degrees*. It was named after the "six degrees of separation" theory and lasted from 1997 to 2001. The evolution of popular social media sites rolled out like this:

- Wikipedia launched in 2001.
- MySpace was founded in 2003.
- Kik was started in 2004.
- Facebook became available to everyone in 2005.
- Twitter was launched in 2005.
- Buzzfeed started in 2006.
- Tumblr got its start in 2007.
- Pinterest began in 2010.
- Instagram was introduced in 2010.
- Snapchat was started in 2011.
- Vine started in 2013.

A whopping 71 percent of teens are on more than one site daily. According to a 2016 Pew Report of middle class and affluent students, ages 12-17:[9]

- 72 percent of teens are on Snapchat.
- 68 percent are on Facebook.
- 66 percent are using Instagram.

Teens now spend more time with digital media than they do sleeping. In fact, many are consuming social media when they should be sleeping. This reality surfaced in every one of our focus groups with young teens. Social media is now the number one time consumer of an adolescent. Teens spend 300 percent more time in front of a screen than they did 20 years ago. Pause and consider this shift. A full 94 percent hop on-line daily. Over half are on-line multiple times a day. Four out of every five teens sleep with their mobile phone next to them. Some shower with their phone.[10]

Here's my greatest concern. During our 2016 research with middle school and high school teens, a common theme continued to surface:

"My parents have no idea what I'm doing ... especially after midnight."

For example, the average teen now spends more than the equivalent of a full-time job on digital media each week. (It's nine hours a day, or about 63 hours a week).[11] However, parents think their child spends about three hours a day on-line. Big deal, you say? It might just be. Over half of U.S. teens are meeting people on-line. Do we know who they are? In a 2011 report, the Council on Communications and Media reveals that cyberbullying is spreading; too many teens have been on one side or the other of digital bullying. One in five has either posted or seen a nude photo of a friend—which is called "sexting." In a report entitled *Bullying, Cyberbullying, and Suicide*, researchers Dr. Sameer Hinduja and Dr. Justin Patchin tell us, "Cyberbullying is quite common, can occur to any young person online, and can cause profound psychosocial outcomes including depression, anxiety, severe isolation, and, tragically, suicide."[12]

I'm not sure we saw these unintended consequences coming.

The PRICE We Pay for Social Media

No doubt, there are plenty of positive growth opportunities with social media. I will cover those later. Here, I want to summarize the price tag our youth culture pays for the ubiquitous presence of social media. The two columns below capture the realities and outcomes we see. Take a glance, then I'll unpack these statements afterward.

Social media offers us…

P— PERSONAL PLATFORM.
This has fostered a narcissistic culture of selfies.

R— REACTIONARY OPINIONS.
This induces a preoccupation with others' judgments.

I— INSTANT UPDATES.
This can make us impulsive with short attention spans.

C— CONSTANT INFORMATION.
This has caused angst and depression in users.

E— EXTERNAL STIMULI.
This can lead to addictive lifestyles with the phone.

The Potential Downside

Let's examine the consequences below and detail the findings for each of them. As I reviewed the results of our research, its clear each introduction of new technology brings unintended consequences with it. I suggest we find ways to counter the negative realities that coincide with the emergence of social media:

1. They can tend to be narcissistic.

Social media has played an enormous role in the narcissistic tendencies of our population, both young and old. Our phones enable us to both take a "selfie" and post it in a matter of minutes. According to a survey from Luster Premium White (a teeth whitening brand), the average Millennial will take 25,000 "selfies" in their lifetime. 95 percent of young adults have taken one. Today, a million "selfies" are taken everyday.[13] I don't believe we'd do this unless we had the ability to post them via social media.

According to Masters in Psychology, the reasons we take so many "selfies" vary. However, "It quickly becomes clear that one thing many people are looking for via their selfies is a boost to their self esteem. From a psychological perspective, it is clear that individuals are looking for an avenue to fulfill this need and they have found it on their social media page. Every like, share and positive comment is a boost to their confidence, and this works to fuel the desire for more selfies."[14]

Our work with student athletes reveals a growing number are consumed far more with their own playing time and their personal brand than what happens to the team. It's about "me" not "we." According to psychologist Jean Twenge in her book, *The Narcissism Epidemic*, a self-preoccupation is growing among students today.[15]

2. They can tend to care too much about what others think of them.
Look around you, at middle class teens. Too often their feelings are represented in the 2015 song by "Twenty One Pilots," that says,

> *I was told when I get older all my fears would shrink,*
> *But now I'm insecure and I care what people think.*
> *My name's 'Blurryface' and I care what you think.*

Our world is constantly critiquing every word or thought we have. Why? Because social media enables it. This can drive students to be obsessed with how others feel about them, constantly checking comments, likes, dislikes, views and shares. Sadly, it's like an evaluation on their identity. An increasing number of students are preoccupied and obsessed with others' opinions, even when they're uninformed. It only matters that they've been posted. Television even imitates social media, as reality TV shows enable viewers to critique and vote on who stays on the show. We've created a population consumed with judging every look, word and act. It stings to be the receiver.

One of the tangible outcomes for this is self-harm, like cutting. The pain of a superficial wound is a momentary escape from the anxiety they're fighting constantly, about opinions, grades, parents and future prospects. One teen explained, "We're the first generation that can't escape our problems at all. We're like little volcanoes. We get this constant pressure from our phones, our relationships, from the way things are today."[16]

I should note that criticism and judgmental attitudes go both ways. Our young can get anxious and preoccupied with the critical comments coming at them. But at the same time, they're proficient at judging others as well, which leads us to the next reality.

3. They can tend to be impulsive with short attention spans.
This reality requires no data. We live in a time of impulsive behavior. We rant and rave on Twitter, even when we are presidential candidates. We react to any information that may diminish our brand, and then we attack the attacker. We cyberbully even if we're celebrities. This tendency may not only lead to addiction, as I will discuss later, it can foster an inability to delay gratification. Let's face it. When something is easy to access and easy to do, we can be impulsive. Social media fits that criteria.

You've likely heard of the Stanford Marshmallow Experiment by Dr. Walter Mischel, done with four-to-six year old children. The kids were told they could enjoy a marshmallow immediately, or if they'd wait for fifteen minutes, they would receive a second one. Predictably, some were able to wait and others were not.

Researchers followed up as the children grew into adolescence. They found the kids who could delay gratification were psychologically better-adjusted, more dependable, more self-motivated, and as high school students, scored significantly higher GPAs. In 2011, the latest study conducted on these same participants showed the characteristics remained with them for life, bad or good.[17] Social media could hinder this ability as they mature. It's far too easy to be impulsive when we can react hiding behind a screen.

Pause and note the connection between social media use and short attention spans. When new information constantly streams at an adolescent, it's tough to pay attention to any one message very long. As I stated earlier, adolescent attention spans have gone from 12 seconds in 2000 to 6 seconds in 2016. Further, when the messages coming our way are limited to 140 characters, teens are not conditioned to read information for very long. Their ability to process information is diminished. Their patience to digest complex information evaporates. Their critical thinking skills atrophy. A lifestyle full of social media pings can foster superficial thinking, rather than deep thinking.

4. They can tend to experience anxiety and depression.

This is the storm on the horizon for which I'm most concerned. The angst that comes with so much information streaming at us 24/7 is overwhelming. As brilliant as I believe our minds are, I don't believe they're hardwired for so much relentless data. Once again, I believe the song lyrics from "Stressed Out" say it best:

> *Wish we could turn back time, to the good old days,*
> *When our momma sang us to sleep but now we're stressed out.*
> *We're stressed out.*

Neuroscientists now report that when we have no margins in our calendar, when information or deadlines are constantly screaming at us, we have less capacity for empathy or creativity.[18] In fact, a noisy, taxing life reduces empathy and raises stress.[19] The noise puts us in survival mode. Life's about coping.

The irony of social media is profound. While many of the messages come from friends we know, the onslaught of information—especially if it appears that the messenger is experiencing a "better life" than the receiver—can lead to FOMO (Fear Of Missing Out) and other such negative emotions. In short, all the happy messages ironically can make us feel sad or anxious.

According to journalist Susanna Schrobsdorff, the rise of depression and angst precisely parallels the rise of social media. From 2006 when Facebook and other sites caught on, we see the bar graph match between social media connections and major depressive episodes. It's either a connection or a major coincidence.[20]

5. They can tend to lead to addictive lifestyles.

Because millions of students have social media posts delivered to them with a notification, their psyche becomes conditioned to react to the ping of their phone. Psychologists remind us that dopamine is released as students become expectant of this ping. It can actually be addictive. I've mentioned before The Pew Research Center reports that college students consider their phone as essential as air and water. It can almost feel as if they're enslaved to the messaging, just like people can be to cigarettes or alcohol.

According to research in the 2013 Journal of Exercise Rehabilitation, cell phone addiction can negatively impact brain development.[21] Further, the data shows that social media addictions can actually pave the way for other addictive behaviors, such as drug or alcohol abuse. It doesn't stop there. Research by Gwenn Schurgin O'Keeffe and Kathleen Clarke-Pearson, in the Journal of the American Academy of Pediatrics[22], suggest a term for the cumulative challenges accompanying social media:

"Compulsive and Problematic Cell Phone use, Cyberbullying, Sexting, and Facebook Depression." They report their conclusions in the April 2015 edition of Pediatrics, which imitate the symptoms of addictive behavior.

In short, it's hard to turn off excessive social media use. When I was a teen, I could hardly wait for the phone to ring. Now teens can't wait for it to ping.

TRAVEL GUIDE:

What symptoms have you observed when students use social media?

What could you do to convince them to use social media in moderation?

What are you doing to leverage social media for constructive purposes?

Let's consider, however, what might be an even more sobering outcome.

STUDENT AMORALITY

We all recognize that social media isn't going away. Most of us don't want it to. More than 9 in 10 adults surveyed acknowledge they are on it themselves.[23] What we may not realize, however, are the moral implications it has on our young.

Spoiler Alert. According to a U.K. poll, most parents believe social media harms their children's moral development. More than half, 55 percent, of people with kids, ages 11-17, "strongly agreed" that social media hinders or undermines moral development.[24] The survey was part of a research project from the Jubilee Center for Character and Virtues at Birmingham University. One researcher, Blaire Morgan, revealed some of the most intriguing findings:

> *"Not least [of these is] the low level of agreement that social media can enhance or support a young person's character or moral development. While parents acknowledged that positive character strengths, including moral virtues such as love, courage and kindness, are promoted through social networking sites, they were reluctant to agree these sites could have a positive impact on their child's character."*

In fact, the observing parents had this to say about their child's habits and attitudes on social media:

- "60 percent said they had seen anger or hostility."
- "51 percent said they had seen arrogance."
- "41 percent said they saw bad judgment."
- "36 percent said they had seen hatred."[25]

The vast majority reported a huge absence of humility, self-control, forgiveness, honesty and fairness. The fact is, social media works like a set of friends. Our kids can be the most mature people when with the right set of peers, but can spiral downward when with the wrong crowd. Somehow, we've got to find a way to foster redemptive and constructive activities on social media if we want to develop virtues in them. It must be our servant not a master. Omar Bradley, former General of the U.S. Army wisely said, "If we continue to develop our technology without wisdom or prudence, our servant may prove to be our executioner."

On the other hand, Steve Ballmer reminds us, "The number one benefit of information technology is that it empowers people to do what they want to do. It lets people be creative. It lets people be productive. It lets people learn things they didn't think they could learn before, and so in a sense it is all about potential."

Perhaps Microsoft founder Bill Gates said it best: "Technology is just a tool. In terms of getting the kids working together and motivating them, the teacher is the most important." Let's play our role.

A Case Study: Where Are Our Ethics and Values Heading?

I'd like to dig deeper on the issue of values, in a technology-filled culture like the U.S.

Our current culture includes a plurality of ethnic groups, worldviews, value systems and spiritual beliefs. Not long ago, the vast majority of Americans were Caucasians of European descent. Today that number is only 63 percent.[26] The rest make up minority groups who are Asian, Arab, Latin American and African American ethnicities. Often, Americans find it difficult to enjoy civil discourse or make any compromises. We feel strongly about many things and often see those who disagree with us as enemies. Yet, today, most of us do agree on one thing.

Something's really wrong.

According to the Barna Research Group, "A majority of American adults across age group, ethnicity, gender, socioeconomic status and political ideology expresses concern about the nation's moral condition—8 in 10 overall (80 percent). The proportion is almost 9 in 10 among Elders (89 percent) and Boomers (87 percent), while about three-quarters of Gen-Xers (75 percent) and Millennials (74 percent) report concern."[27]

Sometimes, this is an issue of faith, but not always. "Practicing Christians are more likely than adults of no faith to be concerned about the moral fabric of the U.S., at 90 percent vs. 67 percent respectively. 72 percent of those who identify with a religious faith other than Christianity say they are concerned about the moral condition of the nation. Though measurable differences exist between population segments, moral concern is widespread across the demographic board."[28] It's what we agree on.

What we don't always agree upon is morality itself. We can't find consensus. What is it based on? Where do you get it? How can someone know what to do when making moral decisions? "According to a majority of American adults (57 percent), knowing what is right or wrong is a matter of personal experience. This view is much more prevalent among younger generations than among older adults. Three-quarters of Millennials (74 percent) agree strongly or somewhat with the statement: 'Whatever is right for your life or works best for you is the only truth you can know,' compared to only 38 percent of Elders."[29]

In 2014, our organization, Growing Leaders, had the privilege of surveying 17,000 public high school students from the state of Georgia. We surveyed students from urban, rural and suburban areas across the state. The results were surprising, even among kids living in the South. Regarding morals and ethics, we discovered the students saw no correlation between a successful life and an ethical life. For them, pragmatism trumps principle. A person must do whatever they feel they must do to get what they want. It was a sobering reality.

Since Baby Boomers became parents, a shift has taken place. Boomers became parents who, by and large, decided they didn't want to dictate morality to their children. Millions of them were "free spirits" during the 60s and 70s, and desired their kids to be able to make up their own minds about what to believe. In many ways, this is a noble idea. Empowering kids to determine what their values are is a good thing. My question is—did parents really empower or acquiesce? When adults refuse to offer ethical direction, history teaches us that civilizations can drift into "amoralism" and even anarchy. Review the fall of the Roman Empire and you catch a glimpse of the ethical vacuum that existed then. So, while it looks so good to leave beliefs up to our children, neglecting to teach ethics or failing to embody values serves only to confuse children. A cursory view of our kids reveals this confusion.

For many of our young, ethics are subjective. There's no plumb line.

Today's Trend: Elastic Morality

As I review statistics on today's students, I'm encouraged to see there are signs of improvement in their conduct. I've written about the downward trends in cigarette smoking, drinking while driving, television viewing and even teen sex. Additionally, youth are drinking more water and fewer soft drinks. This is all good news. However, one expanding reality deserves both our attention and our appropriate response.

Many who'll read this book work directly with students. Perhaps you might work so closely with them, you've not been able to see a trend in the morals of today's high school and college students. This pattern has increased over the last thirty years, and many of us are missing the forest for the trees.

My friends Chris Tompkins and John McAuley have co-authored a book with Don Postereski that puts a finger on the pulse of what's happening. Their research reveals that young adults today experience "elastic morality." Because our culture cherishes qualities such as pluralism and tolerance (which is very helpful), many of our youth have lost the ability to think critically or make moral judgments (which is unhelpful). As we create space for diversity—which is positive—one unintended result is we often fail to prepare them to discern right from wrong. Our culture is marked by:

- Resistance to judgment
- Uncensored acceptance
- Exchanging certainty for ambiguity
- Embracing plurality
- Stretching the boundaries of belief and behavior.

Consequently, what is right can expand or bend. Their interviews with college age students unveil a "dominant view that the 'right choice' is all relative to personal experience, personal convictions and personal opinion."[30]

They continue saying "Profound cultural trends like accelerating technology, and materialism are not just abstract concepts. These trends march into our living rooms, our spending patterns, and our own hearts. We are not separate from strong cultural currents. They swirl around us and even within us."[31]

Five Sources of Morality

Dr. Christian Smith is the professor of sociology at the University of Notre Dame, a lead researcher and author of Lost in Transition.[32] His work details the dark side of emerging adulthood today, and how morals are fading, as American kids become adults. Smith and his team outline five patterns in their study with college students. The patterns demonstrate an evolution in the source of their morality:

1. **Morals are determined by results or consequences.**

   A growing percentage of students possess very fuzzy morals, and when pressed to explain them, the morals developed purely from the results they produce. In other words, it is right to do something if it got you where you wanted to go. The end justifies the means. If you don't get caught, it's OK. It's why 75 percent of college students cheat on tests to get the grade they want; yet when caught, they generally agree it was wrong.[33] It was right only if they got away with it. It's situational morality.

2. **Morals are determined by pleasure or happiness.**

   Approximately 40 percent of students developed a morality based upon how it made others feel around them.[34] Something is judged as right or wrong if your boyfriend agreed with it, or your BFF's felt good about it. In short, it's right if the people around you believe its right at the time. This might be expressed in words like, "If it makes everyone happy, then it must be right." Happiness is the gauge. This, too, is situational morality—just consider how much feelings fluctuate among teens. What's more, there are times when standing for what's right is hard not pleasurable.

3. **Morals are determined by appearance or reputation.**

   The majority of emerging adults professed to believe in right and wrong morals, but have no objective source with which to reference it. Instead, morality is defined by what other people would think of them if they behaved in a certain manner. How would it look if I stole something? How would it appear if I hooked up with her? It's the Facebook Rule, where appearances and reputation govern what we do. This, quite frankly, is a slippery slope, where morality fluctuates with public opinion.

4. **Morals are determined by context or environment.**

   A third of students (34 percent) reported they do believe in specific moral truths, but realize they do so because they were raised in a particular culture that teaches right and wrong.[35] They could not project those morals on all human beings. While I applaud their cultural sensitivity, when we view life this way, we cannot expect terrorists to do anything but continue their mass killings on other nations, nor can we judge them for it, as they developed different values than the rest of the world.

5. Morals are determined by affect or influence.
More than 53 percent of students say they can determine if something is moral if it doesn't hurt someone else.[36] I've heard this before: Yes, I had sex with someone even though they're engaged, but it didn't hurt anyone. Or, Yes, I took some petty cash from the organization, but they're rich. They'll never miss it. It's a subjective compass that allows for immorality solely based on how it affects or doesn't affect others. Again, this is a slippery slope where opinion dictates what's right or wrong.

The Difference Between Relative vs. Absolute Values
The truth is, as culture becomes filled with new realities—including technology, innovations and alternative lifestyles—it becomes difficult for adolescents to distinguish between what is cultural and what is time-less. It has always been "hip" for young adults to be progressive, but today, teens and twenty-somethings are failing to be able to judge anything as absolutely "right" and "wrong." There is, in fact, a moral relativism residing in millions of them.

Let me be clear—some values or morals are relative. They change from culture to culture, from person to person and era to era. But in our desire to be progressive, I'm concerned we've discarded some timeless morals. We have created today an "elastic morality" that shrinks and expands based on expediency. We hesitate to judge anything right or wrong for fear we'll appear intolerant. While societies need tolerance of differing perspectives, tolerance in ethics weakens us all. In our post-modern age today, have we communicated this to our young?

TRAVEL GUIDE:

Can you list some examples of both relative morals and timeless morals?

Have you clearly communicated the difference to your students?

Seven Simple Steps to Start the Conversation

In your Travel Guide, you will find a section called, "The A, B, C's of Guiding Students in Social Media." I encourage you to review it and discuss it with your colleagues.

Consider the following steps you could take as an educator, coach, youth worker or parent with your students:

1. **Ask to meet and talk over the influence and hours consumed by social media.**
   Often, logging the hours a teen spends can be eye-opening for them. Many spend the equivalent of a full-time job on their phones. Talk about how they spend their day.

2. **Ask to scroll through their posts with them.**
   This could be awkward, but actually sit with them and look at the posts uploaded both by them and to them. Discuss it.

3. **Interpret the tone and content of the posts and what it suggests about their character.**
   This may feel cheesy or cliché, but ask what people might conclude if they didn't know them—but saw their posts. Are they different in person than on-line?

4. **Discuss how employers, coaches, instructors or mentors might view their sites.**
   Next, talk about how students (grads) have lost their chance at a job because an employer viewed their social media posts. What does their screen image say?

5. **Ask them if they have ever noticed an attitude change in themselves, after reading or posting on social media?**
   This requires transparency, but discuss how it's easy to experience negative attitudes or impulsive reactions on-line.

6. **Suggest they follow the rule: I will only post what I want my reputation to be ten years from now.**
Finally, give them the long view. Have them ask themselves: What impact does my post have? What reputation will it give me a decade from now?

7. **Balance screen time with face-to-face time.**
Our house rule was: Whatever hours we spent on a screen, we must equal with in person interaction. Kids and adults. This enhanced our Emotional Intelligence.

Leveraging Social Media for Good

I want to be clear in what I am not saying. I'm not suggesting all teens are addicted to social media. I know many who are not. Several actually prefer face-to-face connections. Many possess wonderful interpersonal skills. I love this fact.

I am suggesting, however, that too many emerging adults have not been led well. We, the adult population, did not know how to guide them in a world filled with social media. We are either too busy or ignorant of what to do. Some authors, such as Danah Boyd, say our kids are fine; that the "addiction" problem isn't really addiction. I disagree. If there were no technology addiction, we wouldn't see the level of "withdrawal" symptoms in teens and twenty-somethings when their phone is taken away. The signals that align with addictive behavior are present in too many. What's more, it's easy to look at teens' social media posts and assume they're all happy. Too often, it's a façade for what's really going on inside. One New York Times article said it this way:

> *"Gregory T. Eells, director of counseling and psychological services at Cornell University, believes social media is a huge contributor to the misperception among students that peers aren't also struggling. When students remark during a counseling session that everyone else on campus looks happy, he tells them: "I walk around and think, 'That one's gone to the hospital. That person has an eating disorder. That student just went on antidepressants.' As a therapist, I know that nobody is as happy or as grown-up as they seem on the outside."*[37]

With each new iteration of technology, there are ways to leverage it for good, or to become a victim of it and see it play a destructive role. It's time to redeem it. Below, I offer you some fodder for discussion on the potential upside of social media. What if we capitalized on the potential for good in our schools, homes and teams?

The Potential Upside

Most of us have embraced our 21st century world of technology. We wouldn't want to be without the gadgets, the conveniences or connections they offer us. We adults are often on our phones, tablets or computers as much as the kids are. Let me offer four very real positive outcomes that are possible with social media.

When students grow up in a time of internet connection and social media:

1. **They have enhanced learning opportunities.**
   I believe social media and technology in general offer entirely new ways to gain access to important information. A portable device can be a classroom. I believe this generation of students will actually learn more from a mobile device than they will from a classroom.

2. **They have expanded socialization.**
   Often, a student who's typically introverted or shy in a face-to-face class can be talkative and participatory in an on-line setting. Screens help us connect. We find quiet students instantly feel safe to express themselves on a screen and will contribute brilliantly to a discussion.

3. **They can find solutions on their own.**
   Access to on-line sites can foster a mindset that believes answers can be found without help. Call it a "Google reflex", but it can help kids independently search and discover solutions and information that leads to more discoveries. This autonomy can lead to maturity.

4. **They have opportunities for community engagement.**
   Even in solitude, social media has the ability to beckon kids into the world at large. Exposure to an outside community affords them opportunities to engage. This can broaden their imagination and vision for the future.

HOW CAN WE USE THIS TO TEACH OR TRAIN?

To leverage social media and technology, you can use a variety of methods. Even the least technically savvy instructor can engage students with a screen. While these examples below are elementary in nature, they provide a launching pad for adults to leverage the power of screens and social media to connect with students.

Poll Everywhere

Many teachers utilize "Poll Everywhere," which allows an instructor to survey responses from students in a classroom, by allowing them to use their phone to communicate with the teacher and everyone else in the room. You've likely experienced it at conferences you've attended. (You can check it out at www.polleverywhere.com)

I began seeing this at conferences eight years ago when the hosts used this app from the platform. It enables the facilitator to discover both individual responses and group trends, and then report them live with bar graphs on a big screen. Even if Poll Everywhere merely helps to set up a discussion, it enables students to use their device and enjoy uploading their thoughts or opinions to the group.

Plickers

If you've been in education for any length of time, you've likely seen a classroom set of clickers somewhere. These student response systems were all the rage for a while. They looked like TV remote controls and were designed as a way that students could respond to a quiz or oral question by pressing a button to indicate the answer that they chose. Each clicker was unique to that student so that the teacher could see who answered what and when.

Today you can experience the future of classroom clickers with a free tool called Plickers. It's not a high-tech handset with an HD touchscreen, WiFi and a built-in camera. Your students don't even need a device. Plickers uses paper. Yes, you heard that right. They hold up cards and the teacher uses his or her phone to gather the student responses. (You can check it out at www.plickers.com)

Instagram, Facebook or YouTube

The social media sites most used by students today are Instagram, YouTube and Facebook. Why not employ them. . .rather than complain about them? I know faculty who utilize YouTube by posting their video lecture on the site, and asking students to watch their content at night—since they're on YouTube anyway—which frees up their class time to more experiential and engaging. It's the "flipped class."

Instagram or Facebook can be used for homework projects and classes can form closed groups where only the students in the class can access them. Since such sites are students' natural habitat, this is a normal location for them to interact and learn.

Facing Storms on the Horizon with Clarity

Not long ago, I was conversing with my wife, Pam, about the "storms" we've navigated in our family. We reminisced about how we tried to embody the truths I've discussed in this chapter, even when it wasn't convenient.

Both of my children love technology and both are on social media sites. As kids, they questioned our boundaries, and pushed back against our leadership. As adults today, however, they both recognize the pros and cons of social media and the need for limitations. It is so rewarding to see them master the constructive use of technology to advocate for a worthy cause or to raise money for a need in our community. I also love it when I see them put their phone away to engage with those present with them. And, I love to see them live by their values.

My daughter, Bethany, reminded me that my wife once rolled her shopping cart into the parking lot after buying groceries. Bethany was young enough to be riding in the cart, but old enough to remember what happened when they reached our car. My wife noticed that she'd made it to the car with some tomatoes that were never bagged. She hadn't paid for them.

Bethany watched her mother grab those tomatoes, pick her up and walk right back into the store. Our little girl then watched her mother insist on paying for the tomatoes, even when the clerk replied with astonishment that she couldn't believe someone would return for such a small discrepancy.

Pam responded,

> *"It isn't a small discrepancy when your child is watching."*

CHAPTER 11

TROUBLE BACK HOME

A game plan to face adversity when you return home with brand new maps.

Sometimes I get the feeling the whole world is against me, but deep down I know that's not true. Some of the smaller countries are neutral.

—Comedian Robert Orben

For all of the glory past explorers have received for discovering new land, naming new rivers or founding new nations, many of them have tainted stories. In other words, it wasn't all glitz and glamor for those early pioneers.

Did you know that Christopher Columbus was actually arrested by the Spanish Crown for neglecting the Hispaniola settlement in the New World? Yep. Although he now has a holiday named after him in America, he was stripped of his authority and forced to return to Spain to face the royal court. The charges were later dropped, but Chris Columbus actually lost his title as governor of the Indies and much of the riches he'd accumulated.[1]

Do you remember studying the Spanish sailor Hernando de Soto in history class? He made a name for himself by exploring the "new world" in the 1530s. Sadly for him, one of his ventures led to his untimely and premature death in 1542. The thrill of discovery was eclipsed by a startling encounter with his own mortality.

How about Hernan Cortez? Like other explorers, he didn't follow instructions well. Trouble brewed between Cortez and his commander, Diego Velázquez, in 1518 when he ignored the order to abandon a voyage to Mexico, and sailed to the Mexican coast the following year. His goal to conquer this territory was met with struggle, hunger, pain and death. This was due, in part, to ignoring his authorities.

In short, being a pioneer often means conflict, messy interactions, misunderstanding and lots of learning curves. It's much harder than being a settler.

Are you ready for this?

As you reflect on the truths of his book, we're hopeful you've decided to implement some of the ideas, in your work with the emerging generation. However, you may have to return to your "world" and "sell" someone in authority on your plans. Like Columbus who pioneered in the name of the Spanish monarchs, he had to answer to those in charge who funded his voyages. His ideas were met with resistance at first, just like pioneers today. His trips were years in the making.

Before he could "sail" he had to "sell."

You may be in the same boat. (No pun intended). You may face trouble in a variety of areas as you march off the map, depending on the change you want to orchestrate:

- For some, marching off the map will be changing your pedagogy and delivery.
- For others, marching off the map will be changing lesson plans and content.
- For others, marching off the map will be influencing stagnant colleagues.
- For others, marching off the map will be changing your own poor habits.

So, how will you do it? How will you motivate yourself to replace old habits you've repeated with new ones? How will you get your leaders excited about making these changes? What's the best way to get peers on board with new ideas? After all, far too many leaders gain insights into how they can improve their school or workplace, only to have their ideas shot down when they return home. No one else is excited. Are there "best practices" for selling such new ideas to the old guard? In this chapter, I'd like to discuss three potential trouble spots you may face as you march off the map:

- Improving yourself, building new habits and attitudes as you lead.
- Influencing authorities to allow you to pursue new methods or goals.
- Inspiring students to buy-in to leadership and life-skills.

Improving Yourself, Building New Habits and Attitudes as You Lead

I have discovered two truths about myself in my career. First, like most humans, I am a creature of habit. Second, some of my habits are good and some, not so good. The key is to find ways to substitute antiquated, less effective "addictions" with better ones. Just like programs have been developed for addictive behaviors, including alcohol, smoking, drugs (both prescription and illegal), gambling, food, sex, video games and internet, we need a program too. Over time, I've developed an addiction to poor teaching methods. It can be just as hard to break as one of the habits above. That's why I need a game plan. Let me suggest one for you below.

1. **Identify the specific habit you want to change.**
   We don't change by simply desiring change. Desire must be accompanied by specific targets to hit. Our first step in improving ourselves is to recognize one or two clear habits or attitudes we need to improve. I suggest you even write them down. The more specific you are, the better your odds are of changing your behavior. Once you jot it down, try writing out the specific reason why it needs to change.

2. **Replace the old habit with a new one.**
   Because we are creatures of habit, we usually cannot rid ourselves of a bad habit without replacing it with a new and better one. The key is not to focus on rejecting the bad habit. (If that's all we think about, we're destined to repeat it.) We must spot new behaviors or approaches to our goal and immediately initiate those in place of the previous ones. For example, if my usual approach to instruction is to ask students to open their textbooks to page such and such, and begin lecturing, I must have a new way of launching, perhaps with an activity, video, competition, panel discussion, interview, social media interaction, or insightful question. My new habit has its best chance of succeeding if I utilize the ideas in chapters 6-9.

3. **Re-arrange your environment.**
   According to research I shared earlier, most of us are visual learners. Consequently, re-arranging our classroom, workroom, practice room or environment can go a long way in fostering our desired change.

Different looking environments spark different atmospheres and cultures. These are what ignite and sustain new thoughts and attitudes. If you feel you're not creative enough to know how to transform the look and feel of your environment, find a friend who is and ask for help. Communicate your goal and together alter your space to look new. Retailers and vendors know their products can get a fresh look from customers if the look is new. So it is with us.

4. **Station the new habit next to a current healthy one.**
   When I have successfully replaced "old ways" with new ones, I noticed that I can make the change permanent when I place the new one visually next to an old one. For instance, decades ago when I tried to begin reading every night as a habit, I was more apt to do so when I placed the book I wanted to read next to my toothbrush. I already had a habit of brushing my teeth and now I had a reminder of the new habit I desired. Positioning reminders like this help to launch new lifestyles.

5. **Use new language to accompany the new habit.**
   The late Dr. Hans Selye popularized the discovery that every human being has a "reticular activating system" inside of them. One of the outcomes of this small membrane in the back of our cranial area is to cause us to move in the direction of the dominant thought of the moment. What we think about and talk about, tends to push us toward aligning action. This is why our thoughts and words are so critical to our habits and attitudes. My question is—why not use this reality to our advantage? Why not identify vocabulary and terminology that will guide our conduct and habits? I mentioned earlier, we've leveraged terms at our organization, Growing Leaders, like "pracademic," "edutainment," and "humbitious." They are combined words that spark a feeling and approach to our work.

6. **Give it time. It's a process.**
   We've all heard for years that creating new habits takes somewhere between two and three weeks of daily practice. New practices happen over time not overnight. Don't give up. Don't grow weary. If you've been using a particular pedagogy for decades, you can't expect it to go away quickly. Stay intentional, consistent and conscious of

your new habit for 14-21 days, and you'll likely see the positive improvement you desire. To use one of our *Habitudes®*, you're in a "crock pot" not a "microwave." Give yourself the time, and you're going to love the results.

7. **Invite accountability.**
Positive change is accelerated when I invite other people to hold me accountable for the changes I wish to make. When I know I am going to be asked whether I followed through on what I committed to do—I am much more likely to actually do it. The principle in short is simple: "people do better when they are watched." Right now, I have two good friends (peers that I respect) who I meet with monthly for friendly accountability. We grab coffee and ask each other about the plans and goals we've set and encourage each other to sustain our progress.

8. **Make it fun.**
When humans connect actions with amusement (meaning we like it and perceive it as pleasurable), we experience a dopamine squirt inside of us. Dopamine flows when we sense anything likeable and it nudges in that direction. For instance, many students and adults feel the effects of dopamine when their phone pings with a text message or other social media communication. Consequently, our best chance for change is to find a way to make our new habit feel "fun." The dopamine will help you stick to your new ways. In the words of Mary Poppins, "In every job that must be done, there is an element of fun. You find the fun and snap! The job's a game."

TRAVEL GUIDE:

What change do you want to personally make?

When will you start?

Would any of these steps be relevant?

Influencing Authorities to Allow You to Pursue New Methods/Goals

I began working for John C. Maxwell, upon graduating from college. I count it a privilege to have been mentored by him through the 1980s and 1990s. As a young professional, however, I made the mistake of approaching him with a new idea (more than once) before I was genuinely ready and certainly before he'd been prepared for what I had to say. It's like tossing seed into the soil before it's been cultivated or prepared for the seed. Chances are, those seeds won't take root.

Over the years, I learned that preparation plays a huge role in persuasion.

Winston Churchill said it best: "There is in the act of preparing the moment you start caring." By this he meant, before we ever communicate an idea, we demonstrate that we care for the listener by the amount of preparation we invest. A speaker begins caring for her audience days or weeks prior to the event when she spends time studying both what she wants to say and how she needs to say it to get through. Likewise, you are likely going to have to process just how to communicate the changes you'd like to see happen before implementing them. Every move we make impacts others. Every decision affects others. Every conversation influences others.

The best leaders process what to "say" so it can carry the greatest "sway."

Here are some practical ideas—perhaps even intuitional ideas—for you to consider as you prepare to march off the map. Whether you are a superintendent, principal, teacher, youth worker or employer, at least some of these steps may be helpful:

1. **Summarize your ideas.**
   Collect your thoughts. Summarize the improvement you'd like to make, and the pain you'd like to resolve. For example, as you list the ideas you want to implement, jot down beside each one the pain point it addresses. Every step you plan to take should solve a problem. Most people don't like change for change's sake. Any change should improve a situation. As you jot down this summary, consider your listener's perspective. What may be their objections or struggles with your ideas? Be ready to address them logically. Clarify the "big wins" that can happen if you make a move. This will force you to take measures

to make sure the ideas really are better than your current reality. As you summarize your ideas, remember the two motivators:

Pain—What is the pain people will resolve if they change?

Gain—What is the benefit people will receive if they change?

2. Scout the land.

Before broaching the subject of making changes, begin meeting with your supervisor, asking if they "feel the same pain" and inquiring about what they believe could be done about it. Ask how you can help. This kind of relationship cultivation is vital. It puts "change in your pocket." You earn your right to make suggestions by first listening, empathizing, processing the pain your supervisor experiences and adding value to them. Taking time to converse about important issues, without an apparent agenda, builds credibility with leaders. This step works a bit like a bank account. It's about making lots of deposits before making any withdraws

3. Shoot bullets before cannon balls.

Author Jim Collins suggests this idea when trying anything new. Early American militia first shot bullets to discover exactly where the target was before using a cannon ball, as bullets were quicker and less expensive to fire. Similarly, I suggest you launch a small "pilot" project using the ideas from this book just to test the idea. In fact, it may be wise to involve only a smaller group of students and prepare to collect the data (results) after the pilot is finished. Ohio State Athletic Director Gene Smith taught me years ago, "You have to go slow in order to go fast." By this he meant, start small and move slow to get the action right. Then, you're ready to expand and speed up the pace.

4. Share the results.

Once you've built trust with your leader, and collected some results from a trial project, show them the improvements that occurred. Nothing convinces leaders like good data. In short, when they are ready to hear from you (after conversations and time), and you are ready with some positive outcomes, reveal the progress you made when you marched off the map. After you unveil what's happened with your experimental group, allow them to respond. If the results are clear improvements, you shouldn't have to do much convincing for them to want to scale the project. Leading change works like a bridge. Both relationships and results make the bridge strong enough to bear the weight of tough conversations and serious issues.

5. **Show and tell.**
Let them not only see the data but observe the change in action. For instance, if you're a teacher, invite your administrator into your classroom to observe your new methods or pedagogy. If you're a coach, invite your athletic director to watch practice. If you're a university staff member, invite your dean to see your work. If you're a manager, invite your supervisor to view how you're achieving results with your young team members. I say this because I've learned that while good data is intellectually convincing, observing a change "in person" convinces the heart. You want to sell your leader both mentally and emotionally. This means you both show them what you're doing and you use visuals as you communicate. It's the difference between "hearing" about a news story and being an "eye witness."

6. **Sponsor an event.**
Most significant changes happen over time, but also include a launch event to communicate the "big idea." Once you've experienced a successful pilot, plan an event, a rally, a meeting, or an assembly of some kind that will kindle excitement about this new direction. The event must be engaging and relevant to those attending, whether its students, staff or teachers or leaders. The goal for the event is to introduce the "big idea" and to invite attendees into the journey to join in. At the end of the event, give them an "action step" to sign up for. The event becomes catalytic, while the process afterward, becomes a culture. The event challenges people, but the process they join actually changes them.

7. **Secure a "critical mass."**
Keep in mind that most significant change happens over time not overnight. Be patient and work toward accomplishing "critical mass." By this I mean, growing the percentage of people in your organization who buy into the idea you're proposing until you have a large enough ratio to gain traction with the majority. Often, positive improvements can be made with only a fraction of the whole population, if they

buy in with passion. As your little "movement" grows, choose markers along the way, where you can measure growth and improvement. For example, if you're trying to change the pedagogy (style of delivery) in your classrooms, keep track of every five instructors who make the shift to the new style and mark it down somewhere. Check in with this group in an ongoing way, to maintain momentum.

8. Soften your expectations.

Far too often, those of us who long for change can scare people. We get excited and start running at a breathless pace toward a desired goal, not realizing that others are frightened that we'll spiral out of control. They're afraid we'll be reckless. They fear losing the familiar. They fear losing control. They fear losing what's predictable. They fear discomfort. It's human. I suggest you slow down. Don't scare folks. Talk to them. I learned a principle long ago I call: "growing pains." It means people can handle about 20 percent change a year. When people see more than 20 percent of their world in transition, they often dig their heels in the dirt and refuse to move.

9. Select a champion.

Someone should be chosen to make sure this change is sustainable. In other words, it's easy to get excited about a new idea when it first arrives on the scene. It's more difficult to maintain that excitement, after the novelty wears off. Find the right person (whether it's you or someone else who has influence) to be the leader who waves the flag for this change or this cause and continue to keep it in front of the eyes of everyone. Often a new idea will only take off if the right person is leading it. Be sure you have the right person up front talking about the big idea—one who has the skills, the patience and the time to see it to fruition.

10. Scatter the credit.

As positive improvements are made, don't hoard all the accolades. Make others the heroes, not just yourself. Include anyone you can in the victory lap—literally anyone who tried something new, experimented with you or even advocated on your behalf— call them into the celebration. John Kennedy said, "Success has a thousand fathers, but failure is an orphan." People want to feel a part of victories. Abraham Lincoln once told a Union General to attack an enemy location. When his general balked, he told him if he failed, the General could blame it all on him, as the president. And if he succeeded, he could enjoy all the credit. This empowers others to take a risk.

TRAVEL GUIDE:

Which of these steps are doable for you?

Which will be difficult?

INSPIRING STUDENTS TO BUY-IN TO LEADERSHIP AND LIFE SKILLS

Believe it or not, introducing change to young people can even be a challenge at times. Any person of any age can fall in love with what's familiar, predictable and comfortable. This occurs most often when young adults can't see why they should improve or aren't interested in preparing for the future. They're fine with today. Sometimes they're fine being "stuck." Someone once said, "Growth is painful. But nothing is as painful as staying stuck in some place you don't belong."

So, your job may just be to convince the young to get unstuck.

It may begin with helping students see the current state of culture. With all due respect to the fast food franchise, I call our society today: "McCulture." We keep it light. I believe students benefit from conversations that evaluate our culture's drift into shallow interactions that have little depth or substance. They will either grow into adults who reflect this superficiality—or become counter-cultural.

After watching the news recently, three thoughts struck me. Once a culture rich with depth, democracy, morals and humility, we are now... well, superficial, self-absorbed and synthetic. We are not the American culture that first settled this land. Things are now convenient, quick and easy, like fast food. McRibs. McMuffin, McNuggets...and now McCulture. As I've said before, we live in a culture that is superficial (we value "looks over books"), Self-Absorbed (we put the "self" in "selfie"), and synthetic (we choose "virtual" over "virtue"). So how do you convince the youth you lead to see these same issues?

The Need of the Hour

When I'm in front of high school or university students, I coach them to prepare for the world that awaits them following graduation. I talk about the skills they'll need in the future, regardless of the industry they join. (Skills like the ones I mentioned in chapter six of this book). In short, I cover the "why" before the "what." I explain the importance of life skills and leadership perspective as incentives to jump in to the conversations they need. Then, however, I frequently talk about the times we live in, and the role they'll need to play for our civilization to thrive.

Muscles, Machines, Minds and Morals

In a 2016 commencement speech, Michael Bloomberg gave an interesting summary of the changes in our vocations that have happened over centuries of time. Pause and consider how different a typical job is today than it was centuries ago.

> *"For the first time in human history, the majority of people in the developed world are being asked to make a living with their minds, rather than their muscles. For 3,000 years, humankind had an economy based on farming: till the soil, plant the seed, harvest the crop. Hard to do, but fairly easy to learn. Then, for 300 years, we had an economy based on industry: mold the parts, turn the crank, assemble the product. Hard to do, but also fairly easy to learn. Now, we have an economy based on information: acquire the knowledge, apply the analytics, use your creativity. Hard to do, hard to learn, and even once you've mastered it, you'll have to start learning all over again, pretty much every day."[2]*

As I suggested earlier, we are at the brink of a new age.

I've called it the Intelligence Age, where an essential skill is required of us to maintain our civilization. Artificial Intelligence will reign in the next ten to fifteen years. Many scientists predict our possessions will be smarter than humans. When we are able to invent such smart devices—the critical skill is not our muscles, our machines or our minds any more. It is our morals. Do our ethics and values keep up with our brilliant technology? Cultivating a moral compass in our young will differentiate them. Below are columns illustrating how people differentiate themselves in each age:

Historical Era	How People Differentiate Themselves
1. Agricultural Age	1. Stronger muscles
2. Industrial Age	2. Stronger machines
3. Information Age	3. Stronger minds
4. Intelligence Age	4. Stronger morals.

I believe adolescents and twenty-somethings should recognize how important it is to develop their minds, to learn not merely what to think, but how to think. It will likely be the most important "muscle" they have in their adult life.

Ask your students: Are you ready to redeem technology? Are you prepared to leverage your mind to accomplish something greater than your own advantage?

What to Sell About Life Skills to Students

So, what we'll need to "sell" students on are conversations and experiences that build "life skills." Because a generation of employers have weighed in and let us know too many graduates are unprepared for the workforce, it is time we got them ready.

We're far too ready to spend millions of dollars repairing a broken adolescent (from drug abuse, alcohol, anxiety, addictive behaviors, etc.) but unready to spend time and money up front to prevent the need for those repairs. Preparing beats repairing every time. Let's build a fence at the top of the cliff rather than a hospital at the bottom. Let's talk to them—intentionally—about taking steps to get ready for adulthood, where they'll be spending the majority of their lives.

The reason I created *Habitudes®: Images That Form Leadership Habits and Attitudes* is because I wanted to launch conversations with my own children (and with the thousands of students I got to speak to each year). Each image represents a timeless principle they'll need in life. My wife and I would talk to our kids about an image at dinnertime, discussing if we'd seen any movies that illustrate the principle; if we knew any people who embodied the principle, or had the chance to succeed or fail at practicing it ourselves. Today, thousands of schools, sports teams and organizations use them to spark important conversations and experiences for young people.

They enable an educator, coach or employer to:

- Do "school" differently, getting beyond traditional subjects in advisement period.
- Incorporate "real life" conversations in class that are relevant to life after school.
- Help students build new habits and attitudes that enable them to lead.
- Offer students an advantage as they differentiate themselves from their peers.
- Prepare students to solve current problems and prepare for future challenges.
- Furnish students with clear decision-making skills.
- Provide students with relational skills and emotional intelligence.
- Position graduates with leadership insights and principles to guide them.

Whether or not you utilize the *Habitudes®*, our young desperately need us to launch these conversations. They may not ask for them, nor even know they need them. It's our job to make the "hand off" well. When I noticed my son spending an enormous amount of hours in front of a screen, we simply created an equation: Whatever hours you spend in front of a screen, you must spend equal hours face to face with people, learning interpersonal skills, reading body language, facial cues and building EQ. When our daughter was moving into middle school, we wanted her to be skillful as she interacted with adults, so we had her (and her brother) host a party, when my wife and I had our (adult) friends over. They learned to answer the door, invite people in, take their coat, ask if they knew everyone there, etc. These were simple and practical experiences and conversations that empowered them.

And that can happen anywhere if we are intentional.

Question: Are you ready to sell your students on building life skills?

The Day I Stopped Asking Students the Wrong Questions

I want to make a confession. For years, I have spoken at high school and university commencements and made the classic remarks others have made to students:

- "Find your passion and pursue it."
- "Go after your dreams and don't let anyone deny you."
- "Trust your heart and fulfill your purpose."

These clichés were what I really believed at the time. I wanted to help students figure out what they were supposed to do with their life through self-diagnosis. If they would only look inside—they could discover their calling in life.

It's a sort of self-determination I felt I should encourage in students; I wanted them to be ambitious and I thought this was the right mindset to go after it.

Today—I no longer believe this.

Why This is Bad Advice

Too many students heard this message from parents, pastors and commencement speakers and somehow drew the conclusion: Wow! I can dream up anything I want to do and if I try hard enough, I can do it. Hundreds of thousands began choosing majors in college that our society and economy just didn't need. For a while, the number one goal of college graduates was to be rich and famous. In a survey I mentioned earlier, students reported they most wanted to be the "personal assistant to a celebrity."

For many, the search was autonomous and self-absorbed. It began with: what do I want and what must I do to get it? Even if the search was altruistic, it was still ignited by "self." In the words of David Brooks, it was first about self-investigation and ultimately about self-fulfillment. William Ernest Henry's famous poem, "Invictus," summarizes the sentiment: "I am the master of my fate. I am the captain of my soul."

I believe this has left, perhaps, millions of students with grievances against our culture and their advisors. Why? It didn't work too well. They graduated only to find life wasn't about them; employers weren't interested in their self-fulfillment and money was far too hard to come by in a sour economy.

A Lesson From the Past

During the dark days of World War II, Victor Frankl spent years in a Nazi ghetto and later a concentration camp. It was there he learned that life cannot be evaluated in simple terms of "self." Each of us individuals are part of a larger community, and our success must be measured in terms of that larger community, not in laying personal life plans. We are all part of history, a narrative in which we've been placed to contribute into the specific circumstances and challenges of our day.

For instance, Frankl spent most of his time in the concentration camp laying tracks for the railroad. This was not the life he had planned for himself. It was neither his passion, nor his dream. He could either get lost in depression over it, or he could see that he must figure out his contribution, given the circumstances he was dealt.

"It did not really matter what we expected from life," he'd later write, "but rather what life expected from us." Frankl had been given an amazing intellectual and social opportunity to study human behavior under the most horrific conditions. He had the chance to share what he was learning with his fellow prisoners and, if he survived, with a larger population. It became invigorating to him. "Suffering had become a task on which we did not want to turn our backs," he wrote. Frankl would tell potential suicide victims that life had not stopped expecting things from them. Life "ultimately means taking responsibility to find the right answer to its problems and to fulfill the tasks which it constantly sets before the individual."[3]

A Different Set of Questions

So, as you work with students, may I suggest we make a shift in the questions we're asking? I am making this shift and finding the conversation more invigorating:

Stop Asking...	Start Asking...
• What do you want to major in?	• What problem do you want to solve?
• What do you want out of life?	• What is life asking of you?
• How much money can you make?	• What do you have to give?
• How can you achieve something great?	• How can you add value in this context?
• What do you possess inside?	• What are the needs or opportunities?
• What will make you happy?	• What are you being summoned to do?

Our world is too broken and in need of repair for us to simply ask the trite questions:

- What do you want to major in during college?
- What jobs pay well and can get you a nice house or car?
- What will make you happy?

Happiness comes when I find a great "why" behind a career choice. As Frederick Nietzsche noted, "He who has a why to live for can bear almost any how."

TRAVEL GUIDE:

How could you reframe the questions you ask students?

LEADING CHANGE

This perspective I've described above is certainly different than the one for which adults have conditioned kids today. Ready or not, like it or not, it's time we lead them into positive change. Let's treat them differently. Let's talk to them differently. Let's expect better from them. Eventually, I believe we can shift where history is taking us. We must keep in mind, however, that change usually happens in one of two ways:

- **An Evolution** (Slowly over time)
- **A Revolution** (Surprisingly, overnight)

We must be ready for both, but plan for an evolution. When things change, those in power often feel displaced. They feel like a "new sheriff is in town." They may push back or reject new ideas because the ideas weren't theirs. It's a human reaction.

We must prepare ourselves for the challenges.

Not far from my house outside of Atlanta, there is a greenway. In a beautiful context of trees and foliage, our community paved a path for folks to walk on, bike on, run on or just take a stroll and enjoy the view. When the sun is peering through the branches of the trees, it is just plain gorgeous.

The path, however, doesn't last forever. After about two miles, the pavement stops. The walkway suddenly comes to an end, and afterward it is pretty rough and crude. Weeds and tall grass grow untouched; off to one side you can see an old tire someone left out there, some broken bottles, unwanted boxes and even an old, torn up sofa. In other words, the delightful paved walkway quickly turns into an un-manicured, raw piece of real estate.

This is a picture for us to hold in our minds.

If we're willing to march off the map, we will exit the manicured for the mud. Our current ways are paved; they're familiar systems we've grown accustomed to. We like them smooth. But pioneers move into the untried and untested. It can be scary, but it can also be an experience that awakens our very soul. New territory does this to us.

This untested place is not unlike the one our young experience as they enter the world after graduation. They are nervous but excited. They often feel a mixture of emotions—some are afraid to leave the familiar, but many can hardly wait for the unfamiliar and new. When students graduate from school, they leave a prescribed and pre-planned lifestyle for a completely wide-open field. The path that was once paved, smooth and easy to travel on becomes one that may require a machete to slice their way through.

Perhaps journalist David Brooks put it best in a commencement speech he gave in 2011:

> *"Young Americans today live the most supervised childhoods in American history. The University of Michigan does these time analysis studies and they have found that over the last few decades the amount of time young people spend just hanging around on their own has declined by about a third. The amount of time they spend in adult-structured, supervised activities has risen by about a third: soccer practice, piano practice, SAT prep, LSAT prep. There will be an extreme contrast between the life they led until graduation and the life they'll start afterward, from high-pressure structure to an extreme lack of structure."[4]*

The future could look this way both for them and for us. It's what life is like for those who march off the map. I can hardly wait.

CHAPTER 12

A MOST IMPORTANT FINAL WORD

The single most important leadership practice as you march off the map.

Be the person you needed when you were young.
—Ayesha Saddiqi

Before you close this book for the final time—I feel compelled to remind you of a truth that makes every suggestion in this book actually work. Neglect it, and none of my suggestions matter. I realize it sounds cliché, but if you get nothing else out of this book, please embrace this chapter.

When I think of the below-average instructors that Matt, Zoe, Savannah and Dylan have experienced, I shudder. Each of the four could have been engaged in their classrooms and emerged as focused adults. They're smart and they're gifted. They are ill-equipped, however, due in part to the adults who led them.

They had no teachers or coaches who were willing to march off the map.

Last month, I spoke to Zoe and her soccer coach in two separate conversations. Zoe had just quit her soccer team. Her reason? "I just couldn't handle the yelling and anger from my coaches any more."

When I spoke to Zoe's coach, he said, "I yell because I just don't see any grit in these athletes. That's why I get so frustrated at them."

Both the coach and the athlete were put out with each other. What's most intriguing to me is—I believe at least part of the solution to scenarios like these may just lie in how we lead them.

How We Tend to Lead in High Stress Situations

Some time ago I finished interpreting data on the leadership styles of educators, coaches, youth workers and parents from eight different states across the U.S. It was not surprising to note that these adults were often irritated at the students and dissatisfied with their output. They claimed the kids didn't display resilience; they acted entitled, didn't follow through on commitments and frequently were just plain lazy. This created "high-stress interactions."

Two common scenarios surfaced in the results. In stressful contexts:

1. Most tend to lead out of RELIEF.
2. The successful tend to lead out of BELIEF.

The Motivation of Relief or Belief

Parents often find themselves in challenging scenarios with their children. With tech savvy kids who act confident and entitled, moms or dads can become exhausted; their own children wear them out, especially after a busy day at work. This is when it's tempting to lead out of relief. We want to relieve the current mess and bring peace to the household. Relief sounds very attractive in stressful times.

Teachers often have students who struggle and perform poorly. To remedy the situation well requires all kinds of patience, emotional intelligence, and tenacity (not to mention time). We can opt for the easy route and seek relief: just give them the answers; prescribe the path for them; tell them what's on the test, so you can avoid their parents. It's a quick fix. Recently, I met with some university professors who feared giving students a poor grade because of the retaliation they'd get from the students or their parents. Giving them a passing grade, albeit undeserved, brings relief.

Sadly while these are quicker and easier options, they're not long-term solutions. It's a short-term answer for a larger issue that won't go away until we choose a different leadership approach.

We tend to be motivated by relieving the pain rather than believing in the person. It's usually one or the other—relief or belief.

The Motivation of Relief

Relief is our natural default style. When facing a difficult situation, we seek out a breather for ourselves, or our students. We want to ease the pain; to stop the bleeding; to fix the issue quickly.

At times it's about our relief. We choose the easy route and appease students, giving them their requests. It makes life easier, at least in the moment. And sometimes, we lead out of relief by venting our anger. We go into a rage, screaming and yelling just to feel better in the moment. It feels cathartic. Sadly, it is punitive.

And sometimes, it's about their relief. We want to relieve students of consequences of poor choices or behavior because they're so stressed out. They have so many pressures on them with grades, sports and standardized tests. It feels right to let them off the hook. And while this does ease the pain temporarily, it doesn't necessarily empower students to grow and improve. We fix things up rather than make things right. Sadly, it is permissive.

In short, venting feels good to me and lets me off hook. Caving feels good to them and lets them off the hook. Both, however, compromise good leadership.

When we lead out of "relief" we:

- Send the message that students are "losers" and can't perform sufficiently.

- See and expect only short-term satisfaction but miss long-term success.

- Take a short cut and diminish both their potential as well as ours.

The Motivation of Belief

Belief is the right path. In a challenging situation, we must lead out of belief in the potential of the student. We pull out the best in them when we believe the best about them. Research from psychologist Diana Baumrind at the University of California Berkeley reminds us that students are most productive when we are both:

- **Responsive.** We are attentive to them, supportive and caring. We love them and believe in them.

- **Demanding.** Because we believe in them, we won't let them settle for less than their best. We hold them to standards.[1]

This is what every student needs. We may tell ourselves that our frustration and yelling is all about "belief in these kids" but if they don't sense it, we can have the opposite effect. We actually communicate that we don't believe in them; that they're losers and undeserving of our time and attention. It's a fine line but it's very real.

If today's population of kids is fragile, it's because we have raised them this way. We've not been truthful about their strengths and weaknesses; instead, we've either merely affirmed them, or we became silent, fearing they can't handle the truth.

Author Daniel Coyle reveals that a cadre of psychologists from Stanford, Columbia and Yale set out to explore this issue. They asked middle school teachers to give a writing project to their students, and afterward, offer the students various types of feedback. To their surprise, the researchers discovered there was one particular type of feedback that improved student effort so much, they called it "magical." Students who received this feedback chose to revise their paper far more often than students who did not—a 40 percent increase among white students and a 320 percent boost for minority students.[2] In the end, it improved all their performances significantly. The phrase was simply this:

"I'm giving you these comments because I have high expectations of you and I know you can reach them."

The words themselves are not magic, but the thought behind them is profound. They communicate belief in the student, calling out the best in him or her. This requires tough love from us, with patience and tenacity to follow through. It's effective, however, because our leadership stems from a deep seeded belief in our students.

While our temptation will usually be to lead out of "relief," communicating belief always produces better results. But it's more costly. You'd best not say you believe in a student if your words are hollow. They can smell a fake a mile away. You must be willing to back up your words with actions that convey your belief in them.

When we lead out of "belief" we:

- Call out the very best in the students we are leading.
- Cultivate a new level of expectation and excellence in everyone.
- Produce superior results in student performance as well as ours.

TRAVEL GUIDE:

Can you think of a time when a leader communicated belief in you?

What Does This Look Like in Real Life?

Journalist Jane Ellen Stevens reveals an incredible story about an educator who began to practice this truth and saw his school suspensions drop by 85 percent. It was the story of Principal Jim Sporleder.[3]

When Jim Sporleder became principal of Lincoln Alternative High School in Walla Walla, Washington, he knew he'd have to address the disciplinary incidents at the school. Too many kids, particularly the males, were getting into trouble and getting detentions and even suspensions for poor behavior.

Jim's predecessors may have defaulted to leading out of relief, leveling a penalty and getting back to more important administrative tasks. It's quicker and easier that way. Jim Sporleder, however, decided to handle things differently.

When a student misbehaved or dropped an F-bomb in class (which usually results in automatic suspension), he was sent to the principal's office. Instead of delegating the task of disciplining the student to one of his assistants, Jim took it on himself and chose another route. When the young man entered his office, Jim would motion for the student to have a seat. Often, he would not speak right away, just to allow emotions to cool a bit. Then, Jim would sit down across from the student, calmly look him in the eye and say something like:

"Wow. What just happened in your classroom doesn't sound like you. Are you OK? You really look stressed." Then, if it's still quiet, he continues. "On a scale of 1-10, where are you with your anger? Is something going on with you at home or in your personal life?"

The vast majority of the time, the kid was not ready for kindness or belief. He was ready for a shouting match. He assumed he'd hear, "What is wrong with you!" When Jim led out of belief, the student usually broke down, saying something like:

- My dad just left our family.
- I haven't eaten in two days.
- My uncle beats my sister every night.
- My mom is taking drugs.

From there, a conversation begins about the real issue. There is still a consequence, but authentic belief brings out the best in the student. In fact, because Sporleder believes in them, he wants to send the message—I can't let you off the hook. I believe you're capable of more. Usually, the kid is sent to ISS, (In School Suspension) where they can cool off, talk to a teacher and work on homework. According to Sporleder, when the student returned to the classroom, he'd apologize 90 percent of the time, without any prompting from anyone. That's what belief accomplishes.

Before you say "That's too soft or wimpy," or "It's not the way they did things when I was a kid," check out these numbers below:

2009-2010 (Before new approach)

- 798 suspensions (days students were out of school)
- 50 expulsions
- 600 written referrals

2010-2011 (After new approach)

- 135 suspensions (days students were out of school)
- 30 expulsions
- 320 written referrals

Developmental molecular biologist John Medina, reveals why this kind of leadership, out of belief, is both transformational and essential:

"Severe and chronic trauma (such as living with an alcoholic parent, or watching in terror as your mom gets beat up) causes toxic stress in kids. Toxic stress damages kid's brains. When trauma launches kids into flight, fight or fright mode, they cannot learn. It is physiologically impossible."

"It sounds simple," Sporleder said about his approach. "Just by asking kids what's going on with them, they started talking. It made a believer out of me right away."[4]

It's this belief that must prompt our leadership. By communicating that we care, we convey we believe in them; that their recent misconduct doesn't reflect who they really are; that they're better than this. And that's one great platform to build upon.

So, the next time you're in a conflict with a student, a child, a young professional or an athlete, ask yourself the question:

Are the remarks I'm about to make fueled by relief from the problem or belief in the person?

Believing in someone is the strongest motivator in the world, hands down.

Is it hard? You bet it is. Does it mean we'll be forced to march off the map? Very likely. Is it worth it? Without question.

Taking Some Practical Steps
I want you to imagine a typical conflict you might enter into with your young person at home, or school, or at practice. It matters not if you're a parent, teacher, employer or coach. Perhaps this scenario will be a familiar example:

You: Did you fill out any applications for your scholarship?

Student: Uh, I'm working on it.

You: Well, don't miss the deadlines. They're coming up soon, you know.

Student: I know. I'm on it.

You (still wondering): Have you sent any applications out yet?

Student: Well, not yet. But I am deciding which ones to focus on.

You: Seriously? Aren't all the applications due in two weeks?

Student: Yeah, I think so.

You (now a bit exasperated): How are you deciding which ones to focus on?

Student (now frustrated): I don't know yet, but leave me alone. This is my decision.

You: Yes, but it involves our money. I don't want you missing this important step. Do you even care about the future?

Student: Yes, I care! I know this is super-important! I get it. But, it's my life!

You: Well, you're not acting like it. If you don't get any of those scholarships, you can kiss your career plans goodbye! It's over!

Why Does This Happen So Often?

Too many of us—well-intentioned adults—have been in these kinds of frustrating conversations with young people. And you can see where this one above is going. The interaction begins OK, but both parties sense frustration on the part of the other. In fact, neither the adult nor the student feels any "belief" from the other. This lack of belief leads to negative emotions that don't empower anyone.

Truth be told, you are seriously concerned for their wellbeing. You feel you have a better handle on the big picture and the importance of the decision in front of them. The student is stuck in a cycle of stress, anxiety and fear over a paramount decision. It has begun to paralyze him or her. Seeing their inactivity, we're simply looking for a little assurance from them. Our legitimate fears prompt us to ask questions. To them, this feels like lack of trust or belief. At best, motivation will now be out of carrots or sticks—you offer an incentive or you threaten them with penalties for failing to act. The best case scenario is we achieve behavior modification.

Carrots and sticks work for a while, but they're not the best motivator.

Additionally, too many of these conversations negatively affect the relationship. Patterns of emotion affect our communication. And patterns of communication influence our connection to them. The issues can be scholarship applications, or cleaning their room, or remembering a commitment, or giving their all at practice, or doing homework…you name it. It is important for us to lay tracks of "belief" which will, in turn, measurably improve their motivation.

Taking the Path of Belief

In order to motivate and inspire a student, try this path:

1. Get Clarity.

Before speaking, figure out what's going on inside of you. Are you frustrated? Are you afraid for them? Are you ashamed or disappointed? Or, do you simply not know what's going on in their life? Before talking, get clarity on your emotions and goals. This will foster a clear-headed conversation.

2. Take initiative.

Don't assume the issue will automatically resolve itself or that because it's not your problem directly you can tend to other things. While the problem is likely theirs, avoiding it will just cause emotional build up inside of you. Don't assume your student will initiate and resolve the issue. Get the ball rolling.

3. Begin with empathy.

We're always more effective when we see life from our listener's angle. "Seek first to understand before seeking to be understood," says Stephen Covey. This enables students to be less defensive, believing we "get them." Express empathy for their challenging situation. This is foundational to proceed.

4. Ask the right questions.

Instead of drawing conclusions or offering imperatives—try leading with questions. Ask about their needs. Do they need direction? Support? Steps to be broken down? Be sure the questions communicate you care and that you're confident in their abilities. Ask questions that evoke values or dreams, like: "What are you hoping for at the end of your applications?" Or, "How do you think you'll feel when you get that scholarship?"

5. Seek to help.

Don't blame or shame them. Even when it's totally their fault, let that responsibility surface later. If it appears you want to "fix the blame" more than "fix the problem" it will become a negative interaction, and they'll usually become defensive. Find out what they need. Sometimes I'll simply say: "How can I best cheer you on?"

6. **Express belief.**
   This is the key action on your part. Be sure what you say and do relays belief in them as an emerging adult. Discern what would communicate confidence in them, high expectations of them and hope for them. Strong belief inspires strong behavior.

7. **Talk about "equations" not "rules."**
   No kid likes rules. Equations, however, are how life works: if you do this, then that is the benefit. If you do that, then this is the consequence. (You live by equations every day—just try neglecting to pay your mortgage.) Relay the equation in a positive way to incentivize them. Then, be consistent in helping them live by it.

8. **Follow through.**
   Finally, whatever belief you've communicated, follow through in demonstrating its credibility. Don't undo what you've said with a poor attitude or contradictory words. Be sure your actions match your words. This will help them "own" their life.

I recently spoke to Dr. Meg Meeker, a very successful pediatrician, who surprised me when she told me she failed to get accepted into a medical school on her first batch of applications. As a young student, she was devastated.

She told me, however, that she got over her distress quickly in a most unusual way. As she walked through her parents' home, she overheard her father talking to a colleague on the phone. Without knowing Meg was eavesdropping, her dad said, "Well, my daughter Meg will be attending medical school soon."

It was like a shot in the arm. Her dad affirmed she's going to med school.

Meg told me her father said it very confidently and matter-of-factly. From that moment on, she became confident in her ability to get accepted and to flourish. Years later her dad didn't even remember saying it, which meant it flowed naturally from his belief in his daughter.

May that be our story as well.

THREE STRATEGIC SOLUTIONS

Not long ago, Dr. Henry J. Heimlich, the inventor of the Heimlich Maneuver, got to use his technique for the very first time…at the ripe age of 96.

Can you believe that?

Since inventing the Heimlich Maneuver, Henry had spent decades explaining and demonstrating the life-saving technique on people who were willing to play the role of a choking victim. But in 2016, the 96-year old doctor said he got to do the "real thing." An 87-year old woman started choking at their senior residence community in Cincinnati, and Heimlich immediately sprang into action. He performed the technique on her, popping the morsel out of her mouth. It was a sight to see.

He said later in an interview, "I felt it was just confirmation of what I had been doing throughout my life."

Naturally, he and the woman began seeing each other. What else do you do for the man who saved your life?

I love this story—but far too often it's a picture of us. We spend decades discussing theories about what we believe. We talk and write, and even watch demonstrations. We may even simulate it. But we frequently go too long without practicing what we've learned and what we know.

In this epilogue, I want to turn theory into practice.

THREE PRACTICES TO HELP OUR STUDENTS

Over the course of this book, we've discussed who today's young "natives" are and why they need us to march off the map into new territory—to prepare them for the future. We've examined the data on today's teens and young adults as well as cultural norms. I've tried to offer ideas to employ as you teach and lead them, based on the research. Once again, I want to encourage you to utilize your "Travel Guide" and write down the ideas you plan to implement going forward.

In these last few pages, I'd like to offer you three strategic applications we can make as we guide our young into meaningful and satisfying adult lives. If we will get these three areas right, they'll perform better in the classroom, on the ball field, in the work place and at home. Not only that, but they'll be ready to lead the way into the future. These issues could make or break their happiness and fruitfulness.

1. Integration

Our digital culture today offers an overwhelming number of places to log in, to download, to upload and to consume time. Because social media offers a variety of platforms, students create a variety of personas for themselves. They can pose as an assortment of people, promoting a facade on one platform and a different one elsewhere. I am speaking of more than mere hypocrisy or masquerading. Those have always been around. "For some teens and tweens, social media is the primary way they inter-act socially, rather than at the mall or a friend's house," according to Dr. Gwenn O'Keeffe, co-author of a clinical report issued by the American Academy of Pediatrics (AAP), called "The Impact of Social Media Use on Children, Adolescents, and Families." They are experimenting with their public persona and often have no idea what's occurring inside. "A large part of this generation's social and emotional development is occurring while on the Internet and on cellphones," O'Keeffe added.[1] Add to that the multiple messages they receive everyday from countless sources and it's enough to overwhelm anybody—especially a young mind still forming. This leads to duplicity and complexity that results in angst and fear. Eventually, kids carry the trappings of maintaining a variety of images they want to project on-line; the images others have of them and the image they actually possess of themselves, all of which might be inaccurate. More than any other time, people can experience the burden that accompanies duplicity. We must help them integrate their lives.

This is one of the many reasons that "mindfulness" has become a hot topic today. Therapists, yoga instructors, pastors, school counselors, trainers and psychologists are helping people focus and become mindful. What does this mean? In simple terms it means to be fully present, in the present. To not be distracted from what's in front of us. To not live in angst over tomorrow. To not allow ourselves to be divided in our attention. To not be sitting with people we love and be multi-tasking on our phone instead of giving full attention to our loved ones. Multi-tasking is the opposite of mindfulness. We live in a day where most of us feel we must divide our mind and time in a variety of categories, not giving our full self to any one of them. This does not lead to integration . . . it leads to disintegration. And kids are especially vulnerable. Their lives are often duplicitous.

A recent survey shows that 70 percent of teens hide their behavior from parents, up from the 45 percent reporting this behavior in 2010.[2] Teens access pornography, violent images, and date behind their parents' backs. They achieve this by lying, clearing browser histories, or using other devices left unchecked by parents.

A disproportionate number of young teens say: "My parents have NO idea what my life is like at school or after midnight." Our focus group comments sounded like this:

"Having your parents ask you for your password is one of the scariest things ever. My parents are mostly oblivious to the stuff that's going on in my life, so when they go through my phone and see things they didn't know about, I can't handle it." - 6th grade girl

"My parents worry about me and want to see what's on my phone, but I tell them, 'It's OK, I'm fine!' I have to delete everything off my phone before I show it to them." - 8th grade boy

"I have so many accounts and profiles, I sometimes can't remember who I said I am. I get overwhelmed with it, but I can't stop. – 10th grade boy

"I'm scared that one day my mom will figure out how I hid all of my social media accounts on her iPad." - 6th grade girl

"My mom took away my phone, but she forgot that she bought me a kindle. I just got on my KIK on that." - 7th grade boy

"My mom doesn't like the people I talk to, so I have to sneak my phone out of the house even when I'm grounded." - 6th grade girl

I mentioned in earlier chapters that Growing Leaders surveyed some 17,000 public high school students from Georgia in 2013. Among the results was a stunning revelation that these students did not see any association between their "integrity" and their "success." Meaning, what they do in private has no connection to their public success. They can be or appear to be different people, depending on where they are. The term "integrity" means to be one person, not duplicitous. It's taken from the same root word as integration. If our kids are going to grow up with integrity, we must equip them now to live this way.

What We Can Do
Integration is the smoothest path to overcome stress. And mindfulness is the best path to take toward integration. As I mentioned above, mindfulness has become a buzzword in many circles today. In layman's terms, mindfulness is clearing one's mind of the clutter of multi-tasking and focusing on the here and now. It can go as far as deep breathing and meditation, but it can begin by simply pushing "pause" on the noise and activity of a stressful day. Neuroscientist Moshe Bar, at Harvard Medical School, tells us our brains switch back and forth from activity to recovery mode. We need periods of recovery—but often don't get them. Mindfulness is about putting down our "juggling balls" for a while and recovering. It's about embracing mono-tasking not multi-tasking. The benefits are tangible. The American Psychological Association cites it as a hopeful strategy for alleviating depression, anxiety and pain.[3]

It's a step to combat the:

- OVER-STIMULATED,
- OVER-TAXED,
- OVER-CONNECTED,
- OVER-COMMITTED,
- OVERWHELMED

lifestyles our young have accumulated. The American Psychological Association tells us that 34 percent of Americans say their stress has shot up in the last year.[4] I believe it's even more so among our youth. So, why not begin by helping students:

1. **Balance screen time with face time and alone time.**
Moderation in all things is just plain wise advice. Talk to kids about balancing time with screens, face-to-face conversations and alone time. Depending on their personality, it may not be equal, but several daily hours with each is healthy.

2. **Consume more magnesium.**
This crucial mineral is depleted when we're under duress. It's a catch 22 because when it's low we feel even more emotionally reactive, according to nutritionist Dana James. Magnesium is in foods like spinach, kale, bananas, cocoa and almond milk.

3. **Pause and discuss two questions.**
Host conversations in a safe place where you can ask them two important questions:
    a. What are the advantages of our addiction to technology?
    b. What are the disadvantages of our addiction?

4. **Sit down and do deep breathing.**
This often sounds weird to some, but intentional breathing, where you're mindful of your inhaling and exhaling can do wonders to reduce stress and focus our minds. Have them get quiet, close their eyes and take long, slow breaths in and out.

5. **Take a walk in nature.**
Anytime we exercise, it can reduce stress and help us center ourselves, but strolling in nature is the best. A Japanese study discovered a link between chemicals released by trees, called phytoncides, and reduced levels of stress hormones.

6. **Commit to a regular technology fast.**
Everyone I know who's turned off the technology says the same thing: "At first it was hard, and then it became liberating." Why not choose a weekly period of time and get away from the pinging of the phone. Stress usually drops and peace rises.

7. Get eight hours of sleep at night.

It's common knowledge that teens actually need more sleep than their younger or older counterparts—but often get less, thanks to 24/7 social media outlets. We need to encourage them to actually turn off their phones and sleep deeply.

8. Create environments where multiple generations interface.

Give assignments that force students to interface with people from older or younger generations. When we converse with those different from us we tend to grow in our emotional intelligence and in our communication skills. We also learn to focus.

9. Find challenging work that demands your focused attention.

The research by Hungarian psychologist Mihaly Csikszentmihalyi reveals that we get in a flow when we perform demanding work that forces us to focus our minds on achieving it.[5] We are not distracted but devoted in this period. We are mindful.

10. Build an integrated personal brand.

Remind students that everything they say and do is building their personal brand. Social media posts all play into this—by default or design. Creating an integrated brand is a smart way to align themselves with one persona. More on this later.

The bottom line?

- Integration resolves the issue of duplicity. Complexity becomes simplicity.
- Our action is to equip Generation Z to build an integrated personal brand.

Kendall Ciesemier could have grown up like so many other kids in America—caught up in selfies, social media and multiple personas. But Kendell's journey is different. She grew up with chronic liver disease that affected her lifestyle dramatically. She and her family were constantly afraid for her life, often dealing with hard doctor visits, and not being able to do much but wait. Since Kendall was no stranger to suffering, seeing it in others resonated with her and drove her to help. Even as an 11-year old, Kendall couldn't sit still when she saw others in need.

Her plight helped her integrate her personal "brand" which resulted in serving others.

One night she discovered the plight of orphans with AIDS in Africa and she was astonished by their seemingly unwavering hope. As a 5th grader she started sponsoring a child with her own money, which gave Benite, an 8-year old from Mauritania, newfound hope. Kendall's goals expanded as she realized that, with a little help, she could make a world of difference in other kids' lives.

The next summer she underwent not one, but two liver transplants. As people visited with gifts, she asked for money to help sponsor the less fortunate. With the money she received from friends and family she grew from sponsoring a child, to sponsoring a whole village. People heard of what she was doing and, sure enough, it created a snowball effect. Kids all over started their own fund raisers to help her, because they too started to imagine the struggle these African kids were facing. Some people didn't know how to help, but Kendall gave them that outlet when she started a new nonprofit "Kids Caring 4 Kids."

Kendall now travels around engaging others with these ideas. She leads a movement she started to make an even bigger difference. Little Kendall, the survivor of a deadly disease, surgeries, and transplants, believes her own battle has helped integrate her life and now spends her time cultivating passion within others.

TRAVEL GUIDE:

How are you helping students integrate their lives and practice mindfulness?

---

2. Inspiration

Because the world they've grown up in is full of random terrorism, fierce global competition, poor economies, racial prejudice and tangible uncertainty, Generation Z can become paralyzed with fear. Or, if not fear, they can become jaded and cynical. Along with millions of adults, these young people didn't like either major candidate in the 2016 presidential election. Furthermore, they don't trust corporate America and are leaving organized religion in droves. The combination of fear and skepticism can shut down a teen from action. In past generations, high school and college students possessed some idealism because they were youthfully energetic and naively optimistic. Today, kids know too much. They've watched tragedies and moral crises in real time. Even their heroes seem to have a dark side and they've read about it. It can persuade them to escape; to give up trying to be part of the solution. Too frequently, they have been suffocated from the onslaught of data. They frequently struggle with trust and hope. They don't trust the message society has given them and may not be hopeful they can even make a difference if they act.

Generation Z's constant connection to information and media is causing them to preemptively think about death, pain, suffering, and the world's problems as early as middle school. If you feel like your teens or young adults act too childish, giddy or immature, perhaps it's because they're seeking refuge from the onslaught of tragic news from the media. While I want to see kids mature into healthy adulthood, I have a deep concern they're exposed to too much too soon—leaving them without a sense of childhood wonder and appropriate dreams for their future. Students in our focus groups consistently said things like:

"Every time I watch the news it gets in my head. I have to try to not keep thinking about it." - 8th grade boy

"I think about the world's problems a lot when watching the news, but I just go play games or something to get away from it." - 8th grade boy

"I'm afraid that if people don't learn from history's mistakes, we might allow bad things to happen again." - 6th grade girl

"There are things in our world that are getting better, but most of it is getting worse." - 8th grade boy

"I think about the world's problems on a daily basis." - 9th grade boy

"We are more depressed than generations that have come before us." - 6th grade girl

"I know so many people who are in this school right now and can't handle their life. They've told me that they want to kill themselves because they don't know what's going to happen." - 6th grade girl
"The society that we are in is disgusting. It leads us to have a lot of scary thoughts." - 6th grade girl

Because of the overwhelming amount of options and problems, students can get bogged down in a morass of details and dilemmas. We must grow hope inside of them. We must equip students to find a passion and take initiative. Aspiration and inspiration always go together.

What We Can Do
To gain some insight on inspiring students, I'd like to explore some answers that come from a surprising place—the incredible growing population of ISIS.

I have been asking myself a question since 2001, when the World Trade Center and the Pentagon were hit by jet planes and nearly 3,000 Americans died. After the Paris and Belgium attacks and the mass shooting in San Bernardino and Orlando, I found myself perplexed again. I am asking the same question. I know it sounds crazy, but what can we learn from these radical groups?

Why are young people drawn to Islamist extremism?

The main target for groups like the Islamic State is said to be young people between 16 and 24 years old. We should understand, however, the radicalization process can start as early as 11 or 12, says Daniel Koehler, director of the German Institute on Radicalization and De-radicalization Studies (GIRDS).[6] BBC Journalist Jasmine Coleman suggests her own list on what draws youth to terrorism and says: "The number of under-18s arrested for alleged terror offenses in the UK almost doubled from 2014 to 2015. The total number of arrests for all age groups increased by a third over the previous year."[7]

So what is it that makes such a destructive organization so appealing? Why would a young person be attracted to this kind of thing, and further, are their lessons for us to learn, as we work with students this same age? Based on Coleman's article and leadership interviews I've done recently, let me offer five reasons below.

1. **Social Media Connection**

   It's important to remember, ISIS usually connects with young people first through social media. The Internet is essential, according to Koehler. Their goal is to produce 30-40 high quality videos a day in almost every language. "They have an estimated 30,000 to 40,000 Twitter accounts and guides for carrying out jihad or how to join the Islamic State are easily available on-line."

   Our Take Away: As you enlist students, do you leverage social media well? Or, would students say your "brand" is antiquated and "tired?" Do you create engaging videos? Do you recruit through original and compelling ideas ... and interact via the Internet? Have you created a community on-line for them to join?

2. **Contrarian Viewpoint to Mainstream Thought**

   Students have always been drawn to ideas that reject the "status quo" and combat what's being done by mainstream adults, who've bought into the establishment. Do you remember the Baby Boomers in the 1960s? Islamic extremists are contrarian, and while unhealthy in their methods, they furnish a way for youth to express themselves while taking on the perceived "unjust system" wherever they live.

   Our Take Away: Would students view you as merely "status quo?" Or, do they see you as an organization (or school) that challenges the status quo? Do you think for yourself and offer fresh solutions to today's problems? Have you found ways to communicate to students that while you're established you still can be contrarian?

3. **The Offer to Become Someone Significant**

   One practice the Islamist State does well is pitch the idea that to join them, your identity will improve. You will be somebody important. You will know people who are important. Experts say one of the greatest draws for young followers is the promise of belonging to a significant collective. Members tell their stories of impact and the stories can be heard in schools, in communities and on-line.[8]

   Our Take Away: What do you offer that would make a student feel significant? How do you improve a young person's identity? If they join you, do they feel better about themselves? Do they get to do something significant, or do they simply fill a position that feels like "going through the motions?" Are you about maintenance or mission?

4. Grievances Against Society as a Whole

The Islamist Jihadists attract those who experience negative emotions. They appeal to those who are disenfranchised and they franchise them. Many causes throughout history have drawn the marginalized young person who feels they have nothing to lose and they engage them. Charlie Winter, an expert in jihadist militancy says, "Real or perceived grievances in the hands of a recruiter can reach fever pitch."[9]

Our Take Away: Do you attract students who are marginalized or mainstream? Does a kid on the fringes feel welcome? Do you engage students to turn their negative emotions into positive ones, helping them channel depression into hope?

5. The Challenge to Invest Your Life in Something Big

They offer a cause to join. "Ideology is very important but it is also about how people feel about the society they live in," according to experts.[10] The appeal doesn't begin with violence. It begins with doing something significant, focusing on being someone important. Once a young adult buys in big time, they're willing to take extreme measures on behalf of the cause. They want to prove they belong.

Our Take Away: What do you provide that makes a student feel like they're doing something very important and almost impossible? Are you up to something big? Are students compelled to join your organization or club because it calls the very best out of them? Is your vision easy to understand but challenging to achieve?

Perhaps we have a new measuring stick for what we do with students.

TRAVEL GUIDE:

What can we learn from even unhealthy movements or organizations around us about reaching kids? Are we inspiring Generation Z as well?

Brittany Wenger was only 13 when she became fascinated with artificial intelligence. Curious and passionate, she began teaching herself to code and experimenting with artificial neural networks, mostly for amusing purposes. After all, she was a young teen. Things changed for her at 15. Brittany's cousin was diagnosed with breast cancer, a disease affecting one in eight women around the world. When this problem hit so close to home, Brittany wanted to find a way to use what she'd learned to help somehow.

Undaunted by the size of the task in front of her, she took her first steps on a long journey. After a year of research, five years of working with neural networks, two failed projects, and 7.6 million test trials, a new project found success. Brittany wrote a code that could detect breast cancer in tissue samples with an astoundingly high accuracy rate of 99.1 percent. Using Brittany's code, doctors can diagnose cancer in the cheapest, quickest, and least invasive way possible. Her work continued to grow with the release of an app called Cloud4Cancer. It allows doctors to enter their own findings in an effort to constantly fuel cancer research.[11]

Brittany faced huge challenges along the way. Despite her young age and the size of her goal, her perseverance did not falter. Millions of people have been positively impacted by her work. Cancer patients have a stronger chance of winning the fight, all thanks to an inspired 15-year old girl. Brittany works tirelessly on her programs to advance cancer research and detection, while simultaneously getting her MD and PhD in pediatric oncology at Duke. Wow. Anything can happen with an inspired kid.

> TRAVEL GUIDE:
>
> How could you inspire hope and vision within the students you lead?

3. Identification

Identity is a third paramount issue for Generation Z. One could certainly argue that identity has always been a big issue for adolescents, but it's more complicated today thanks to social media. Navigating identity is much more complex than it was even twenty years ago, now that our world is connected and we can derive it from so many places. Remember the personas I mentioned when I spoke about integration? Multiple personas can create a split sense of identity—including differing cliques, genders, family connections, ethnicity, faith and spirituality.

In 2016, a Global Survey of Millennials (18-35) asked young adults what they derive their identity from (the survey listed several categories—family, nationality, gender, faith, etc.). The response from young adults around the world was intriguing. The top response far and away was: "I am a citizen of the world."[12]

Pause and consider the challenge of a clear sense of identity today. Over the course of human history, we've experienced a variety of eras regarding the origin of identity. My colleague, Andrew McPeak, suggests this identity issue has evolved over the years. Note his theory of how identity is more complicated in today's era:

- **Tribal Era.**
  Centuries ago, the issue of identity was simple. It was about family origin and name; it was about tribe and community. You got a sense of who you were from the people in front of you. The values were: ancestry, community, ethnicity and family. You were part of a small circle. An example was the tribal crest, where families had a symbol representing their name.

- **Gatekeeper Era.**
  By the Renaissance, identity issues were broadened. Why? The introduction of the printing press. People with power and voice decided what ideas got published and broadcasted. Think: books, TV, radio. We connected less with tribes and more with culture and society. You had an ideal with which you wanted to identify. The value: Key leaders. For example, communist governments determined the ideals of a society of people.

- **Digital Era.**
  Today, technology plays a central role in where kids derive their identity—and it's from all over. The Internet age allows everyone to have an equal voice. No one person's opinion is more important than others. Further, we can derive our identity from a variety of global

communities. The value is: Tolerance. We clarify our identity by what we invest in; 13 year olds have a platform on line and can speak to issues and become whomever they wish.

If you don't recognize how challenging identity is today, just listen to what kids are saying about it. The students in our focus groups communicated these realities:

> *"I am afraid of being alone and feeling lonely with no one there. Before I started school I was always lonely because my parents were never there. I was in the dark by myself." - 6th grade girl*

> *"I make up who I am on most of my social media sites, but sometimes I forget who I decided to be on some of them." - 9th grade girl*

> *"I'm always afraid that I am going to see someone from school outside of school. I don't like going out because of that." - 7th grade boy*

> *"My dad is so addicted to Facebook." - 7th grade girl*

> *"I just got a physical because I turned 13. They asked me how many days a week I feel stressed. I marked "several" because I don't wake up hearing the birds chirping every morning. That's just not what happens in life." - 7th grade girl*

> *"My mom and dad think my siblings and I spend too much time on our phones, so they took it away one time. That night I didn't get to do my normal ritual of surfing the Internet and YouTube for 3 hours. I do it every night, and I can't sleep until I do it. I couldn't sleep that night and I felt really incomplete until I got my phone back the next day." - 8th grade girl*

If this generation presents problems as young adults, it won't be because they try to take over the establishment, like Baby Boomers. It may be because there is no establishment. Our culture of uncertainty and complexity have changed the rules of engagement. To publish a song, you need no record label. To publish a book, you need no traditional publisher. To gain ideas you need only to go online. The system is so chaotic and transient, identity can be dynamic and unstable. At age 62, actor Sean Connery was asked why he continued acting, when he needed no more income. His response was telling. He said, "Because I get the opportunity to be somebody better and more interesting than I am."

Do our young today experience this same feeling? Are they experimenting because they have no sense of identity or because they're unhappy with the one they have?

What We Can Do
What can we do to equip them with a robust and appropriate identity? I believe we can begin with conversation surrounding our four human needs for identity:

Four emotional needs people have:

A Sense of…	If Missing, they Feel…
• Worth	• Inferior
• Belonging	• Insecure
• Competence	• Inadequate
• Purpose	• Insignificant

Do they have a place where these needs are met in a healthy way?

Four Components to Healthy Identity
Let's discuss their application of these four components of identity:

1. **Awareness:** I need to know my personality, traits and gifts that make me unique.
2. **Association:** I need to feel connected to a family or community. I need to belong.
3. **Achievement:** I need to face challenges and see I can add value through my gifts.
4. **Affirmation:** I need to hear others affirm my value and learn to affirm myself.

Have they fulfilled each of these four components in a healthy way?

Guidelines for Establishing a Healthy Sense of Identity

When I teach college students on this topic, I always end the discussion by offering this list of essential guidelines for building a healthy sense of identity:

- It revolves around the characteristics inside you.
- It's based on something that cannot be taken away.
- It's built from beliefs that will last a lifetime.
- It involves solving problems and serving people.
- It fosters satisfaction when you live up to it.
- It furnishes a platform to leave a legacy.

Are they constructing their identity from these healthy foundations?

We can help students develop a healthy, integrated and inspired identity by equipping them to create a Personal Brand. Everything a student does is either developing or damaging their personal brand. When Growing Leaders speakers address students about their future we talk about one of our *Habitudes*® "Brands and Labels." Products have them. People have them. This particular image is helpful way to think about identity for students. You might explain it to them this way:

Whether you know it or not, YOU are building your own brand, as well. Right now. You have a reputation; you have a style of your own; you have a personality, experiences, talents and passions—all kinds of assets to offer to a future employer. Whether you know it or not, you communicate your brand on Instagram, in your Facebook profile, through texts or emails you send and even through the clothes you wear. Those are like labels. In the same way a label is a tag on a piece of clothing that customers can see and identify the brand, all your actions and words are the ways people see and hear you, and come to think of you. Labels usually communicate the logo and image of the product, while the brand is all about the reputation.

If your brand isn't good, it doesn't matter how nice your label looks.

The key is to be aware of it, and to build your brand on purpose. For instance, ask them: If you did a job interview and your potential employer decided to visit your Facebook page, what would he or she find? Would it be something that might cause them to avoid you and move on to the next candidate?

It works a little like a toolbox. You carry an imaginary toolbox with you each day. You are filling it with knowledge, experiences, skills and relationships that will make you more valuable or less valuable to the marketplace. You are either preparing for the future or you are just surviving, living from day to day. Your toolbox is either filling up or remaining empty. When you fail to get ready for tomorrow, you end up with much more work to compensate for later. My warning is this: if you are not preparing today, you will be repairing tomorrow.

As you can imagine, building a brand doesn't happen overnight. It took Coca-Cola decades to become the number one brand in the world—and they are still managing their name. Similarly, managing your brand takes a lifetime. It requires:

- Choosing a career path based on your strengths and interests.
- Deliberating to see each job and relationship as an opportunity to grow.
- Keeping the big picture in mind as you convey your personal image.

Kyle Weiss would claim to be an ordinary kid growing up. He was into games, friends, technology and very much into soccer. Wanting to expand their children's horizon's, his family took his brother and him to the World Cup in Germany in 2006. He was fourteen years old and it would forever change his perspective. He realized how big soccer was globally, to both affluent and underprivileged kids. He saw how soccer offered an incentive for impoverished children to survive. A year later, he and his brother took a big step and started FUNDaFIELD. They targeted youth in at-risk areas where there was great conflict or trauma and few if any resources. They reached out to victims of civil disputes and war, and those infected with disease. He knew that even with food and medicine, people need help to stay focused and positive in their quest to live and thrive.

In order to participate in the program, students must attend school regularly, using soccer as an incentive. With locations in South Africa, Kenya, Uganda, and Haiti, they now have over ten fully operational soccer fields (with more in production) and over 3,200 students registered to play in more than 15 tournaments. All it took was a teen and some caring adults who helped him identify his love for soccer and gaming and inspire him to do something redemptive with it around the world.

Helping Students Write a Better Story

We can do this. We can enable students to climb out of the traps and avoid the landmines our current maps contain and march forward and into the 21st century. And we can empower them to do it their way, taking plumb lines with them.

Every student or young adult in front of you is writing their own story, as they create their brand. Each year is a chapter in that story, and we are the guides who help them create a better story with each year. We can play a vital role if we'll stay alert and adaptable to their needs.

As a young girl, you might have pegged Gillian as a student with ADHD. She had a difficult time sitting still and was hopeless at school. She so consistently distracted her classmates, that two of her teachers suggested to her mom that Gillian might have a learning disability. So, her mother took her to see a doctor for a diagnosis, and after careful conversation and examination—he had a hunch.

He took Gillian to an empty room and told her to wait there, while he spoke to her mother. When he left, her turned on the radio. At that point, both her mom and the doctor watched her through a window. Gillian immediately began to dance. And dance and dance and dance. After some time, the doctor turned to her mother and said, "Your daughter isn't sick. She's a dancer."

Gillian Lynne went on to attend the Royal Ballet and later became one of the most successful dancers and choreographers of our day. She choreographed Phantom of the Opera, Cats, Aspects of Love, and Chitty, Chitty Bang Bang, among others. She's directed television shows. She's danced in ballets and musicals, and produced shows all over the world. I think she's done quite well, don't you?

All it took was someone who saw what others couldn't see. Someone with a new map.

What do you say we start marching into new territory?

END NOTES

Chapter One

1. "Welcome to the Exponential Age The New Industrial Revolution." Equitas. N.p., n.d. Web. 22 Mar. 2017.

2. Ibid.

3. Ibid.

4. Ibid.

5. Ibid.

6. Ibid.

7. Ibid.

8. Postman, Neil. The Disappearance of Childhood. New York: Vintage, 1994. Print.

9. Ibid.

10. "Life after college for many means returning home." Tribunedigital-baltimoresun. N.p., 20 June 2010. Web. 22 Mar. 2017.

11. Berman, Jillian. "Millennials Now Bringing Their Parents Along On Job Interviews." The Huffington Post. The Huffington Post, 13 Sept. 2013. Web. 22 Mar. 2017.

12. Gann, Carrie, and Abc News Medical Unit. "Study: Significant Number of Young Americans Get Arrested." ABC News. ABC News Network, 19 Dec. 2011. Web. 22 Mar. 2017.

13. "30 Mindblowing Statistics About Americans Under The Age Of 30." ZeroHedge. N.p., 04 Oct. 2013. Web. 22 Mar. 2017.

14. "A Breakdown of Millennial Debt & What the Numbers Look Like Now." Credit Sesame. N.p., 26 July 2016. Web. 22 Mar. 2017.

15. Christeson, William, Amy Dawson Taggart, and Soren Messner-Zidell. "Ready, Willing, and Unable to Serve." Mission: Readiness (2009): n. pag. Mission:Readiness. Mission:Readiness, 2009. Web. 22 Mar. 2017.

16. Elmore, Tim. Artificial maturity: helping kids meet the challenge of becoming authentic adults. San Francisco: Jossey-Bass, 2012. Print.

17. Halpern, Jake. "THE FAME SURVEY." Jake Halpern :: Famesurvey. N.p., n.d. Web. 22 Mar. 2017.

18. Ericson, Mona. "Towards a Sensed Decision-Making Approach: From Deja Vu to Vu Jade." Management Decision 48, no. 1 (2010): 132-155.

19. "Leadership as enabling function for flourishing by Design." Emeraldinsight. Journal of Global Responsibility, 2010. Web. 22 Mar. 2017.

20. "When Cosmonaut Lands On Earth, He`ll Find Himself A Man Without A Country." Tribunedigital-sunsentinel. N.p., 19 Feb. 1992. Web. 22 Mar. 2017.

Chapter Two

1. Howe, Neil, and William Strauss. Millennials rising: the next great generation. New York: Vintage , 2000. Print.

2. Kelly, Kevin. The inevitable: understanding the 12 technological forces that will shape our future. NY, NY: Viking, 2016. Print.

3. Mead, Margaret. People and places. Toronto: Bantam , 1970. Print.

4. Kelly, Kevin. The inevitable: understanding the 12 technological forces that will shape our future. NY, NY: Viking, 2016. Print.

5. "U.S. college enrollment is dropping. Bad sign?" CNNMoney. Cable News Network, 20 May 2016. Web. 22 Mar. 2017.

6. Campos, Paul F. "The Real Reason College Tuition Costs So Much." The New York Times. The New York Times, 04 Apr. 2015. Web. 22 Mar. 2017.

7. "U.S. Student Loan Debt Statistics for 2017." Student Loan Hero. N.p., n.d. Web. 22 Mar. 2017.

8. Christensen, Clayton. "Innovation Imperative: Change Everything." The New York Times. The New York Times, 02 Nov. 2013. Web. 22 Mar. 2017.

9. Schaffhauser, Dian. "Survey: Professors and Employers Find High School Grads Unready for College or Work." THE Journal. N.p., 27 July 2015. Web. 22 Mar. 2017.

10. "Bridge That Gap: Analyzing the Student Skill Index." Chegg. Chegg, 2013. Web. 22 Mar. 2017.

CHAPTER THREE

1. Williams, Casey. "Surprising Number Of Americans Would Chop Off A Finger To Stay Online." The Huffington Post. TheHuffingtonPost.com, 25 Apr. 2016. Web. 22 Mar. 2017.

2. Anderson, Monica. "6 facts about teen romance in the digital age." Pew Research Center. N.p., 01 Oct. 2015. Web. 22 Mar. 2017.

3. Jackson, Alexis. "Half of teens admit addiction to 1 item." AOL.com. AOL, 14 July 2016. Web. 22 Mar. 2017.

4. "More Young People Are Moving Away From Religion, But Why?" NPR. NPR, 15 Jan. 2013. Web. 22 Mar. 2017.

5. Sederer, MD Lloyd I. "Addiction: America's Most Neglected Disease." The Huffington Post. TheHuffingtonPost.com, 26 June 2012. Web. 22 Mar. 2017.

6. Sederer, Lloyd. "A Blind Eye to Addiction." U.S. News & World Report. U.S. News & World Report, 01 June 2015. Web. 22 Mar. 2017.

7. "Teenage Drug and Alcohol Abuse | Teenage Substance Abuse Facts." Summit Behavioral Health. N.p., n.d. Web. 22 Mar. 2017.

8. Korry, Elaine. "Addiction Among Teens Can Be Prevented." Youth Today. N.p., 17 Nov. 2015. Web. 22 Mar. 2017.

9. Sparks & Honey. "Meet Generation Z: Forget Everything You Learned About Millennials." LinkedIn SlideShare. N.p., 17 June 2014. Web. 22 Mar. 2017.

10. "Childhood Obesity Facts." Centers for Disease Control and Prevention. Centers for Disease Control and Prevention, 25 Jan. 2017. Web. 22 Mar. 2017.

11. "Census: More people identify as mixed race." CNN. Cable News Network, n.d. Web. 22 Mar. 2017.

12. Elmore, Tim. "Contrasting Generation Y and Z." The Huffington Post. TheHuffingtonPost.com, 15 Aug. 2014. Web. 22 Mar. 2017.

13. Cohn, D'Vera, and Jeffrey S. Passel. "A record 60.6 million Americans live in multigenerational households." Pew Research Center. N.p., 11 Aug. 2016. Web. 22 Mar. 2017.

14. Sparks & Honey. "Meet Generation Z: Forget Everything You Learned About Millennials." LinkedIn SlideShare. N.p., 17 June 2014. Web. 22 Mar. 2017.

15. "Generation Z: Rebels With A Cause." Forbes. Forbes Magazine, 28 May 2013. Web. 22 Mar. 2017.

16. "Coming Soon to Your Office: Gen Z." Time. Time, n.d. Web. 22 Mar. 2017.

17. Elmore, Tim. "Seven Shifts as Generation Y Becomes Generation Z." Psychology Today. N.p., 21 Sept. 2015. Web. 22 Mar. 2017.

18. Sparks & Honey. "Meet Generation Z: Forget Everything You Learned About Millennials." LinkedIn SlideShare. N.p., 17 June 2014. Web. 22 Mar. 2017.

19. Blair, Josh. "Innovative learning project takes on bee crisis." Cincinnati.com. N.p., 07 Feb. 2016. Web. 22 Mar. 2017.

Chapter Four

1. Fry, Richard. "Millennials surpass Gen Xers as the largest generation in U.S. labor force." Pew Research Center. N.p., 11 May 2015. Web. 22 Mar. 2017.

2. Arthur Levine, Diane Dean, Generation on a Tightrope: A Portrait of Today's College Student, San Francisco, CA: Wiley Press, 2012.

3. Poushter, Jacob. "Smartphone Ownership and Internet Usage Continues to Climb in Emerging Economies." Pew Research Center's Global Attitudes Project. N.p., 22 Feb. 2016. Web. 22 Mar. 2017.

4. Rundle, Michael. "Half Of All Jobs Will Be Automated By 2034." The Huffington Post. The Huffington Post, 25 Jan. 2014. Web. 22 Mar. 2017.

5. Corey Seemiller and Meghan Grace, Generation Z Goes to College, San Francisco, CA: Wiley, 2016.

6. Matthews, Christopher. "More Than 11 Million Young People Have Fled Facebook Since 2011." Time. Time, 15 Jan. 2014. Web. 22 Mar. 2017.

7. Kadakia, Crystal. "72 Percent of HS Students Are Entrepreneurial and Corporate America Just Doesn't Get It." The Huffington Post. TheHuffingtonPost.com, 03 Aug. 2015. Web. 22 Mar. 2017.

8. "Here Comes Generation Z." Bloomberg.com. Bloomberg, 18 June 2014. Web. 22 Mar. 2017.

9. Corey Seemiller and Meghan Grace, Generation Z Goes to College, San Francisco, CA: Wiley, 2016.

10. Ibid.

11. Ibid.

12. McGrath, Ellen, Barry Sears, Ph.D., Hara Estroff Marano, and Stephen A. Diamond, Ph.D. "How Big a Problem Is Anxiety?" Psychology Today. N.p., n.d. Web. 22 Mar. 2017.

13. Fottrell, Quentin. "Babies younger than 2 are using smartphones and tablets." MarketWatch. N.p., 03 Nov. 2015. Web. 22 Mar. 2017.

14. Kingston, Anne. "Get ready for Generation Z." Macleans.ca. N.p., 11 Aug. 2014. Web. 22 Mar. 2017.

15. Ibid.

16. Nekola, Adam. "America's morphing age pyramid." Pew Research Center. N.p., 10 Apr. 2014. Web. 22 Mar. 2017.

17. Ibid.

18. Ibid.

19. Abrashoff, D. Michael. It's your ship: management techniques from the best damn ship in the Navy. New York: Grand Central Publishing, 2012. Print.

20. Noman, Natashanoman. "The Exact Year You'll Finally Feel Like an Adult Has Been Declared." Mic. Mic Network Inc., 10 Aug. 2016. Web. 22 Mar. 2017.

Chapter Five

1. "Georgia's Teacher Dropout Crisis." Georgia Department of Education (2015): n. pag. Www.gadoe.org. Dec. 2015. Web. 22 Mar. 2017.

2. Ibid.

3. Strauss, Valerie. "Why so many teachers leave — and how to get them to stay." The Washington Post. WP Company, 12 June 2015. Web. 22 Mar. 2017.

4. Rizga, Kristina. "Why so many teachers quit, and how to fix that." Los Angeles Times. Los Angeles Times, 23 Aug. 2015. Web. 22 Mar. 2017.

5. Weale, Sally. "Four in 10 new teachers quit within a year." The Guardian. Guardian News and Media, 31 Mar. 2015. Web. 22 Mar. 2017.

6. Richmond, Emily. "Teacher Job Satisfaction Hits 25-Year Low." The Atlantic. Atlantic Media Company, 21 Feb. 2013. Web. 22 Mar. 2017.

7. Heitin, Liana. "Survey: Teacher Job Satisfaction Hits a Low Point." Education Week Teacher. N.p., 29 Apr. 2016. Web. 22 Mar. 2017.

8. "Poll of America's Attitude toward Public Schools." PDK International. N.p., n.d. Web. 22 Mar. 2017. <pdkpoll.pdkintl.org>.

9. "Fosbury flops to an Olympic record." History.com. A&E Television Networks, n.d. Web. 22 Mar. 2017.

10. "Roger Bannister breaks four-minutes mile." History.com. A&E Television Networks, n.d. Web. 22 Mar. 2017.

11. "Carlisle Indians Made It A Whole New Ballgame." The Washington Post. WP Company, 13 May 2007. Web. 22 Mar. 2017.

12. Wilson, James Q., and George L. Kelling. "Broken Windows." Atlantic Monthly (n.d.): n. pag. Manhattan Institute. Web. 22 Mar. 2017.

13. Hartung, Adam. "GE: A Total Leadership Failure." Forbes. Forbes Magazine, 16 Apr. 2015. Web. 22 Mar. 2017.

Chapter Six

1. Jaschik, Scott. "Data on Helicopter Parents." Inside Higher Ed. N.p., 15 Mar. 2007. Web. 22 Mar. 2017.

2. Toppo, Greg. "Techie tykes: Kids going mobile at much earlier age." USA Today. Gannett Satellite Information Network, 02 Nov. 2015. Web. 22 Mar. 2017.

3. Kabali, Hilda K., Matilde M. Irigoyen, Rosemary Nunez-Davis, Jennifer G. Budacki, Sweta H. Mohanty, Kristin P. Leister, and Robert L. Bonner. "Exposure and Use of Mobile Media Devices by Young Children." Pediatrics. American Academy of Pediatrics, 01 Oct. 2015. Web. 22 Mar. 2017.

4. Postman, Neil. The disappearance of childhood. New York: Vintage , 1994. Print.

5. Ibid.

6. "These Are the Job Skills Employers Want but Can't Find." Bloomberg.com. Bloomberg, 2015. Web. 22 Mar. 2017.

7. Sheet, Megan Elliott The Cheat. "5 skills college grads need to get a job." USA Today. Gannett Satellite Information Network, 03 May 2015. Web. 22 Mar. 2017.

8. "Employers More Interested in Critical Thinking and Problem Solving Than College Major." Association of American Colleges & Universities. N.p., 10 Apr. 2013. Web. 22 Mar. 2017.

9. Wolpert, Stuart. "Is technology producing a decline in critical thinking and analysis?" UCLA Newsroom. N.p., 27 Jan. 2009. Web. 22 Mar. 2017.

10. "75 to 98 Percent of College Students Have Cheated." Study.com. N.p., 29 June 2011. Web. 22 Mar. 2017.

11. "Developing Students' Creative Skills for 21st Century Success." Education Update:Reading First:Developing Students' Creative Skills for 21st Century Success. N.p., Dec. 2015. Web. 22 Mar. 2017.

12. "A Social Change Model of Leadership Development." Higher Education Research Institute (n.d.): n. pag. Heri.ucla.edu. Higher Education Research Institute. Web. 22 Mar. 2017.

13. "Pressure on the Provosts: 2014 Survey of Chief Academic Officers | Inside Higher Ed." 2014 Survey of Chief Academic Officers. N.p., 2014. Web. 22 Mar. 2017.

14. "What America Needs to Know About Higher Education Redesign." Gallup.com. N.p., 25 Feb. 2014. Web. 22 Mar. 2017.

Chapter Seven

1. Donovan, Suzanne, and John Bransford. How Students Learn. Washington, D.C.: National Academies Press, 2005. Print.

2. Maats, Hunter, Katie O'Brien, Lindsey Gary, Andrew Goulet, and Travis Stanberry. The Straight-A Conspiracy: Your Secret Guide to Ending the Stress of School and Totally Ruling the World. Los Angeles?: 368 Press, 2012. Print.

3. www.theindependentproject.org

4. "Climbing a tree can improve cognitive skills, researchers say." ScienceDaily. University of North Florida, 29 July 2015. Web. 06 Apr. 2017.

5. Cook, Susan Wagner, Zachary Mitchell, and Susan Goldin-Meadow. "Gesturing Makes Learning Last." Cognition 106.2 (2008): 1047-058. Science Direct. Web. 5 Apr. 2017.

6. Making Science Make Sense. Rep. Bayer Facts of Science Education, 2015. Web. 5 Apr. 2017. <http://s3.amazonaws.com/rdcms-pta/files/production/public/Images/Bayer_Facts-Exec_Summary-2015.pdf>.

7. Wilde | April 2, 2015 Print article, Marian. "Global grade: How do U.S. students compare?" Great Schools. N.p., 2 Apr. 2015. Web. 05 Apr. 2017.

8. Engaging Schools: Fostering High School Students' Motivation to Learn. Washington, D.C: National Academies Press, 2006. Print.

Chapter Eight

1. Paul, Annie Murphy. "Your Brain on Fiction." The New York Times. The New York Times, 17 Mar. 2012. Web. 05 Apr. 2017.

2. Ha, Thu-Huong. "What happens in the brain when we hear stories? Uri Hasson at TED2016." TED Blog. N.p., 18 Feb. 2016. Web. 05 Apr. 2017.

3. Miller, Tessa. "The Science of Storytelling: Why Telling a Story is the Most Powerful Way to Activate Our Brains." Lifehacker. Lifehacker.com, 05 Dec. 2012. Web. 05 Apr. 2017.

4. Sapolsky, Robert. "This Is Your Brain on Metaphors." New York Times. New York Times, 14 Nov. 2010. Web. 5 Apr. 2017.

5. Gutierrez, Karla. "Studies Confirm the Power of Visuals in eLearning." SHIFT eLearning Blog. N.p., 08 July 2014. Web. 05 Apr. 2017.

6. The Future of 3D Education. N.p.: Sensavis Education AB, n.d. Cision. Sensavis Education AB, 2013. Web. 5 Apr. 2017. <http://mb.cision.com/ Public/8227/9478258/b567878833acc4ce.pdf>.

7. "Active Learning." Changingminds.org. N.p., n.d. Web. 05 Apr. 2017.

8. Lane, Robert, and Stephen K. Kosslyn. "Show Me: What Brain Research Says About Visuals in PowerPoint." Cedma-europe.org. Microsoft, 2008. Web. 5 Apr. 2017.

9. Pant, Ritu. "Visual Marketing: A Picture's Worth 60,000 Words." Business 2 Community. N.p., 16 Jan. 2015. Web. 5 Apr. 2017.

10. Pink, Daniel H. A Whole New Mind: Why Right-Brainers Will Rule the Future. London: MC, Marshall Cavendish, 2012. Print.

11. Jensen, Eric. Brain-based learning: the new paradigm of teaching. Thousand Oaks, Calif: Corwin Press, 2008. Print.

12. Vogel, Douglas R. , Gary W. Dickson, and John A. Lehman. Persuasion and the Role of Visual. Publication. Minneapolis: WORKING PAPER SERIES | U of Minnesota, 1986. Persuasion and the Role of Visual. University of Minnesota and 3M. Web. 5 Apr. 2017. <https://www.misrc.umn.edu/workingpapers/ fullpapers/1986/8611.pdf>.

13. Jensen, Eric. Brain-based learning: the new paradigm of teaching. Thousand Oaks, Calif: Corwin Press, 2008. Print.

14. "How To Retain 90% Of Everything You Learn." Psychotactics. N.p., 13 Aug. 2015. Web. 05 Apr. 2017.

15. Houts PS, Doak CC, Doak LG, Loscalzo MJ. The role of pictures in improving health communication: a review of research on attention, comprehension, recall, and adherence. Patient Educ Couns. 2006 May.

16. Miller, Jennifer. "Science Says Art Will Make Your Kids Better Thinkers (and Nicer People)." Fast Company. Fast Company, 09 Dec. 2013. Web. 05 Apr. 2017.

17. Postman, Neil, The Disappearance of Childhood, Vintage Books, New York, NY, Reprinted in 1994.

Chapter Nine

1. "What is a Sooner?" OU Athletics. N.p., n.d. Web. 07 Apr. 2017. <http://www. soonersports.com/ViewArticle.dbml?ATCLID=208806115>.

2. "LAND RUN of 1889." Archive.org. N.p., n.d. Web. 07 Apr. 2017. <https:// web.archive.org/web/20060214202906/http://www.ok-history.mus.ok.us/enc/ landrun.htm>.

3. "SOONERS." Archive.org. N.p., n.d. Web. 07 Apr. 2017. <https://web.archive. org/web/20060218001824/www.ok-history.mus.ok.us/enc/sooner.htm>.

4. "Why Water? Impact of the Global Water Crisis." Impact of the Global Water Crisis | charity: water. N.p., n.d. Web. 07 Apr. 2017. <http://www.charitywater. org/whywater/>.

5. "Compassion International: Who We Are." Christian Child Sponsorship - Compassion - Child Charity Organization. N.p., n.d. Web. 07 Apr. 2017.

6. "Darrow | Our People." Darrow School. N.p., n.d. Web. 07 Apr. 2017. <https://www.darrowschool.org/Our-People/ Profile?ProfileID=60&20160113-140403.156>.

7. Smith, Jenn. "Darrow School students learning to 'think outside the box'" The Berkshire Eagle. N.p., 26 Jan. 2016. Web. 07 Apr. 2017.

8. Werberger, Raleigh. From project-based learning to artistic thinking: lessons learned from creating an unHappy meal. Lanham: Rowman & Littlefield, 2016. Print.

9. Smith, Jenn. "Darrow School students learning to 'think outside the box'" The Berkshire Eagle. N.p., 26 Jan. 2016. Web. 07 Apr. 2017.

10. Ibid.

11. Tyre, Peg. "The Writing Revolution." The Atlantic. Atlantic Media Company, 19 Feb. 2014. Web. 07 Apr. 2017.

12. Ibid.

13. Ibid.

14. Ibid.

15. Ibid.

16. "2014 Women's Basketball Class Rankings." ESPN. ESPN Internet Ventures, n.d. Web. 07 Apr. 2017. <http://www.espn.com/high-school/girls-basketball/ recruiting/class-rankings/_/class/2017)>.

17. Pappano, Laura. "The Year of the MOOC." The New York Times. The New York Times, 03 Nov. 2012. Web. 07 Apr. 2017.

18. Chafkin, Max. "Udacity's Sebastian Thrun, Godfather Of Free Online Education, Changes Course." Fast Company. Fast Company, 19 Apr. 2016. Web. 07 Apr. 2017.

19. Tamburri, Rosanna. "An interview with Canadian MOOC pioneer George Siemens." University Affairs. N.p., n.d. Web. 07 Apr. 2017.

20. Smith, Clint. "The Power of Pell Grants for Prisoners." The New Yorker. The New Yorker, 30 June 2016. Web. 07 Apr. 2017.

21. "Who We Are." The Petey Greene Program. N.p., n.d. Web. 07 Apr. 2017. <http://www.peteygreene.org/who-we-are/>.

22. "What Is Autism?" Autism Speaks. N.p., 30 May 2012. Web. 07 Apr. 2017. <https://www.autismspeaks.org/what-autism>.

23. "Tsunami of Young Adults with Autism Face Uncertain Future, Unemployment Crisis." Extraordinary Ventures. N.p., 14 Feb. 2014. Web. 07 Apr. 2017.

24. NationSwell. Meet the Gutsy Dad That Started a Car Wash to Help His Son Find Purpose. Youtube.com, 29 Jan. 2015. Web. 07 Apr. 2017.

25. "2015 Academy Fellows ." National League for Nursing (n.d.): 11. Nln.org. Web. 7 Apr. 2017. <http://www.nln.org/docs/default-source/default-document-library/2015-academy-fellows-(ppt).pdf?sfvrsn=0>.

26. Baquero, Gabby. "UCF professors use innovative, unusual teaching methods." (n.d.): n. pag. Central Florida Future. 21 Oct. 2015. Web. 7 Apr. 2017.

27. Cpetagno. "UCF Professor Recently Honored has Died, Leaves Legacy for Nursing Students." UCF News - University of Central Florida Articles - Orlando, FL News. N.p., 17 May 2016. Web. 07 Apr. 2017.

28. "Student Affairs." Because This Is Auburn . Auburn University, n.d. Web. 07 Apr. 2017.

Chapter Ten

1. American College Health Association, National College Health Assessment Spring 2007, reference group data report 55, no. 4 (January-Februrary 2007):195-206

2. "College students' mental health is a growing concern, survey finds." Elements of Behavioral Health 44.6 (2013): 13. Apa.org. Web. 7 Apr. 2017.

3. Ibid.

4. "20 Percent of Teens Suffering From Anxiety." Addiction Treatment | Elements | Drug Rehab Treatment Centers. N.p., 16 Dec. 2016. Web. 07 Apr. 2017.

5. Hutchison, Courtney, and ABC News Medical Unit. "Today's Teens More Anxious, Depressed and Paranoid Than Ever." ABC News. ABC News Network, 10 Dec. 2009. Web. 01 May 2017.

6. "20 Percent of Teens Suffering From Anxiety." Addiction Treatment | Elements | Drug Rehab Treatment Centers. N.p., 16 Dec. 2016. Web. 07 Apr. 2017.

7. Susanna Schrobsdorff, "The Kids Are Not Alright," TIME magazine, Time Inc, New York, NY: p. 44-51.

8. Hutchison, Courtney. "Today's Teens More Anxious, Depressed and Paranoid Than Ever." ABC News. ABC News Network, 10 Dec. 2009. Web. 07 Apr. 2017.

9. Lenhart, Amanda. "Teens, Social Media & Technology Overview 2015." Pew Research Center: Internet, Science & Tech. N.p., 08 Apr. 2015. Web. 07 Apr. 2017.

10. Ibid.

11. Ibid.

12. "About the Cyberbullying Research Center." Cyberbullying Research Center. N.p., n.d. Web. 07 Apr. 2017. <http://cyberbullying.org/about-us>.

13. Buchanan, Lauren. "Staggering Stats on Selfies." Staggering Stats on Selfies. N.p., n.d. Web. 07 Apr. 2017.

14. Steele, Ann. "What Do #Selfies Say About The Psychology Of You?" What Do #Selfies Say About The Psychology Of You? | MastersinPsychologyGuide.com. Masters in Psychology Guide, n.d. Web. 07 Apr. 2017.

15. Twenge, Jean M., and W. Keith. Campbell. The narcissism epidemic: living in the age of entitlement. New York: Atria Paperback, 2013. Print.

16. Susanna Schrobsdorff, "The Kids Are Not Alright," TIME magazine, Time Inc, New York, NY: p. 44-51.

17. Casey, B. J., Leah H. Somerville, Ian H. Gotlib, Ozlem Ayduk, Nicholas T. Franklin, Mary K. Askren, John Jonides, Marc G. Berman, Nicole L. Wilson, Theresa Teslovich, Gary Glover, Vivian Zayas, Walter Mischel, and Yuichi Shoda. Behavioral and neural correlates of delay of gratification 40 years later. Rep. PNAS, 26 July 2011. Web. 7 Apr. 2017.

18. Lewis, Thomas. "The Neuroscience of Empathy" | Talks at Google. YouTube, Google, 17 Dec. 2007. Web. 07 Apr. 2017.

19. Bergland, Christopher. "The Neuroscience of Empathy." Psychology Today. N.p., 10 Oct. 2016. Web. 07 Apr. 2017.

20. Susanna Schrobsdorff, "The Kids Are Not Alright," TIME magazine, Time Inc, New York, NY: p. 44-51.

21. "Teen Cell Phone Addiction." Teen Cell Phone Addiction. N.p., n.d. Web. 07 Apr. 2017. <http://www.psychguides.com/guides/teen-cell-phone-addiction/>.

22. O'keeffe, G. S., and K. Clarke-Pearson. "The Impact of Social Media on Children, Adolescents, and Families." Pediatrics 127.4 (2011): 800-04. Fit.edu. Web. 7 Apr. 2017.

23. Greenwood, Shannon, Andrew Perrin, and Maeve Duggan. "Social Media Update 2016." Pew Research Center: Internet, Science & Tech. N.p., 11 Nov. 2016. Web. 07 Apr. 2017.

24. Burns, Judith. "Social media harms moral development, parents say." BBC News. BBC, 18 July 2016. Web. 07 Apr. 2017.

25. Ibid.

26. Kayne, Eric. "Census: White majority in U.S. gone by 2043." U.S. News. N.p., 13 June 2013. Web. 07 Apr. 2017.

27. David Kinnaman and Gabe Lyons, Good Faith, Baker Books: Grand Rapids, MI, 2016.

28. Ibid.

29. Ibid.

30. Tompkins, Chris, Don Posterski, and John McAuley. Elastic morality: leading young adults in our age of acceptance. Bloomington, IN: West Bow Press, 2011. Print.

31. Ibid.

32. Smith, Christian. Lost in transition. New York: Oxford U Press, 2011. Print.

33. "Cheating Fact Sheet - RESEARCH CENTER - Cheating Is A Personal Foul." Cheating Fact Sheet - RESEARCH CENTER - Cheating Is A Personal Foul. N.p., n.d. Web. 07 Apr. 2017.

34. Smith, Christian. Lost in transition. New York: Oxford U Press, 2011. Print.

35. Ibid.

36. Ibid.

37. Scelfo, Julie. "Suicide on Campus and the Pressure of Perfection." The New York Times. The New York Times, 27 July 2015. Web. 07 Apr. 2017.

Chapter Eleven

1. "Christopher Columbus." Biography.com. A&E Networks Television, 16 Nov. 2016. Web. 09 Apr. 2017.

2. Bloomberg, Michael. "Here's Your Degree. Now Go Defeat Demagogues." Bloomberg.com. Bloomberg, 30 Apr. 2016. Web. 09 Apr. 2017.

3. Frankl, Viktor E. Man's search for meaning. Boston: Beacon Press, 2014. Print.

4. Brooks, David. "Keynote address by David Brooks." Brandeis.edu. N.p., 22 May 2011. Web. 09 Apr. 2017.

Chapter Twelve

1. Divecha, Diana, Ph.D. "The Only Parenting Model You Need." Developmental Science. N.p., 28 June 2015. Web. 09 Apr. 2017.

2. Yeager, David Scott, Julio Garcia, Patti Brzustoski, William T. Hessert, Valerie Purdie-Vaughns, Nancy Apfel, Allison Master, Matthew E. Williams, and Geoffrey L. Cohen. Breaking the Cycle of Mistrust: Wise Interventions to Provide Critical Feedback Across the Racial Divide. Rep. American Psychological Association, 2013. Web. 9 Apr. 2017.

3.   Stevens, Jane Ellen. "Lincoln High School in Walla Walla, WA, tries new approach to school discipline — suspensions drop 85%." ACEs Too High. N.p., 30 May 2015. Web. 09 Apr. 2017.

4.   Ibid.

EPILOGUE

1.   "Social Media and Kids: Some Benefits, Some Worries." Aap.org. American Academy of Pediatrics, 28 Mar. 2011. Web. 09 Apr. 2017.

2.   "Take the Rated 4 Kids Online Personality Quiz." Rated 4 Kids. N.p., 28 Apr. 2016. Web. 09 Apr. 2017.

3.   Time Special Edition, "Mindfulness: The New Science of Health and Happiness, Editor Lisa Lombardi, Time, Inc. Books, New York, NY: 2016.

4.   Ibid.

5.   "Mihaly Csikszentmihalyi." Pursuit of Happiness. N.p., 10 Sept. 2016. Web. 09 Apr. 2017.

6.   Coleman, Jasmine. "Islamist extremism: Why young people are being drawn to it." BBC News. BBC, 10 Dec. 2015. Web. 09 Apr. 2017.

7.   Ibid.

8.   Ibid.

9.   Ibid.

10.   Ibid.

11.   Kiefer, Elizabeth. "This 19-Year-Old College Student Built an Artificial Brain That Detects Breast Cancer." Teen Vogue. TeenVogue.com, 19 June 2015. Web. 09 Apr. 2017.

12.   "Millennials Uphold Ideals of Global Citizenship amid Concern for Corruption, Climate Change and Lack of Opportunity." World Economic Forum. N.p., 22 Aug. 2016. Web. 09 Apr. 2017.

ACKNOWLEDGEMENTS

I am compelled to say thank you to the significant people who participated in the vision for this book. It was the work of many hands:

Andrew McPeak—who helped to craft the sequence of thought, lay out the chapters, host our focus groups with students and write chapter nine. Andrew was an invaluable partner in crafting this book, as both a sounding board and practitioner.

Anne Alexander—who was our copy editor, making sure our grammar, spelling and sentence structure was accurate and didn't distract readers from comprehension.

Matt Litton—who was our line editor and offered incredible guidance to this book's clear messaging. Matt was a cheerleader as well as a surgeon.

My outside reading team—consisting of Joe Castiglione, from Oklahoma University, Mary Gerardy, from Wake Forest University, Nicki Moore, from the University of North Carolina, Danny White from Virginia Tech, Jason Lane from Millcreek High School, Mary Lynn Realff from Georgia Tech and Amy Zulauf from Greeley West High School.

Clari Mercier—who consistently worked to find regular writing times for me in between meetings and travel this last year. She was a care-taker and a life-saver.

Chris Harris—who helped to ensure the message of this book was clear and compelling. As our marketing director, he worked to make sure we added value to others.

Evan Donoho—who did research for various chapters of this book, making sure we had valid data and current statistics on students, teachers, parents and culture.

Jim Woodard—who formatted the copy and graphics for this book, so that the thoughts could find their way into the minds and hearts of everyone who read it.

Ricky Warren—who designed the cover and all the surrounding graphics. Ricky is a gifted artist who, having taught university students, understands their needs as well.

Holly Moore—who pushed me to create this manuscript, knowing that educators, coaches, employers and parents need new maps for the future. Holly is a partner in our cause of equipping the emerging generation and I am eternally grateful for her.

Finally, our **Growing Leaders team**, who embody the truths of this book. Most of them are young, and believe we must be both timely and timeless as we equip students.

MARCHING OFF THE MAP
. . . AND INTO YOUR SCHOOL, OFFICE, OR CHURCH

Hear Dr. Tim Elmore, Andrew McPeak, or one of our other amazing speakers share the insights, ideas, and strategies from *Marching Off the Map* at your next event.

While it's true that today's students present a host of new challenges for those who mentor and lead them, we have hope that they can succeed in life, and like you, we are determined to help them fulfill their potential.

Available as a customized 90-minute, half-day, or full-day presentation, our *Marching Off the Map* in-person event will further educate your team on the unique characteristics of this generation, and provide an in-depth look at what methodology needs to change in order to engage them. And, perhaps most importantly, it will empower your team with practical applications and solutions.

We have previously brought Growing Leaders concepts to
schools,
organizations,
athletic departments,
businesses,
and churches.

With the right resources to help educate, lead, and parent young adults better, we can all be a catalyst for emerging generations that will truly change the world.

So, while we all love a good book, this discussion-based workshop can be the catalyst to spark long-term change with your group. We're willing to venture into this uncharted territory for the sake of our teens. Will you join us?

Contact Speakers@GrowingLeaders.com
for more information, and to book your guide today.

A WORD ABOUT  GROWING LEADERS

Real-life challenges call for real-life leadership.

Imagine a world improved, even transformed, by the next generation. That's our vision at Growing Leaders.

Founded in 2003 by Dr. Tim Elmore, Growing Leaders is a global non-profit that encourages and equips young adults to take on real-life opportunities and challenges in the classroom, in their careers, and in the community.

We do this by partnering with organizations like yours to teach practical life and leadership skills using real stories, intriguing images, and engaging experiences that are relatable and memorable.

Our process and resources are grounded in research and a unique understanding of the emerging generations, and recognize that leading others at any level begins with learning how to lead yourself. These tools include:

- Life and leadership skills curriculum for educators and trainers
- Leadership resources for mentoring communities
- An annual National Leadership Forum
- Conferences held at your organization or campus

Some of the organizations that use our training resources include:

- The U.S. Department of Justice
- Boys and Girls Club of America
- National Future Farmers of America Organization
- The Kansas City Royals Baseball Club (minor league affiliates)
- University of Texas
- University of Alabama
- Stanford University
- University of North Carolina
- Pepperdine University
- Georgia Institute of Technology
- University of Oklahoma
- Duke University
- The Ohio State University
- Auburn University

Tim Elmore and the Growing Leaders team are available to help you invest wisely in the next generation. For more information, please visit:

www.GrowingLeaders.com

ABOUT TIM ELMORE
& ANDREW McPEAK

Dr. Tim Elmore, President of Growing Leaders, is a best-selling author and international speaker who uses his expertise on Generations Y and Z to equip educators, coaches, leaders, parents, and other adults to impart practical life and leadership skills to young adults that will help them navigate through life.

He educates adults to help them understand the challenges and experiences today's generation faces and connect with them in a way that resonates. Dr. Elmore believes, by cultivating leadership abilities in young adults and encouraging the adults who guide them, Growing Leaders can be the catalyst for emerging generations that will truly change the world.

Dr. Tim Elmore teaches leadership courses and speaks at schools, universities, businesses, and athletic programs. He has trained thousands of leaders in partnership with nationally renowned schools and organizations like the Kansas City Royals, Stanford University, Virginia Tech, National Football League, University of Texas, Chick-fil-A, Cici's Pizza, and more.

Dr. Elmore has also authored more than 30 books including: *Habitudes®: Images that Form Leadership Habits and Attitudes, Artificial Maturity: Helping Kids Meet the Challenge of Becoming Authentic Adults, Generation iY®: Secrets to Connecting with Today's Teens & Young Adults in the Digital Age, 12 Huge Mistakes Parents Can Avoid*, and *lifeGIVING Mentors*.

Andrew McPeak is a next gen researcher, speaker, and curriculum designer for Growing Leaders. He works with schools, universities, and sports teams on implementing *Habitudes®* as a teaching tool for life and leadership skills. He excels at helping these leaders craft their message to connect with today's student.

HABITUDES®

IMAGES THAT FORM LEADERSHIP HABITS & ATTITUDES

Every person is faced with unique obstacles and possibilities throughout his or her life. What makes someone a leader is how they manage them and leverage those experiences to positively influence others.

Habitudes® is a curriculum and training system that combines images, relatable stories and experiences into leadership lesson plans that resonate with today's young adults, equipping them to navigate through life's challenges and opportunities.

Grounded in established research, they are a fun, creative, and engaging way that helps young adults:

> Take initiative and set the pace to influence others in positive ways.

> Overcome complex problems through creative persistence.

> Capitalize on personal strengths to be career-ready after graduation.

> Develop critical thinking skills that produce better life choices, such as choosing healthy friends, improving study habits, and setting meaningful goals.

Habitudes® has been used in over 8,000 schools and organizations across the world for:

> Secondary School Advisement Periods

> Athletic Programs (high school, college, and pro)

> College Freshmen Programs

> Corporate On-boarding Programs for Young Professionals

> Leadership Classes

> Youth Groups

❝ Tim Elmore's masterful usage of visual, cognitive, and experiential learning tools makes Habitudes one of the best teaching tools available. ❞

- Dr. L. Keith Whitney, Former Chairperson of the Business Division, Pepperdine University

For a FREE Sample and Case Studies, visit
GrowingLeaders.com/Habitudes